**THE YEAR THE TREES
DIDN'T DIE**

THE YEAR THE TREES DIDN'T DIE

One Mother's Memoir

Mary J. Koral

TWO HARBORS PRESS • MINNEAPOLIS

Copyright © 2015 by Mary J. Koral

Two Harbors Press
322 First Avenue N, 5th floor
Minneapolis, MN 55401
612.455.2293
www.TwoHarborsPress.com

All rights reserved. No part of this publication may be reproduced, stored in a retrieval system, or transmitted, in any form or by any means, electronic, mechanical, photocopying, recording, or otherwise, without the prior written permission of the author.

Names have been changed in order to preserve some privacy. Time has been conflated. Nothing has been invented. It is the story as I remember it.

ISBN-13: 978-1-63413-657-0
LCCN: 2015911741

Distributed by Itasca Books

Cover Design by James Arneson
Typeset by Mary K. Ross

Printed in the United States of America

For Ken and for the children. You are my world.

Following my footprints
walk home
following my footprints
Come home, happily...

Leslie Marmon Silko, *Ceremony*

Chapter 1

THE GRADUATION

I saw the steady, careful look the woman gave us, a look I knew from other times, other places. She was a stranger who paid no mind to the silver trays laden with desserts and didn't talk to anyone around her. She concentrated on us.

Pretty soon I'd have to explain my family to her. I would have placed money on it. I had explained my family many times over the years. Still I allowed myself a hope that she'd stay on her side of the room and content herself with watching.

Somebody in the room pointed to the éclairs, brownies with chocolate ganache, cream puffs, cupcakes frosted in school colors. Blue and orange for Hope College, a small, private college on the western side of Michigan. "What a spread!"

I loved the spread. If anyone had asked, I'd have said, "Lay it on! All this and more!" Sung, our youngest, was graduating. It was May, a miserably cold May in 2004. But who cared? Not me. Sung had not only graduated from college, he'd won a Fulbright. A Fulbright! The reception for the graduates was held in one of the college's big-occasion reception rooms replete with dark paneling and Oriental rugs. Faces of past presidents lined the walls; the room was meant to reassure parents they had spent their money wisely. We were convinced. Sung's graduation would have been enough to reassure us, but the Fulbright made it feel like our family had summited, every one of us standing on top of the mountain, flags in hand, waving, all of us together.

Nobody missing. Nobody in distress.

It had not always been like that. There were plenty of times

1

I could not have imagined all of us together and happy. Plenty of times I could not have imagined Sung triumphant. Times I could not swallow a thing for fear.

But we *were* together, and Sung *was* triumphant. So.

"I can't believe it. When your mom phoned and told me, I cried." My sister Rosie teared up when she hugged Sung. He smiled at her, embarrassed by the emotion. But I'd heard him choke back his own tears when he called and said, "Your son just won a Fulbright."

It struck me, what he didn't say: "*I* just won a Fulbright." He said, "your son." Like the grant was something he'd managed for *me*. I felt the old need to assure him. He didn't have to prove himself. We loved him, would always love him, with or without reflected glory.

How many times had I sworn that was true? And still, there it was, those two words, *your son*, seeming proof that Sung, maybe every one of the kids, would never believe it. "Your son won a Fulbright," he said. And I heard: *See? You didn't get a bad deal when you said yes to me*. He said as much to somebody congratulating him; I'd just bitten into my second éclair:

"They didn't get such a bad deal when they took me," he said. He was laughing, joking, but I winced. Couldn't he ever just relax into life? But no. He was a worker and worrier, our youngest, forever proving himself. Those nights he struggled to learn math facts! Although he has mastered German and is conquering Spanish, he still can't multiply, not without a calculator—"Thank God for calculators," he says when he goes to leave a tip—but he walked off with a big-deal award. Maybe, finally, things were spinning in the right direction.

Maybe we could all stay together: happy, no distress, nobody ever gone missing again.

* * *

The woman set her cup down, picked up her purse, and headed our way just the way I thought she would. *No*, I thought. *I don't want to deal with you. Leave us alone.*

She'd want details: everything I was willing to give about the graduate and his family. On a purely objective level, her curiosity was not unreasonable. One glance and a person could see we didn't fit normal family groupings in the room, in most rooms. We're a nonmatched adoptive family. First time seeing us, somebody usually says to me, "That's some family you've got, a regular United Nations."

Our color palette varies.

We, the parents, are white, sort of champagne colored. Two of our kids, Sung and his brother, Minh, have skin the color of weak tea and are usually identified as *some kind of Asian*. People like to guess. *Chinese? Japanese?* They are surprised when we don't nod yes; they blink and try to think of other Asian countries. Our Indo-Asian daughter with her espresso-brown skin—people don't try to identify her. *What is she?* they ask.

She stood next to her dad, close. He'd look out for her; she never liked crowds, didn't interact easily with people, wanted backup. She held a very small child with skin her shade, maybe a little darker. The child was her Afro-Indo-Asian baby boy.

There was more.

A little girl in a swishy purple dress came up to Minh. He picked her up and gave her a kiss, somewhat awkward in his movements, still acquiring a patina, still surprised to find himself in the role of parent. But that little girl didn't mind. She smooched him right back, his little Afro-Amer-Asian daughter.

And that was our family, all of us together in the room

drinking punch, admiring the flowers, huge vases of tulips and yellow roses, exulting over Sung's triumph. We were a group I had never fully pictured when I first thought about a family. How could I have?

    Our family. On the occasion of our younger son's college graduation. We took his picture next to a vase of tulips, red, blue-black, and magenta. We took another one with his siblings and their children. Somebody offered to pose all of us. "Say Fulbright," the guy joked. And we did.

* * *

I could see the highlights in her blonde hair, the navy-blue purse that she used as a wedge to make her way through the crowd. I looked away from her, looked back at the graduate—but I was caught, as if she'd lassoed me and thrown me to the ground. I was never good in those situations. Most of the time I came across as defensive. Even the graduate told me to chill once. We were an unusual family, he said. People didn't mean to be rude. I should expect that people would want to know about us.

    Maybe. But what I most loved, my family, wasn't easy to explain. Most times, I didn't want to. Explaining felt like reducing the children to quality and quantity, like the purchase of a house or car. Something with a column of plus and minus signs. It was never like that.

    I wanted to be in that room, taking pictures, eating and drinking. Period. I wanted to look around through the slick of my own happy tears and absorb the fuss and glory, store it someplace inside me. I wanted to keep every one of us in that room as long as I could. All of us together, breathing free and easy at the summit.

"Sung," I said, "honey, I'm so glad."

"Bro," his older brother said, "you did great."

"I can't believe I got it, not with that redo on my record." He meant the microeconomics course he'd failed and had to retake one wretched semester. "Still," he added, "I do have it." He shoved his hand into his pants pocket like he was checking for a receipt. "Off to Austria come fall. Two more years of German! Man!"

* * *

I felt her touch, caught the scent of vanilla. She'd probably eaten a cupcake.

I turned to her. She looked like somebody I might talk to in line at the grocery store. We'd complain about the packaged baby carrots that always went bad before we finished them. We'd agree that since the store had been remodeled, it was hard to find things. We might be friends for the space of time we stood in line.

I waited.

Her hand rested lightly on the sleeve of my linen blazer.

"Is he yours?" she asked, pointing to Sung, her index nail red as one of the tulips. "Is he your son? Did you adopt him?"

There was an easy answer to that question. I might have said, "Yes," if that would have been the end of it. "Yes." Just that, no more. But I was pretty sure it wouldn't have been the end. Likely she would want to know *why* and *how* and *what was it like?* Probably she would want to know about the other son, the daughter, their small children. And then she'd want to know how we came to be a family. What was it like?

And how would I answer her?

Chapter 2

YELLOW DRESS

To begin, I will tell you there was a plane crash. We got our first child after the plane crashed. I won't start with that part of the story. It won't even be the biggest part. But there was a plane full of babies that crashed. Most of the babies on board were killed. We were never told whether our baby was on that plane or not, but he definitely came to us after we had lost hope. It was a very circuitous route to get that baby. He came to us by way of a phone call, a whole month after the plane crashed.

It seemed like it would be any normal phone call, maybe my mother or one of my sisters, a little verbal exchange, some connection. We were separated by hundreds of miles. I was in Ann Arbor, home to the University of Michigan, the school where Ken had taken a job, in a town that liked to bill its university as the Harvard of the Midwest. My family was in Saint Marys, a remote town in northwestern Pennsylvania. A person has to leave the highway and drive for an hour on hilly back roads to get there. Saint Marys. Founded by German nuns, Mariendstadt, City of Mary: city of churches, bars, and factories.

Likely we'd catch up on news and say how much we missed each other. But it wasn't that kind of call. I answered the phone in May of 1975, and after that, nothing was the same. "Mary," Ken said, when I told him the news. "Are you sure?" I was. We were going to be parents. Out of the blue, just like that. Parents of a baby come all the way from Vietnam, a baby who had made it out of chaos and then spent a month in a San Francisco hospital. A might-not-have-lived baby, so sick from complications of chicken pox that he'd spent weeks in intensive care. But he was fine by the time I took the phone call. He'd gained weight, weighed about fourteen pounds, and was maybe eight or ten months old. We would need to make sure a pediatrician saw him right away, but he could be our baby if we wanted him. He would arrive at Detroit Metro Airport in two days.

We hadn't even known he existed. I rattled off the news to Ken, who was at work, and took a breath.

"Yes, yes! It's unbelievable. Come home as soon as you can." We passed kisses through the phone, and I hung up to call our families, mine in Saint Marys, Ken's in Cleveland. After I'd talked to everyone I could think of, I went out to buy a dress. I wanted something that would signify my new life, the same way my wedding gown had. I wanted a dress that signaled new mom. I wouldn't shop at Moms To Be. I wasn't that kind of mother. I bought the dress from the old Goodyear's on Main Street in downtown Ann Arbor. A yellow sundress, exactly what I wanted. I tried it on for Ken when he got home. He swore I'd be the prettiest mother ever to get a baby at an airport. Such a nice thing to say. And then, on the way to collect that baby, I slammed the car door on my dress. A piece of yellow flew down the highway with us, flapping in the wind, like a pennant. I never noticed until I got out of the car. A line of dirt ran across the bottom, just above the hemline.

"Too bad," said Ken.

"I don't care," I said to him, grabbing for his hand, dismissing my new dress as if it mattered not at all. What was a dress? We were getting a baby. Ken squeezed back and we broke into a run-walk as we made our way to domestic flights.

* * *

It was something like that when I left town on my wedding day, almost ten years before we drove from our house to the airport. I was so eager to move out into a new life that I never changed from my wedding gown, just walked away from the reception and jumped into the secondhand Impala Ken drove. My wedding dress caught in the door, and my veil flew behind as we drove off, windows open, waving backhanded to my parents standing on the sidewalk, Ma in her green chiffon, Dad in his tux. I watched them from the rearview mirror, never turned to look back. My parents stood there waving. My dress was caught in the door, my veil was whipping in the wind, and then Ken turned the corner, and my parents disappeared.

The day we left to get the baby, it felt like leaving Saint Marys all over again, that same kind of urgency. *Whoosh I left Saint Marys and went off with Ken. Whoosh I answered the phone, and we went off to get a baby.*

Less than forty-eight hours after that phone call, I turned to look back as we ran out of the parking structure. There was our car with a blue infant seat in it. We'd bought it at Sears. Before we slept that night, someone would claim it.

We stood in the lounge waiting, dead center.

Ken's fingers wrapped around mine. "Are you all right? Do you want something to drink, tea, water?" He sounded like a birthing coach. I loved his earnestness, loved standing with him in the terminal at Detroit Metro, a full two hours early, neither one of us willing to risk a mess-up. We were to look for a flight attendant wearing a nametag that said Dusty. She'd have our baby.

A drink? No. I wasn't going to have Ken leave our spot for a minute. We stood still, locked in place. We studied the walls, the rows of blue plastic chairs, memorized the industrial gray carpet, stray pages of newspapers, and somebody's lost or left-behind copy of *Looking for Mr. Goodbar*.

People went by. They pushed luggage carts, scanned the crowd for someone they couldn't find. Not one of them had a clue about the couple who held a navy-blue gym bag between them filled with diapers, a bottle, a blanket, and a stuffed bear that played Brahms's *Lullaby*.

We watched fluorescent light shine on vending machines, heard the chink of coins dropping, cans falling. Everything around us was magnified, and nothing had relevance.

What mattered was somewhere in the sky.

It was almost time and then it was time.

I took a few ragged breaths and squeezed Ken's hand. He pointed to the sign that blinked to let us know the plane had landed. "This is it. This is it. This is it."

A guy wearing brown cords walked up and stood near us. He held a bouquet of red carnations in front of him and smiled at me. I gave a smile back to him. He was waiting for somebody too. Ken wasn't looking at anybody by then. He stared straight ahead, stiff smiling.

* * *

I loved that smile, his nervous smile. He smiled like that when he came to fetch me, the small-town girl living in Saint Marys, PA, the girl who would go off to Cleveland with him. The town had a sign at its entrance back then. *Saint Marys, The Carbon Center of the World*. Carbon factories made bearings, seal rings, bushings. Carbon smoke rose up and over everything. A washing hung on the line in the morning was coated with soot by afternoon. Women learned to look toward the smokestacks and gauge the amount of time their washing could be left outside. I didn't want to do washing underneath smokestacks. I wanted to leave the town and its factories, and I was leaving. Ken had come to marry me. He had reservations for Honeymoon Haven and a ring in a black velvet box. He showed me brochures of the place where he proposed to spend our honeymoon: a small-time resort in the Pocono Mountains. Wherever he wanted to go was fine with me. I read the brochures and licked my lips at pictures of piled-high shrimp, baskets of strawberries, a bathtub shaped like a heart. I had never eaten shrimp, was more than ready to lower myself into a red porcelain heart.

I was travelling with nuns when I met him. I was fifteen years old, a reluctant student in a Catholic high school, a dreamer who lived in the town library and wrote for the school paper. There was a conference for high school journalists, at Saint Bonaventure University near Olean, New York. Not an important conference for sure, but Sister Anita was eager and she was mentor to the paper. Off we went: we writers, Sister Anita, and her companion, Sister Imelda. Travelling a whole three hours away. I'd never been that far from home. My family made do. We did not travel. I lay awake the night before we left, wild with excitement. I wore a green dress with a flared skirt, which I hoped would be adequate for the occasion. I went to the morning sessions and took careful notes. Lunch was in the dining hall. Six of us writers sat at a long table eating chicken and rice. The nuns dined separately.

And that's when I met Ken. He smiled at me. Maybe, he noticed my green dress, my blue eyes. He was a boy still, although I didn't see that. What I saw was somebody who seemed assured, grown up. Somebody wearing a navy-blue suit. Back home guys wore suits for weddings, proms and graduations, and funerals. Some older men wore suits to church Sundays. Ken looked: not handsome, but arresting, like a young Daniel Day- Lewis. I listened to him laughing with his friends, talking about the conference, and, just that quick, I decided that he was somebody I wanted. *Mine.* I saw this guy who said he was from Cleveland, seventeen, a senior in high school. He'd driven to Olean, New York, for the conference, he and his friends from high school. That impressed me. I had been only to places within range of Saint Marys: Toby Valley, Clear Fork, Dubois. And the woods; I'd been in the woods because Saint Marys is at the edge of the Allegheny National Forest. If Ken had needed me to identify a rattlesnake, I could have done that. If he had wanted me to talk about the Brontë sisters or Nathaniel Hawthorne I could have done that too. But I didn't know much else. Not everyone growing up there was so insular, so ignorant of the larger world, so—there is no other word—naive. I was. I lived in the books I read and ignored almost everything else.

 Ken didn't need me to identify a rattlesnake, but he didn't seem shocked by my lack of sophistication either. He pulled a map from his pocket and showed me the route from Cleveland to Olean. I studied it earnestly. He talked about the college he planned to attend, easily, casually:, Case Institute of Technology in Cleveland. "He's a nerd," said one of the guys, nodding at Ken. "He's got a full ride to college, and he's majoring in physics." College? No one in my family talked about college. Physics? I failed algebra my freshman year. Ken smiled and waved the comment aside. "What are you interested in?" He was asking me and he seemed to want to know. Well, I read and I memorized words, collected them. "I like words," I said. "I like to have more than one word at hand." He nodded as if he understood.

Then he finished his chicken and polished off a plate of Neapolitan ice cream.

I watched him eat his ice cream and considered my options. I knew something about hunting. I'd listened to my father talk about tracking deer, bear, turkey; a person had to be both steady and quick to come home with game. I thought for the smallest minute, and as soon as Ken was done with his ice cream, I offered him mine. Then, when he took it, I smiled and called him greedy, my voice low and as sexy as I could make it. He laughed. He knew I had him in my sight line and he seemed fine with that. The truth is, no matter that it seems unbelievable, maybe appalling, I think I'd have gone with him right then, if he had asked me. Driven off with him that day, wearing my green dress, leaving Saint Marys and its hills behind. Abandoning my family, the place I lived in just like that, no note, not even a backward glance.

I was eager for living and had no idea what it costs to leave people and a place behind. I had only an obscure vision of what life *might* be. That's what I was like back then. "A hick," I tell my friends and Ken's amused family. I was an ignorant hick. Completely naive. My friends protest, disbelieving, say I'm exaggerating, but I'm not.

Ken had sense. He did not suggest that we take off together, no matter that he liked my green dress and blue eyes. "Let's be patient, get to know each other," he said. He was headed back to Cleveland. He leaned close and gave me a little half hug, not even a kiss, nothing rushed about the guy. He sniffed at the smell of my Avon Skin So Soft. "Nice," he said. He drove off in his blue suit, back to his city and his high school. I went back to Saint Marys with the nuns. I returned to my mostly bad grades. I rarely did my schoolwork. It didn't compel me the way the Brontë sisters did; school did not allow me to escape. I wanted a world that held possibility and I couldn't find it in school. I brooded all the way home, convinced I would never see Ken again. Why would he, a city guy, a brainy guy, head into the wilds of Pennsylvania to see me?

But he did. He drove into those woods and he found me there. He kept making those trips to see me while he went on to college and I finished high school. After that, I spent two years working in a lamp factory, testing light bulbs. A continuous row of bulbs went by on a conveyer belt. My job was to check every one for broken filaments or an incomplete solder. I was waiting for Ken to finish his undergrad degree. The attic of our house holds five full cartons of letters we wrote in those years. The letters are full of plans for our life, the progress of Ken's studies, the books I read when I got off work. It was nothing for us to write nine- and ten-page letters, using both sides of the paper. The letters, plus some phone calls and occasional visits, carried us through those years. When I read those letters now, it's clear how naive we were, but it's also clear how we managed to figure out *who* we were. One of the letters I wrote to Ken describes my dislike of the job I had. "No one is mean to me," I said. "It's not even that the work is hard, but it's boring. I want to go to school and learn to do something interesting." He had no problem with that. It would require strict budgeting, but Ken had been a saver from the time he got his first paper route, and a community college, the only place that would accept me with the grades I had, would not be expensive. I could probably manage a work-study program.

As soon as Ken graduated from college, we married. We held hands walking back down the aisle to the foyer of the church and we called out to everyone there, "We did it!" Our parents exchanged commiserating looks with each other: *too young, too young*. But we paid them no mind. We had waited it out and had married each other—we could do anything at all. I married Ken, and then, about a year after we were married, with his encouragement, I enrolled in college.

* * *

"We'll do this," Ken said to me, still looking straight ahead, still smiling in his serious way, his hand tight in mine. The arrival of the baby's flight was announced. "This is going to change our lives," he said, "but we'll do it." I believed him. He was the guy with a PhD in nuclear physics by then, a researcher at the University of Michigan. No longer the boy-man who sped me out of Saint Marys. He was a man who drove cautiously to the airport to meet our son who was coming to us straight down from the sky.

The baby came off the plane in a little portable cave. A flight attendant held the carrier and looked around. That had to be Dusty, had to be our baby. I fretted that she'd hand the baby to someone else. Maybe she'd give the baby to the guy with the carnations. He was snapping somebody's picture as she walked toward him, hair clipped back from her face, black leather purse slung over her shoulder. They made a good-looking couple. Dusty might give the baby to the guy with the carnations, the woman with the black leather purse. Besides, they had a camera, and we hadn't remembered a camera. What kind of parents wouldn't have remembered a camera?

And we had no proof! No papers, no signatures, not even a sign to hold. Surely we should have had proof. Something!

But no proof was needed. Recognition took no time at

all. Only one couple looked as if they were about to implode. Dusty—I could read her nametag—walked up to us and said, "You're the couple, right? The Koral couple?"

We reached for him.

I could see his eyes in that cave, dark with the epicanthic fold.

* * *

We were told that this baby was found in the Delta and taken upstream. V823367 were the numbers assigned to him for identification. He was called Nguyen when he arrived at the hospital. We called him Jason. He is so cheerful. He rarely fussed even when he was sickest. Everybody loves him. He will be missed.

That was the note that came with him; it must have been intended for us. But it wasn't addressed to us, not even a generic *Dear Parents*. It was a quick note, possibly written by a nurse in that San Francisco hospital, somebody who had been fond of the baby and stopped midshift to write about his cheerfulness and his two names. He had been there long enough for someone to grow attached. But who told the nurse he had been taken up from the Mekong Delta? Was it fact or supposition? Had he been on the plane that went down? Did he leave Saigon at the very last minute, shoved into a bus by his desperate mother? We never knew. Still, I was grateful for that note, a scrap of our baby's story.

Our first child.

The one who came happy, unexpected, like free fall, like

he had no story beyond that scrap of paper. A child who would want to know all of his story later on, searching, grabbing whatever he could find, unable to find the smallest satisfactory bit. All of his past, when he was born, where he was born, whether he cried a lot or a little, the story of who he was, lost somewhere in Vietnam. Our baby who came to us by way of a phone call and a plane ride. The very last baby that our adoption agency, Friends for All Children, had to offer. It couldn't happen that way now. It required a war.

Saigon was in panic mode in the spring of 1975. Every day brought more terror. In fact, V823367 might have been the identification tag of the baby we took from Dusty in the airport. Or not. Who knows if someone trying to get the babies out of a land gone crazy didn't grab any available identification and attach it to a baby needing ID? Who would have cared at that point? Reliable information about the babies, what happened to their birth parents, had never been easy to come by. Mothers who are desperate enough to leave their babies don't usually include information about the baby; so many times information went missing; disaster was the only reliable thing to believe in. Even Operation Babylift, which was supposed to avert disaster, became a disaster.

In April of 1975, as Saigon collapsed and Americans fled, people worried that babies in orphanages that had been run by Westerners would be killed by the Viet Cong. So adoption agencies, ours included, persuaded then-President Ford to fly the babies out of Saigon. It might be, not okay exactly, but necessary, to leave adults behind, but not babies! We couldn't leave the babies. Ford agreed. How could he not? And that's how the Operation Babylift happened. A C-5A Galaxy cargo plane left Vietnam April 4, 1975, with babies strapped three and four to a seat. Babies in cardboard boxes on the floor. Babies held in laps. *Get the babies out! As many as possible!* Forty miles from Saigon, the rear cargo doors of that plane blew off, and the plane crashed in a rice paddy.

Babies fell out of the sky and drowned in the mud. They burned to death or were crushed by plane parts. We killed the babies we intended to save. When we heard the news, Ken sat on the back steps of our green house, his shoulders heaved inside his maroon shirt. I held his arm and cried with him. We had no idea if a baby meant for us was on the plane, so we couldn't cry for a *specific* baby. We cried for loss: dead babies, dead workers, our hopes. A weeping volunteer from our agency, Friends for All Children, called about three days after the news broke to say that because of the crash we were unlikely to ever get a baby. "You understand that we have to try to replace the babies that were already assigned," she said. "Although, we can't replace them. You hadn't been assigned a baby yet, so I don't hold out much hope." We didn't either. We moved around inside the house like we were in mourning, a strange kind of miscarriage.

So how did we get our baby? We got him because he wasn't supposed to live. He wasn't in the "baby inventory" that the worker had available when she called us after the crash. He was in intensive care. A might-not-live baby. Hard to believe that something like chicken pox can do that to a baby, but it can.

Beverly was the one who called with the good news a whole month after the plane crash. We were just coming out of our grief, had no plans for a baby. The biggest thing on our agenda was a movie that night. I answered the phone and heard her offer the managed-to-live baby to us.

"It was close," she said. "There was another family ahead of you on the list, but I pleaded for you. I pointed out the other family had children. You do not have kids and it says right on your file that you're unlikely to be able to. It just seemed fair. The board agreed with me. I felt like cheering."

So did I. We would get to have a baby!

Who was he? Maybe he was a baby who had been shoved through the window of a bus leaving Saigon, his mother wailing as she handed him over? You can see pictures of those scenes if you want. You can Google them, but they're hard to look at. There is still controversy over the adoption of those Vietnamese children and the baby lift. There are accusations that the children had families in Vietnam, that identification was inaccurate, that the adoption agencies acted in haste. Those babies should have been left in Vietnam! But our baby was not left in Vietnam. We had him and that was everything.

We sat in one of the blue plastic chairs and looked at him. Would we be good parents for him?

The baby laughed when we lifted him to us, a wrapped-up bundle of eyes, four teeth, and masses of pockmarks. And although he had been a might-not-live baby, he was more than ready to live when he was handed over to us. He was a little underweight for American babies, but he looked alert and eager. He laughed and we were his, gone over the edge into crazy love. Although, I remember wondering, just for a second: What if the pockmarks didn't fade? What if he was scarred? Right then, he looked like a picture in a medical textbook, every inch of him covered in pockmarks. I shoved the thought aside. Once that baby came off the plane, handed over to us by Dusty, who looked at the two of us standing there shaking with fright and excitement and said, "You're the couple, right?" —it was a done deal. We were his parents. Parents of a baby we had never even heard of two days before—could not have imagined.

* * *

Birth is physical, a process begun and ended in the body. Adoption relies on the evanescence of *one word*, "yes." One word and we became parents.

We took a child we didn't know; we never gave it a second thought. Ken looked down at our son, who was staring at us, waiting to see what would happen. "You know," Ken said, "you are a pig in the poke, Baby Pig in the Poke. That's what you are. I've spent more time buying a car, a pair of shoes even. But, you're here!" The baby didn't cry. He looked while Ken pointed out things in the waiting room, the chairs, the carpet, the copy of *Mr. Goodbar*. "This is our place," Ken said. "It's where we start our life together."

* * *

"It worked out?" people ask us. They asked that question for years, still ask it. Their incredulity irks me, even though I suppose the question's reasonable enough. I know the coming of our first child and the two who followed are not the way most people make a family. Most of the time, two people meet; they love each other; they imagine the baby they'll make: *My nose, your forehead. My flexibility, your skill at tossing a ball.*

We imagined nothing beyond a child. If we could have a child, we'd take the child, no questions asked. Maybe now, after all that has happened, we, ourselves, are taken aback by our impetuousness. So naive! How could we be so naive?

But back then, if we stopped long enough to think at all, back then, we thought of the arrival of our son—as if the sky had lit up over the entire Detroit metropolitan area and out of that light had come our son. "Yes," we wanted him. "Yes," and he came home with us.

We drove back from the airport with the complete-stranger-but-ours baby, *Nguyen*, the name he was called in Vietnam. We tried the name. "Nguyen, baby boy, Nguyen." Nguyen is pronounced like *when*. Was it the name his birth mom gave him? Maybe. Or not. I imagined kids calling to him . . . *Nguyen, Nguyen, big fat hen*. A name likely to give grief on the playgrounds of Ann Arbor, Michigan.

No, no, no. "How about Minh?" I'd stayed up late studying Vietnamese male names before he came. Had no idea whether or not he had a name. Minh was easy on American ears. He'd still have to tell people how to say his name, but it was an easy fit.

"Later," we said to each other, "he can take the name he wants."

Minh. He has kept the name. It means peaceful. It suits him, our smiling oldest son.

"Hey, baby boy, Minh," Ken called over his shoulder as he drove us home.

I turned around to look at our baby. He looked lost back there, so I climbed over the seat to sit with him. I held his hand and he seemed to like that.

We were so dazed with him, traveling *home with him*, that Ken missed the turnoff for Ann Arbor and we headed west toward Jackson. We laughed and agreed it was typical of the way the whole process of adoption was for us, bad roads, detours, missed turnoffs, and then the baby like a stretch of brand-new road.

I could not carry a baby to term.

We had been trying for almost two years to adopt by the time

The Year The Trees Didn't Die

Minh came to us; we'd found the agency that worked in Vietnam by luck. Pat, a friend of ours, an Amer-Asian doctor, had volunteered in an orphanage run by Friends for All Children in Vietnam. She'd met people who knew how to start the process and she gave us the contact information when she came back home. Why did we choose international adoption? There's an easy answer to that. The seventies had seen a rise of single mothers and abortions, which resulted in a years-long waiting list for domestic babies. So, international adoption was appealing. Babies and toddlers were available. The wait for a child was nowhere nearly as long. And it felt safer. The birth mom would be unlikely to appear at our door asking for her baby back. That's what I thought. I don't know that it's to my credit, but it is what I thought. Harder to explain is why we picked Vietnam and not Korea or even, say, the Dominican Republic. We knew Maria and Felipe from Santo Domingo. We had met them when Ken was in grad school, and they offered to help us with an adoption. They were sure they could find us a baby in the Dominican Republic. We were grateful, almost ready to go ahead with the Dominican Republic, and then we didn't. So much is nebulous when I try to understand why Vietnam, not someplace else. Why do we pick one place to live and not the other? One person to love and not another? We give what we think are solid reasons, but a lot is amorphous. Pat had come back from Vietnam, in love with the country and the children. Once she handed us the name of that agency, we moved forward with the process of adopting from Vietnam. We got a home study, had background checks, sent off information to the agency, and waited. We watched the horror of the news every night. Then the plane crash, the phone calls, and the baby.

  When we pulled into the driveway, it was still light, spring edging to summer, and there was a yard full of neighbors, friends, some people we didn't know at all. *Everybody* wanted to see the sky kid. They looked at him as if he were Jesus in the Nativity scene. They reached for him, wanted to touch him, his arm, a hand, a foot. He was a helpless thing, that Vietnamese baby. So, all those people did exactly what people do with babies. What I suppose even the Magi did with Jesus. They crooned to him, begged to feed him, to hold him. They offered him soft new blankets in blue and butter yellow.

The agency mailed us a guide sheet for new adoptive parents. It came in the mail a few days after Minh came home with us. The sheet was generic and mimeographed—no computers and printers in 1975. We read it every day for a long time. One of us held Minh and the other one read aloud. I needed to hear the words; they soothed me.

> *Go slowly. Do not expose the child to many strangers. These children have been traumatized. Keep foods simple. Do not introduce too many toys or people at once. Be sensitive to changes in routine or environment. Be aware that the child misses the familiar. Be patient. Do not expect too much, too soon.*

Sometimes the words felt vaguely like instructions for a television or a toaster oven. This baby we already loved so much had such a *small* story. But we were glad for what we had and we studied the lines one by one. We wanted to be good parents, so glad that he was sitting in a high chair in our kitchen. Only a fool would ask for more. Who could want more than a child who let us rock him, walk with him, feed him? A child who grew more teeth, whose pockmarks slowly faded, who laughed when we poked his belly?

Chapter 3

ASIAN BABY VISITS SAINT MARYS

I had planned for my life to be filled with kids and the wealth of the everyday. I could hardly wait. And then I surprised myself. I, who couldn't leave town fast enough, cried in those early days for what I had left behind. When I called home teary, Ma answered. "Oh Mary," she said, "I knew you'd miss us." And I did.

In the very early days of our marriage, we lived on savings. Ken was great at managing money, far better than I was. He had studied hard, won a full ride to college, worked summers and saved, saved, saved, so he could come to get me with his brand new bachelor of science degree and a savings account that would allow us to be married. It was a game for us to see how little we could spend that first year; we didn't want much, completely enamored with each other. Ken applied to the PhD program at Case while I spent that first year in Cleveland looking in store windows, wandering around learning how to use the bus system and the Rapid Transit. We had a tiny box of a place. I was given three keys, one to unlock the outer door, which let me into a small lobby, then, after I climbed three flights of steps, another to unlock our apartment door. There was, also, a very small key to unlock the mailbox in the lobby. It was all new to me. We didn't lock doors in Saint Marys.

I made roast chicken, which was cheap. I learned to cook it with rosemary. I read nonstop. At night, I saw shapes of people in windows across the way. People who ate, smoked, put their feet up, sipped something from a cup, not one of them close enough to touch, no one I knew. How was it possible that I was where I wanted to be and ached with loneliness? But that's how it was. I had just turned nineteen and had yet to figure out how to make that world of possibilities that I wanted. Oh, I had some ideas. I loved much of the world I inhabited in Cleveland, the books, the days I could order any way I wanted. I loved Ken, but I had an undercurrent of uneasiness.

I missed home. I wanted to see my father, a carpenter, who would come in the back door every night and yell for someone to pull off his Red Wings. He never said "please." He never said "thank you." He expected us to be ready to pull his boots off and we lined up to do it. He worked two shifts six days a week, roofing, nailing houses together, pouring concrete. That's what it took to keep us fed. When I think about my father back then, he is sitting on a kitchen chair, his legs stretched out straight, waiting for someone to pull off his boots. I see my mother handing him a plate of potatoes and eggs, with a side of bread. He breaks the yolk of each egg over the potatoes and dips the bread into the yolk. He eats in silence. I see him pull his Red Wings on again, the leather sweat salted. My father was demanding, a person to issue commands, not requests. But he came in the back door every night; I missed that. I missed him and his Red Wings.

I missed my mother and the way she hung her wash on the line: white sheets, then towels and washcloths, green work pants, green work shirts. Everything perfectly graduated in length and color. I missed my brothers, both of them. They were always gone hunting or fishing, but I missed them anyway. I missed Rosie and Barb, my closest sisters. I missed the younger kids, Kathy, and Raye Ann, the baby—the one with a brown eye and a blue eye. As if Ma and Dad were worn out making babies and put the last of the seven babies they had together the best they could.

I missed what I *had known*.

Later on, I saw that loneliness in my kids sometimes. They were where they wanted to be. They loved us; they did not want to lose us; did not want to leave their home with us. Still, they grieved. I would learn to allow the ache. Allow them to be sad for what they *couldn't know*.

So, after we got our baby, I was crazy to take him back home, introduce him to the hills and the family I had left behind. Three months after he came to us, we took Minh back to the hills. He was exotic back there, unusual, worthy of comment. People talked about him the way they talked about a week of weather that was ninety degrees plus—something that almost never happened in the mountains. He was a rarity.

My mother was shocked when I told her we were trying to adopt a child from Vietnam. She had stood still, a hand raised to pin a sheet to the clothesline, and said to me, "Blood is thicker than water." I felt as if she'd kicked me. I knew what she meant all right. She was only saying what almost everyone else in town would have said to me. But I hadn't expected her to say it. What if she didn't accept our baby? Well, if she didn't, she didn't. I *was* going to adopt, no matter what.

But, my mother could not resist a baby. She came across the yard clicking two wooden clothespins together when we arrived with our son, luring the Vietnam-born baby to her. He was, even then, eager to grab. He reached for Ma's clothespins and she let out a yelp. "Ha," she said. "You said he'd be scared but he's fine. Give him to me." I held on to him, ignoring her and Minh's willingness to go to her, his eagerness to grab her clothespins. I wanted to be sure he knew I was the mom. The mom with her arms forever open, the mom who cared nothing about blood or water.

* * *

My mother was a woman who seemed to be alive only when she was having a baby. Something about an infant made her smile, but the minute the baby lost its newness, started to grow into a child, Ma became sad.

Was it because one of her babies had died, living only for a day? Ma grieved for the brother I never knew. "He's an angel," she said to Rosie, to me.

Was she sad because her mother had died giving birth? What name might be given to her grief? No one ever tried to name my mother's sadness, but it dominated our lives. As a kid, I wanted my mother to reach for me, the way she reached for Minh the day I brought him to see her. I'd come home from school and stand by the side of her bed waiting for her to get up. She'd lie there, her face pressed into a pink chenille spread, hands underneath the pillow, a person who had gone and left a mannequin behind.

She hid herself.

She hid things too. She hid boxes of crackers and sticks of meat in the back of the cupboard behind the cast-iron fry pans. She left her room in the middle of the night to find her secrets. I heard her scuffling in her slippers, scrabbling in the cupboard. She ate her crackers and meat in the dark of the kitchen, a shape, a blur. I watched sometimes from the doorway.

There came a time when I watched, not my mother, but my children stash food away, turn their faces away from me. The time came when they hid secrets way back where I couldn't find them, when they became shapes I sought to define. They blurred and moved away from me. I watched my kids do that and, sometimes, I wondered if they had been coached by my mother.

The Year The Trees Didn't Die

In my kid years, I decided I didn't have a mother, no matter that my mother insisted she did the best she could, talking to me facedown on her bed, her words flattened. "You don't know how good you have it." She pulled a hand out from under the pillow and pointed in the direction of the kitchen toward the bread she'd baked, the floors she'd scrubbed, pointed to my new Easter coat hanging in the hallway. What more did I want? She never had bread or coats when she was growing up. Her mother died when she was seven. "Seven," she said. "Seven. I'd have given anything to have a mother." I never believed her, a hard-hearted girl wanting an ideal mother. Maybe we all want that mother, the mother who makes so much food, such delicious food, that we eat it and want for nothing more. If we don't have that mother, we spend years hunting her, bereft when we don't find her. My mother mourned the absence of her mother. The best she could do most days was to bury her face in her pillow and take long naps on top of pink chenille. When she raised her face from the pillow, the shape of a rose was imprinted on her cheek. I yelled at her, "Get up! Get up!" She blinked at me and burrowed deeper. I yelled louder, my voice thick with fear and rage, "You think bread's enough?" I was sick of bread. She replied, calm and distant, as though she were halfway to dead, close on the trail of her mother, "Bread's enough."

Even if the rope that connects the mother to the child is made of flesh, twisted in blood and sweat, it can be cut. If need be, it can be bitten. I ate bread and bit the rope of flesh between my mother and myself, determined to be nothing like her.

I reconsider now, a grown woman who's had her share of mothering troubles. I've learned some generosity, a bit of humility: Ma did not *plan* to leave her kids hungry, yelling by the side of her bed. Grief had her by the throat. She lived all of her life as if she were newly orphaned. Maybe all such a person *can* do is to lie still, facedown, hands under the pillow.

During the visit to Saint Marys, when we took Minh back for Ma to see, she reached for the new Vietnamese baby, all smiles and her face wide open, no mannequin in human form then. She reached for my baby and I didn't want to hand him over to her. I was his mother and I was going to be a *good* mother. Maybe such intensity created its own complications, but there it was.

Of course, Ma paid no attention to my fussing. She held out her arms to Minh, all the while clicking those clothespins. And Minh grabbed at her, or the pins, or both. He stuffed a clothespin in his mouth; Ma took the other end in her mouth and growled like a bear.

I continued to fuss. The baby was not *hers*.

Ma glanced at me and said, "I never needed a set of instructions to tell me what to do. You don't need guidelines." She meant the sheet of paper that had come with Minh, the one Ken and I had learned by heart. She scorned those guidelines. She lifted Minh up over her head, and he squealed.

"But it says to be careful, Ma, to take it easy with him. It's not like he's ordinary." What did I mean by that? Because he *was* ordinary: a baby boy with skin and teeth and hair and eyes, somebody willing to play with whatever came his way.

Ma brought him back down to her lap and raised her shoulders ever so slightly, the smallest confident shrug.

I shrugged back, smiled at Minh and held out my arms, waggled my fingers until he returned to me. Ma frowned. Then she suggested that we go take Minh to feed the bear.

I agreed.

Ken didn't want to. "What's the point?" He looked baffled, as if I had turned into someone who would feed our baby to the bear. Bear watching was what people *did* in Saint Marys, I said. Whole families piled into their cars with bags of day-old bread and drove out to the dump to feed the bear. They tossed bread out their windows and waited.

"We have to," I said.

Dad drove. It was a Sunday. He didn't work on Sundays. Ma sat up front. Ken and I and Minh were in back. Once we got there, it didn't take long before the bear came out of the woods, chuffing and pawing at donuts and bread. "Bears have a right to territory," said my father. "It's not the fault of the bear if a person gets mauled. It's the fault of the fool who got too close to the bear." I listened and shivered. I did not want to get mauled. I certainly did not want my father to call me foolish, so I kept my door locked, the window up while I watched the bear eat bread we had tossed out the window.

"Bear, Minh," I said, "bear." He looked, and then went back to playing with the clothespins Ma had brought along.

The next day, a reporter from the local paper came to see us, wanting Minh's picture, eager for a story about the Vietnamese baby visiting Saint Marys. He'd been at Pfaff's market when he heard someone say we were in town with a Vietnamese baby. He had never seen a Vietnamese baby before. He thought Minh was cute with his dark hair and dark eyes. "I've never even met a person from outside of Pennsylvania," he said, "and now I get to see a baby from Vietnam." He looked at our child as if we had brought a miracle into my parents' living room, as if he couldn't believe that actual babies lived in Vietnam. "Imagine," he said. "I can't believe he survived. What with the war and all," he added. Minh's picture was placed next to a picture of the bear underneath a headline that read, "Asian Baby Gets to See Local Wildlife."

Ken called it racist. I didn't want to think so, although I had no idea how I'd explain the headline to Minh later on. What would he think of it? The headline wasn't the kind of overt racism that refuses a person service, denies a person entrance. But Ken objected to the attitude that points out *otherness*. I could not articulate my sense of uneasiness though, much less explain it. Who would have understood? No one in Saint Marys, not even Barb and Rosie, my sister-friends. They would have been sad that I questioned the picture, distressed that Ken was upset. They wanted us to be happy to be home. I was happy.

I'd taken our son back to Saint Marys so he could claim a piece of what I had to give him. A complicated place, insular, not at all familiar with Vietnamese babies, unsure how to receive them. The place where Minh would always be *the other*: in the store, at the local pool. Still we went back three or four times a year, glad for the cocoon of family. And every time we went, Minh went home with pieces of the place: hand-knit afghans Rosie or Barb made, bread Ma baked, scrap lumber from Dad.

One time, a hammer and a box of nails. "Might as well teach him early," said Dad to Ken. We drove away, the three of us. Ken turned to wave. He honked, two quick beeps, and called out that he'd teach Minh how to hammer a nail. He'd teach him how to hit a nail straight on, hard and true.

* * *

I have to explain how it was that the girl who grew up with babies and her baby-crazy mother never insisted on making a baby herself. I was okay with writing "can't have children" on our adoption application. Why was that? Why didn't I try harder to make one? Isn't that what most women do if they want a baby?

What seems to be underneath that impulse is—*your own, one of your own*. If I can explain how I felt about making a baby, it might make the rest of the story easier to untangle.

It was early 1972. Everything was supposed to be natural, green and growing. Even shampoo smelled like apples. Ken and I liked rolling around together and something often took hold—there was an intake, a breath, a faint twitch—but every time, three or four months after the start, there it was, the same story all over again: splotched dark like spilled coffee, a smear of old blood gone brown, sometimes clots. Sometimes cramps and a trip to the hospital. Unlike my mother and the baby-crazy friends she had, women who sat in her kitchen and cried if they did not get pregnant, I would *not* cry for a baby. I wanted kids and the wealth of the everyday, all right. But. I didn't require a baby we made ourselves. I didn't feel that way at all.

I was willing to try though, so I lay on an examining table while a doctor searched around inside me. Like I was a defective part in one of those carbon factories back home. Ken had passed his test, so I was the culprit. "We could try surgery on your fallopian tubes."

"No," I said to the OB-GYN, who was doing his best to help us make a baby.

Even now, I am not sure when the idea of adoption took shape within me. Still, it was there that day in the examining room and I held to it. If I wanted children, what I had to do was reach out. I didn't have to cry or have procedures or wash out any more nightgowns. I could be a mother if I adopted, and there were children around. People were adopting children from Vietnam. Sometimes there would be a picture in the paper, a shot on the news. So, if I could love a child who emerged from someone else, I could be a mother. I didn't explain that to the doctor though. I thanked him and went home. "Give it another try," he said. "I'm not holding out much hope, but you never can tell."

* * *

"We should adopt," I said to Ken one morning while I ran water in the tub, put my creamy silk nightgown in to soak, the bloodstain drifting out over the water. We had given it another try, but the baby hadn't even taken hold that time. Ken leaned closer to the mirror to check on his shave and stayed quiet. Maybe he was puzzled by me. But I think he was willing. I think he took my idea in and made it his own. He turned from the mirror and gave me a hug.

He never said "infertile," as if I were a bad patch of ground, non-arable land. "You aren't infertile," he said, "you just lose your grip." I loved when he said that. And he was willing to begin the search for a child already born—to a woman who could grow a baby. Her problem was that, although she could birth the child, she couldn't keep the child. I could keep a child, but couldn't birth a child. We needed to find the woman and the child she could not keep. We could solve each other's problem. So straightforward, so simple. That's what I thought in my ignorance.

I was almost thirty. Ken was thirty-two.

I figured I'd be good at finding a baby because I'd grown up around hunters, in a place edged by woods. I knew how to search. I had used those skills to capture Ken, was sure that I could find a baby.

It surprises me that people often think of the adoption process as no kind of work. They seem to think adoption is the easy way to get kids, no trouble at all. As if a person filled out an order form and a kid was delivered. No work at all. It's true that the adoption itself, the acceptance of the child, requires only one word, *yes*. But there is work to get to the point where you can say, *yes*.

Still people mostly think of the work of *birthing* a child.

Lots of women told me over the years that the physical act of birth was one of the most intense experiences a woman could have. They were not being mean. They were only sharing what they saw as the universal experience. They were sorry that I didn't have that experience. They found it hard to understand why I did not work harder to have a baby. They would have had every test possible, considered any kind of medical procedure in order to be able to give birth. Sometimes, they reached to finger their stretch marks when they described the effort required to move their child down the birth canal. They held the memory of that effort within their bodies, relived the memory standing in parking lots, in line at Kroger—wherever women came together.

"Hours of pushing!" They cupped their hands over their stomachs while they talked. "They were almost ready to cut me. I don't know how I managed. Never again!" The women would smile and nod at each other.

But it was brag talk. Those women didn't believe that anybody climbing Everest or over-wintering in the Arctic had a thing on them. *They* knew what hard meant. They had experienced life. And they'd have done it over again, no matter what they said. Like the climbers on Everest gasping for air at high altitudes, struggling to stay upright, in pain, but going higher and higher, birth women remained in love with birth. I listened. It was the story of most mothers, but it was never my story. When I wanted to exchange nods with mothers who understood my story, I found other adoptive moms.

Chapter 4

LIFE IN A CAVE

When I look back at the time right after our first child came, I can see that we were unreasonably happy. We lived as though the center of everything was in our laps. Whatever else there was to be had in the larger world was peripheral.

We had him. We didn't need anything else.

Holding Minh, his laugh, the ease with which he loved us, made us blind to anything else. We went reeling through those days slugging down happiness.

The summer after Minh came off that plane, I stopped looking at him just long enough to begin work, in the smallest sense of the word, toward my MA in creative writing.

I had managed to get my undergraduate degree.

"What do you think?" I had asked Ken a couple of months after we settled into that apartment in Cleveland Heights. "Remember what I wrote to you? Although, I'm nothing like you. I have not been a good student. Do you think I could make it in college?"

"Do it," he said. He had the undergrad degree and had been admitted to grad school at Case Institute of Technology. He was going for a PhD in physics. "Do it," he said. "You're smart. You just need to believe it." I did it. I became an ace student, a woman who found a way to use those books she loved. I got my degree, no problem. "See?" said Ken.

Then we left Cleveland for Ann Arbor. Ken went to work as a research physicist in nuclear medicine at the University of Michigan. I considered the idea of earning a graduate degree. Maybe in literature? Creative writing?

I wasn't at all sure that I could manage a graduate degree though. Right after the move, while Ken went off to work, I spent lots of time thinking about what I should do. Maybe I should bide my time and work retail? There were plenty of used-book stores. I could be happy working in a used-book store. Then I met Ann, a woman who lived up the street from us. She had a two-year-old. She pushed the little girl in a red-plaid stroller around the block, while we carried mugs of coffee I'd made and discussed my life. The little girl tugged at me. I told Ann I wanted a child. I was ready. Ken and I wanted to make a family. So where were the children I was so sure I could find? "It'll happen," she said. "Then, we'll both be pushing strollers. We can take the kids to the lake and spend the day there." I liked her confidence; it gave me hope. So I waited, almost held my breath.

After Minh arrived, I reconsidered things. It was the seventies. Women were *supposed* to be able to manage babies and a career. I found a fiction-writing class at the University of Michigan, which would point me toward a graduate degree in creative writing. But I was pretty sure I'd never get into UofM's creative writing program, not with a baby. They only took students full time and I could never manage that. I went to class, worked hard, and went back home to the baby. And every chance I got, I reread the worn guide sheet that had come with our baby. I read it as if I thought that sheet would allow me to shape the story I wanted: beginning, middle, end. A graduate degree couldn't compete with Minh.

"I can't concentrate," I said to Ann. "I haven't written much at all that's worthwhile."

"I'm not surprised," she said. "Kids just come right on in and take over. Why don't you give yourself time?" So I did that. I held the baby and sang to him. I let the graduate degree drift off.

Mary J. Koral

* * *

He remembers the songs I made up. He sings one of them sometimes when he comes around, and then, teasing me, he says, "Pineapple tree!"—as if it's the dumbest thing.

> *Long time ago in Vietnam, a little boy named Minh*
> *climbed up, up. Up to the top of the pineapple tree*
> *and he picked pineapples and he threw them down*
> *and he gave them to his mommy*
> *and she made pineapple pie.*

It *was* dumb! But he fell asleep while I sang to him, lying under a quilt of multicolored elephants, purple, green, and blue, their trunks hooked one to another, his name, *Minh*, stitched across the trunk of the purple elephant. While he slept I watched him and wondered. How attached did I want him to be to Vietnam? Did I want him to think of Vietnam as home, his Vietnamese mother as his real mother? I did not. I wanted him to know about Vietnam; I wanted him to love it, but always to remain, by choice, with us in Ann Arbor, Michigan.

I wanted him to be happy: in our house with me, his mom, singing my made-up song. Isn't that what most of us want—a good strong cord that wraps around us, parents and children, and holds us together? We talked about his birth mother. "Birth mother" was the expression of choice. You could also say biological mother. But that was way too cumbersome. For a short time, when Minh was around two, we called her the pineapple mother. That made sense to him. But I worried that the expression made light of her. It was a made-up song, after all. I knew nothing about his mother. But we always, always said that his birth mother had done the best she could.

I still believe that the birth moms of my children made the best plans they could for the kids. Sometimes, one of the kids would snort in disbelief when I said this. When they were older. "Yeah, abandoning me was a good plan." But we'd always say they did not know the mother's story. After all, the kids were not thrown down a well. They were not tossed into a garbage can. The birth moms made the best plans they could. "Your Viet mom made the best plan she could for you," I told our oldest. "She wanted you to be safe and happy."

And it seemed as if we had managed safe and happy.

Did we never once anticipate *trouble*? Trouble was the warning of the adoption workers. In one guise or another it appeared on every application sheet we ever filled out, *no guarantee, no guarantee*. You had to be willing to take a chance. There would be no records of any kind. There would be no promises of a healthy, happy child. I remember sitting down with our very first social worker after we started the process to adopt from Vietnam. We sat there in her office all nervous, knowing she had the job of approving us for adoption in the state of Michigan. If she agreed that we were sound and stable, we could send our application off to Friends for All Children and they would begin the process of finding a child for us. She seemed distressed by our adoption choice. She wanted to know why. Why Vietnam? We told her about Pat who had given us a connection. It didn't take more than that for us. And maybe that seemed uninformed, as if we were so without a clue we shouldn't have even been trusted with a baby. But that's how it was. Plus we had met a child who was adopted from Vietnam.

One evening in the middle of winter, with old snow

hard-packed on sidewalks that somebody hadn't bothered to shovel—that kind of weather—we went to visit a couple who had adopted a little girl from Vietnam. We were introduced through friends at our church. "You should get to know each other. They've already adopted and you want to." We met them for the first time sitting in their living room on Ann Arbor's west side, the increasingly fashionable side of Ann Arbor. The section of town where artists and writers liked to live. We drank coffee and ate Pepperidge Farm cookies while we looked at photos of their child. They actually had pictures of her in her orphanage. We wanted a child like that! Is that so different from saying you want a child who has, say, your husband's good nose?

We watched their daughter, about six, maybe seven—with them for nearly two years at that point—go upstairs to bed in her pink robe over a pink Barbie nightgown, a perfectly happy child who blew kisses to her parents as she went up the stairs. And that was as far as we could see, only to the top of the stairs. Once the little girl reached the top of the stairs, she disappeared from view.

After that visit, I waved worry away like wasps buzzing around the plum tree in the yard where I had grown up . . .

"You can't be at all sure what you will have to deal with," reiterated the social worker. She had left her office and come to see us for the obligatory home visit. She sat in our living room nicely ignoring the fact that we had only one piece of actual living room furniture, an orange overstuffed chair from Ken's parents' house. We'd had it in Cleveland Heights and we'd taken it with us to Ann Arbor. Ken and I sat on kitchen chairs, straight and unyielding. Marilyn. The woman's name was Marilyn. She was earnest, sincere, and had never been involved with a foreign adoption before. She said she wasn't sure if we should go ahead. "You are young yet. If you can wait maybe two to five years, you could have a domestic baby. What you are planning to do is chancy. You will know nothing about the baby's background if you go the international route. It's not like a domestic adoption. With a domestic adoption, you would have some information about the prenatal care, an accurate health report, and probably some information about the parents." But we weren't persuaded. Somewhat doubtfully, she signed off on our home study.

Well, there are never guarantees. Not with birth, not with domestic adoption, not at all. Plus, after Minh arrived, we didn't think about a lack of a guarantee. If we thought about the future at all, we brushed it off like dust, weightless. Which only shows how little we knew. But we couldn't get enough of Minh and he never acted like a traumatized baby: no refusal to eat or middle-of-the-night terrors. It seemed as if he decided, the moment he got off that plane, that he was ready to be put into our story. Whatever we gave him was fine with him. It was all good stuff for Minh. It was as if he got up mornings figuring he would swallow pieces of happiness with his pancakes. So, we relaxed and ate the pancakes with him. We swallowed sweet ease.

* * *

He grew older though, and he started to reconsider those pancakes.

Once when he was four, he plopped down on the sofa between us and asked if we could make our eyes like his. I would have done anything for him, but I couldn't do that.

"I'm stuck with round eyes," I said. "You have a round-eyed mother." He fell flat on his back, stretched between Ken and me, laughing.

"Round eyes," he said. "Round eyes!" He played with the words, funniest thing he'd heard, kept saying them.

But then he stopped. And he asked about his other mother. What about her eyes?

He sat up between the both of us when he asked that question, waiting for our answer.

* * *

I always pictured her this way, still picture her this way:

Me. The word means mother in Vietnamese. She has a long wash of hair, the same eyes as his, the same skin; her feet are carved statues. She is swimming all the way from Vietnam, her lovely feet kicking water. She is beautiful, and she wants her baby back. She points to the high arch of her feet, the high arch of his feet. Their eyes are the same; their feet are the same.

Listening to my son call out, "Round eyes," I sniffed the smell of lemongrass, cilantro right there in the living room of the green house.

I looked at my kid, so completely *my* kid, Ken's kid. What if his Vietnamese mother materialized? What if she came for him? Impossible. Still. My stomach clutched. She *did* have first claim. I got up and took my son by his shoulders. Ken took his feet. We picked him up and swung him between the two of us.

"Your Vietnamese mother has eyes that look like yours. She has Asian eyes for sure. But you are stuck with round-eyed parents. You're stuck with us."

The answer barely masked the fact that I was afraid of the birth mother. She was always around, a whisper or the last bit of my dream, someone I could never be. Minh's question about our eyes was the beginning of all the questions that would follow through the years: about biology, adoption, identification.

If you are my mother and father, why don't we look like each other? Who is my mother? Where do I belong? Why did she leave me?

People like to say that little kids don't recognize physical differences. I wonder if it's not truer to say they don't know how to process what they see. We always talked about adoption with the kids, even when they had no way to understand the word. "We're an adoptive family," we said. We wanted the word to be easy to say, not a loaded word. There was never a moment to choose to tell them they were adopted. Our physical differences were clear. They always knew they had a mother who had not been able to take care of them. They always knew we were wild to take care of them.

"I wish you were my birth mother." Every one of the children said that at some point. "But then you would not look like yourself," I'd say. And sometimes they wouldn't care if that were so, and sometimes they wanted their other mother, the lost one. Mostly they decided that adoption was okay.

Adoption, we told them, was saying *yes*. Adoption was a choice to be a family, on their part as well as ours. It wouldn't work otherwise. And it *has* worked, even with the pain.

Minh was plenty happy. He was good at saying yes to family.

Every time we went out the door though, there were questions that cast doubt on the authenticity of our family. Questions that sometimes felt aggressive.

Does he know his real mother? Where is he from? Will he go back? Does he want to find his mother? I had not developed toughness, and the questions left me feeling that if there were medals given out for good mothers, I'd come in as an honorable mention. So wimpy. Always thinking of the perfect answer way too late.

Adoption does center on that one word, *yes*. "Yes, I will parent this child." That's the easy part. Adoption also centers on loss and that's the hard part.

My son's birth mother had to give up her child in order for me to say *yes*. She said *no*, and I said, *yes*. So, when people asked questions, I felt uneasy, maybe guilty. She was sad and I was glad. I didn't want her to be sad. But I wanted her child.

No matter that we knew nothing about her, we always told Minh that his birth mom was a *good person*. Somebody we would be in debt to all our lives. But I never said, never *thought* of saying, "She can have you back if she wants you. She has the best right." That little boy was *our* child.

He drew pictures of us. He colored our skins, half white and half brown. He gave us mixed eyes, one eye round, one eye slanted. He drew us that way. He understood, even then, that we were a mixed family. He came into our room and put the pictures on our pillows in the early morning. I woke to find strangers on my pillow.

We read books about Vietnam to him. We read *A Thousand Years of Vietnamese Poetry*—poems that promised good fortune to obedient sons, poems that sung the beauties of the country or wept for it, so often pillaged. We read until Minh looked up and asked us to stop—he'd had enough.

At the beginning of every Vietnamese New Year, we gave lucky money to our son inside a red envelope. We exploded firecrackers into a winter-white Michigan sky, ate spicy noodles, soup, and egg rolls. We arranged oranges in a pyramid, peeled and bit into them, bitter spray stinging our eyes. White faces of my husband and me, darker face of our son, whoever else we could gather. Two flags of Vietnam flying, the old and new. Minh was gifted the old flag from friends. We got the new one from a store.

One time, it was probably the year that Minh was four, the oldest member of the Vietnamese community in Ann Arbor came to visit us for the new year.

The Vietnamese in Ann Arbor were tight, a group of people who kept close tabs. They helped each other, found substitutes for foods they craved, negotiated bus routes. The old man heard about our adoption from friends, and he wanted to meet the boy who came as such a surprise. The old man used to *be somebody* in Vietnam, a scholar who had status, an elder. In Ann Arbor, he lived in a so-so apartment just off Packard on the south side of town. He spent his days doing his best to remain a scholar, living, I think, a kind of ghost life, somewhere in between Ann Arbor and Vietnam, eking out his relief check. We knew his visit was an honor, so we were plenty nervous. What if he thought we were a bad deal for that Vietnamese baby?

I consulted my friend Mui. We'd met each other at the library the summer after Minh came. She was roaming the stacks of the library looking for books to help her learn English when she spotted the two of us. "Vietnamese baby, right?" she said. "You have Vietnamese baby." I eyed her cautiously. Was she going to complain or, worse, thank me for taking her country's child, like I was somebody who refurbished drop-off kids? She did neither thing. She smiled at me, at the baby. She wanted a friend, somebody to help her with English. She was young, maybe early thirties, small and very thin, trying to learn how to live in the place where she'd landed. We hung out together. I learned how to make pho. She learned how to run a washing machine and live in an apartment that was painted white. Which made her nervous. So much white was dangerous. It invited death. She masked the color with plants: coffee cans with philodendron, old milk jugs cut in half with sweet potato vines growing up and around everything. I offered her an elephant ear plant, a big thing that she shoved into the mix. The white of the walls blurred to green and Mui breathed easier, the same way I did when I was with her. If plants blurred the white for Mui, she eased my newness as a mom to a Vietnam-born child.

 We were a good pair, the two of us, especially at the grocery store. I took her to Kroger, taught her about coupons and good deals. She was quick and paid attention to things like a sale on chicken breasts, but what she loved was Pepsi. She tossed two or three six-packs into her cart every time. I warned her that she had too much; she would rot her nice white teeth. She said the teeth weren't her own anyway. Her teeth had been pulled in a refugee camp. I reached across the cart to hug her, my friend who had lost her teeth, who didn't mind that I was parenting one of her country's children, who always called me Minh's real mother, who hated white walls. I loved her and she loved me back. She'd keep that love, even though years went by and we didn't see each other. She'd offer it to me one day when she saw me in a coffee shop. I would be emerging from my own kind of refugee life, learning how to live in the world again, and I'd be very glad for that love.

 Before the new year party, I headed to her apartment to make sweet rice cakes. I intended to serve them with the best green tea I could buy and mounds of oranges. The two of us worked in her kitchen, which smelled faintly of nuoc mam sauce, a narrow bit of a room with a gray-tiled floor that showed rust marks. Minh played with his Matchbox cars in the living room, then moved into the kitchen to pull things from her cupboards.

She let him take out the empty margarine tubs, the blue plastic bowls given to her by a local church group. She waved to us when we left with the rice cakes, calling after us, "Fine, fine, fine." Meaning I did a good job with the rice cakes.

The elder arrived. He removed his shoes and sat on our teal-green sofa in his black socks. He ate five rice cakes and an orange. He took Minh on his lap, sniffed his hair, his cheeks, and told him that he had to be a credit to two countries, South Vietnam, the mother country, and America, his adopted country.

We took pictures, and in the best picture, the old man's traditional scholar's beard is just behind our son's dark head. He has his arms wrapped around Minh and the long fingernail on his little finger, an old sign of a Vietnamese scholar, is clearly visible.

He reached into his pocket and gave Minh a red envelope. Inside the envelope there was lucky money, a new dollar bill folded into the shape of a green bird. Almost, it could have flown.

Chapter 5

BABY STEALER

Eventually, we have three children, and not one of those children comes with physical labor on my part. All three of them come to me by way of other women's labor.

When I think about that, it weighs on my mind, even after all these years. I remember what it was like in the years before the children landed in my arms: I was a woman waiting for the birth mothers to give birth in those years. I didn't think about adoption in those terms. But the description is more than a little accurate. While those birth mothers went into labor, pushing, sweating, crying out, having their babies in places I had never seen, I waited in Ann Arbor, in a house we had painted green, on the banks of the Huron River, ready for the babies to come and live in the house.

Initially, the move to Ann Arbor was not one I wanted at all. I had thought we might remain in Cleveland, have a family there. What was I going to do in Ann Arbor? I heard comments before we moved to the effect that even the mail person had a PhD. Cleveland was strange to me at first, somewhat intimidating, but it had become familiar, almost laid back. We had been happy there, going to movies, cooking with friends, camping. We were the crazy couple back there, the couple who decided to hike from Cleveland to Saint Marys. One hundred ninety-eight miles. When we talked about doing it, we imagined taking a couple of weeks, hiking ten miles a day. We were good walkers, skinny and strong. We bought topographical maps of our proposed route and set out with backpacks, hiking boots, a lightweight tent. The guy who sold us the tent and the maps looked doubtful.

"It's harder than you think," he said. "You'll be on highway some of the time; it's not like you're using a trail. Plus you have to consider water and food." We ignored his caution, but he was right. We hiked two days, during which we were accosted by dogs three separate times while their owners looked on unsure whether they should allow their dogs free rein or help us. We both got bad blisters that made walking excruciating and ended the whole thing about twenty miles from Cleveland. A friend came to pick us up and take us home. We tossed the gear into our car and drove off to camp at Heart's Content high in the Allegheny National Forest. "So we'll hike the Appalachian Trail," said Ken. "Maybe the highway was a bad idea." We were inside our lightweight tent, about to fall asleep. "Okay," I said, glad to be holding his hand, happy my blisters didn't hurt anymore.

Well, we did move to Ann Arbor. Whatever children we'd have would live in a green house on the banks of the Huron River. I wanted those children to show up, fast.

I was not generous in my waiting and wanting. I didn't even picture what the birth mothers might look like. In fact, the faces of those birthing women are visible in my children's faces. They look out at me from my children's eyes.

But I never knew one of those women, and I did not want to, not then.

Now is different. I could meet those women now and tell them the stories I have about their children, all of them grown. But back then I wanted to be the only, best mother. They could be the other mother, far away and nicely blurred.

Sometimes I am ashamed of myself. Other times, I think it's the nature of parenting. I was bear-like, growling and rearing at anything that might come between me and those children. I held on to those children with both hands while I practiced saying *mother, adoptive family, interracial, international adoptive family*, a list of words that took a while to roll off my tongue.

There were people who felt I had done a bad thing, people who felt that I used those women like machines, allowed them to make babies for me, handed over some cash and walked away with their babies, like the women were so many vending machines. I flinched at that, was defensive, but at least no one was bold enough to say it in front of the kids. But one time someone was plenty bold. He called me a *baby stealer*.

I was out walking with Minh. It seemed he'd been with us forever, but it had only been about four months, so it was probably late summer, August. He rarely cried, was laughing almost all of the time by then, and he made his way across the room to take a toy if we held it out to him. We hardly thought about the war anymore, the circumstances that had given us our child. But other people did. Once a guy looked at Minh when we were grocery shopping and asked me if Minh was from the north or south of Vietnam. Why did he ask me that? Nobody else had asked me *that*. How could he be from the north? "He's from the Delta region," I said and moved on to find tomato soup.

The day I was walking with Minh, a much younger guy, almost a kid really, wearing a Black Sabbath T-shirt and riding a bike, passed us on the Broadway bridge. He looked at me and my son, easy like, as if he planned to say, "Nice day." But he didn't say that. He stopped, straddled his bike, and said, leaning toward me, "You should be ashamed of yourself. Baby stealer!"

His words hit hard. I held my hand against my chest as if I were stopping up a hole. I looked at the baby who was busy chewing on a bagel and seemed not to have noticed.

When I met the guy on his bike, I was thinking only of the baby riding in his stroller. I was not thinking of the other mother.

I was not thinking of all that trauma in Vietnam or picturing myself as a stealer of babies. It was more likely that I thought, just then, that someone had pulled the world close for the baby and me to meet. I was happy with the baby who smelled faintly of the Desitin I had spread across his bottom. I talked to him, pointed out trees and dogs and the bike. I said, "That's a bike, honey," as the guy came toward us.

And then there was the face of that guy leaning in toward me, an angry face with a spread of acne, breath a little rank. *Baby stealer!* I wanted to defend myself, our family, the baby in the stroller, and I wanted to knock that guy off his bike and stomp on him with my red sandals. I leaned over Minh like I was a bullet shield. I would have died for him and considered it a bargain, would have killed anyone who tried to hurt him, no guilt. But I stood there, my hand over my chest, mute with anger and fear. Why did I fear a skinny punk? He *was* skinny. It would probably have been a pretty equal fight. I was strong with walking and lifting the baby. Did I think that Minh would hear and agree with the guy—if not then, later on? Did the absent birth mother tug at me? I turned away and pushed the stroller on over the bridge to the park where we played on the swings: "Up high, high, touch the sky. That's where you were, Minh. You flew all the way from Vietnam to Michigan."

I pushed the baby swing and considered the idea of adoption all over again. Should Vietnamese babies be in Michigan? Vietnamese adoptions had peaked the year before Minh had come to us; there were a thousand children adopted from Vietnam by US families in 1974. And it's true that great pieces of their culture were lost to them. Minh speaks only the smallest bit of Vietnamese. He can make pho. But he's American Viet, not Vietnamese. Still, I believe children have a right to family, however that family is shaped. They don't do well in institutions or selling plastic flowers on the street. So how do we make the choices? Should adoption be based on similar ethnicity, country, religion, education? Should white people adopt black babies? Black people adopt white babies? Should an Asian couple adopt a Caucasian baby? *Should* we have adopted Minh? He seemed to think he was fine where he was, moving back and forth in a swing at the bottom of Broadway hill. He had lost his Vietnamese culture. I knew the baby in the swing hadn't absorbed that loss yet. He only knew his life of milk and bagels and sometimes a spoonful of ice cream. It would be some time yet before he knew what was lost.

That would be true for all our children.

Ken was furious. He had none of my angst. He scoffed at *baby stealer*. "We didn't steal anybody's baby. No one handed a child over to us for cash. We could never have paid for a baby, even if we had wanted to. Plus, we had police check us out, for God's sake. We had to be fingerprinted before we could even be approved for adoption! Remember going to the police station? We had that whole long process of a home study. Baby stealers don't do that." He slapped his paper on the arm of the sofa, incredulous, *baby stealer?* He couldn't believe it. Who would say such a thing? It was ridiculous. Had we travelled to Vietnam and plucked a baby from its mother? No. Had we dealt with a shady agency and handed over a packet of cash? No. His voice rose with his anger. "Who is this guy?" he yelled. "What does he even know?"

"Hush," I told him. "Hush. You'll scare the baby." He picked Minh up and held him close. "Look, baby, we didn't steal you from anybody." He checked him over as though he were looking for damage, pulled me close and gave me a hug. "Maybe the guy was strung out, Mary." But it was half comfort. For a time, I wheeled Minh the long way around. I would not cross over the bridge.

But what if I had been in Vietnam in April of 1975? What if I had been wandering through the orphanages filled with babies? Would I have picked one up and headed off, not knowing if there were parents in the background? Maybe I would have told myself it was the right thing to do. How could I know? Would that have been stealing a baby? Had that happened to *our* baby? What if someone said they had proof that Minh had a living mother?

I thought about those things, mostly in the middle of the night while Ken and the baby slept. I went into the baby's room and looked at him in his red sleeper, his hands open and easy, a dribble of milk at the corner of his mouth. I would have to give him back if his birth mom claimed him. I would be forced to. I would never willingly hand him over though, living birth mom or no. So I could be a baby stealer. It would be possible.

How else could I love? I could not love conditionally.

Ken always saw us as parents. Just that. Parents. He never gave much thought to the idea of *birth father*. He has never imagined a birth father in the background, a father who might appear and demand his child. He still doesn't. So we adopted. So was I a baby stealer?

I don't know.

* * *

One afternoon when the kids were young, so probably in the early eighties, I was reminded of the encounter with the kid who called me baby stealer. The kids and I went looking for turtles by the river. We ate sandwiches; the kids put crayfish in a bucket and we walked back home uphill. I found it at the top of the hill, almost in plain sight, just a little obscured by the grass and weeds: a Swiss Army knife, the same one I still have in my dresser drawer. I had always wanted a Swiss Army knife, and there it was, complete with can opener, nail file, screwdriver, and tiny saw, perfect and no way to find the owner. I scribbled a note and poked it on a tree branch.

Item found: Thursday 6/4. Please contact: 762-9390 with description of lost article.

Meanwhile, I had the knife and held on to it, a red knife inside my white fingers that made a bony cave.

Finders keepers.

"So what do you want a knife for?" the kids asked. "You don't fish except for taking us to the river. You don't go camping anymore; you just put up the tent in the backyard. Will you give it back if somebody finds the note? What will you do with the knife?"

I would have to give it back if somebody found the note and claimed it, yes. What would I do with the knife? I didn't know. Leave it in my drawer probably. Put it in my pocket when we went on hikes. Not much. I wouldn't do much with it. But I wanted one. Someone lost one. And no one phoned to claim it, so it was mine. I put it in my pocket when we went hiking and used it once or twice, but mostly I was just glad to have it. I looked at it when I opened my drawer; I picked it up and felt its heft, my red Swiss Army knife. I still do that. I kept the knife happily, no thought of trying really hard to find the owner.

I didn't find my children lying in the grass. Their birth mothers and I were always separated by so much space and time that if I had left a note describing those children, it would never have been found. The children would stay with me, just like the Swiss Army knife.

My children came out of the sky, pieces of gladness that I reached for and held on to. They carry with them, in every cell of their bodies, pieces of those birthing women. When I hug my children, now grown children, and I think of that, it makes me catch my breath—like my children are a mystery, both true and untrue, mine and, yet, not altogether.

Every birthday that I scooped ice cream into bowls for them, lit candles on a cake, I could only be glad, with the kind of gladness we own when we have what can never be earned.

Chapter 6

LUCK AND LOSS

Because I was someone who drove away from Saint Marys, nineteen years old, without stopping to change from her wedding gown, because I left my family and everyone I knew for someplace that promised different, I often thought of myself as someone who escaped. A kind of refugee. I did not end up working forever in a lamp factory or a carbon factory back in Saint Marys. I did not bide my time until one of the boys on the corner offered me a ring and a roof. I was lucky—which is exactly what people told my children later on. They told them they were lucky, lucky children, their lives were so much better than they might have been. They had escaped poverty and things worse than poverty.

    Escape is complicated. Of course, I was grateful not to be living such a hard life. I was glad to be in what I believed was a better place. I slept with the guy I wanted to sleep with in a bed that held just the two of us. Which had not been the case back home. Rosie, Barb, and I had shared a bed, fighting over covers and space, close enough in age for one of us to walk off with the only pair of clean socks or the lone pencil, leaving the other two with yesterday's socks, a stub for a pencil. The two youngest girls, Kathy and Raye Ann, a baby and a toddler, were packed into a crib. They could not take anything. Could only cry for milk or a dry diaper. I did not want to go back to that. But escape and survival can leave a person ashamed to look into the mirror. I wanted the life I had with Ken. Still, I felt as if I had left my family in Saint Marys to survive as best they could. My children were never sure how to view their lives either. Of course, they were glad to have so much plenty. But, did they have to feel continually grateful? Should they be glad they had come to us, or sad?

"You are so lucky." Every time someone said this, I watched the kids shrink inside their skins. We'd be standing on some sidewalk somewhere, a stranger in front of us telling the kids, "You are so lucky." I would say that I was the lucky one, but who ever believed me? A teacher wrote to my youngest son once. *You are so lucky,* she wrote. *You made it here.* I widened my eyes when I read that. When I protested her remark, she was hurt and defensive. She had no idea why I might object, why it might hurt my son, after all he had been lucky to leave that orphanage, hadn't he? "You're too sensitive," said Ann, who thought the teacher's comment innocuous. Maybe so. Still, as children, in the seventies and eighties, my kids often felt their way, uncomfortable sometimes, worried that they'd invite comment. Which they did. People came down from their porches, stopped us in the street, and looked at the kids as if the kids might share some of their mythical luck, the luck of a survivor, somebody who beat the odds.

But it was never luck. If I had to name it, I might call it *willingness*. My children were mostly willing to accept their lives. They were willing to live in the day-to-day. That might seem obvious, but it isn't. Because sometimes they were not so willing.

When they were easy in their skins, the kids loved their life, didn't want any other life. They were happy! But then, sooner or later, they complained that they felt uneasy; they ached; they wondered who there was, what there was, before they met us. They felt guilty even though their past was nothing they could know, nothing they could find; they missed it. They worried if their other family was okay. Shouldn't they look for them? Shouldn't they try to help them?

I could not know what they felt. And yet, I had a sense of what they meant. Whenever I went back home and it was time to say good-bye, my sisters waved from the front porch, my mother stood at the window and waved past the curtains she shoved aside. I was ashamed all over again to remember the ease with which I had left with Ken all those years ago, just slammed the car door and drove off. And I continued to leave. Every time, I made the same choice all over again.

Was that how my kids felt? Like they'd just taken off? Left without a good-bye? Did they think they kept making the same choice over and over? Did they feel guilty about loving us, the parents they knew, even though they might have living parents someplace else?

Things are left behind all the time. Big things like a family or a child. Small things like the garden rake we intended to put away, but forgot. Sometimes it's okay. We find the rake lying in the grass and we put it away. We go back to see the family we left behind. We eat and laugh together. But sometimes, the loss is forever and all that luck people talk about is distilled from loss.

* * *

Loss. Ken's parents died when he was young, still in his early twenties. First his mother, then his father, in the space of two years. He was shocked and grieved. Ken's older brother John and John's wife, Mary Ann, plus their two children, became the center of our Cleveland life after the death of Ken's parents. They lived in a sprawling ranch in a suburb of the city. They had a woods outside their floor-to-ceiling windows. There were bird feeders, a little pond, a deck with a gas grill, lounge chairs. There were no hunters because their woods did not harbor bears or snakes. There was a path through the woods that led down to tennis courts and a playground. Down the road was a swimming pool where the kids floated in warm blue water. In Cleveland, Ken and I were offered everything John and Mary Ann had to offer. I could sit on the deck in summer, by the fire in winter, drinking oolong tea from a china cup with a butterfly printed just inside the rim. All of Ken's family welcomed first me, strange girl from the hills, and later each of the children, as if they had been waiting for us.

One Thanksgiving we drove to Cleveland from Ann Arbor. We sat at the table and watched the purple light of the sky bend in on itself. We had all three children by then, but they were still young, probably ten, eight, and three. Ken and John drank coffee and ate two pieces of pie each, banana cream and pumpkin. I drank my oolong tea from the butterfly cup. Minh said, to no one in particular, that he wanted to see the deer that he knew roamed the woods. He went to the window and looked out. I smiled and drank more tea, but Phyl, Ken's older sister, was there and she heard Minh. Phyl is a person who believes in miracles. She'll make one if she has to. That day she said to Minh, "Well, wish hard." Then she added, "No, ask Saint Anthony. He's the patron saint of lost things. Tell him you want to see a deer. He won't mind. You might be stretching it a bit, but go on: *Tony, Tony, look around. Something's lost and can't be found.*" She looked at Minh, waiting.

Phyl was someone Minh needed to defer to, plus she was persistent, so he mumbled: "*Tony Tony, look around. Something's lost and can't be found.*"

She forked up the last of her pie and said, "Okay, but you have to be patient. It takes Tony time to do the job."

"Maybe a deer will come," I said to Minh, stressing the

maybe. I left to join a game of Clue. They were big game players in Cleveland: cards, board games, tennis, golf. I found that unsettling at first. Shouldn't we have been minding a baby or scrubbing a floor? I played Clue that day though and came close to winning. Phyl watched the game for a while, then put on her coat to head home and asked for kisses. And that was when she took Minh by the shoulders and turned him around. A doe stood outside the window looking in at us. Two more deer joined her. "See," Phyl said. "That's what happens when you ask." Her smile was wide; it covered the five of them, Minh, Phyl, the deer. She left in glory. "That's what happens," she called over her shoulder to her nephew.

Chapter 7

REASONS

Seven years before the Thanksgiving of the deer in Cleveland, East Indian friends—Subhendu, one of Ken's good friends from grad school, and his wife, Leela—came to visit in the late summer of 1978. They told us about the hundreds of little girls in India available for adoption. We should adopt one, they said. We were out back in the yard drinking iced tea and shelling peanuts. "You should have a little girl. She will take care of you later on when you are old."

"Girls don't grow up that way here. Girls make their own lives here." We offered more tea while the thought of a little girl took hold, rose in our minds like the tea filling glasses.

We knew nothing about Indian adoption, but they had connections. They knew Kathy Sreedhar, who worked with Mother Teresa's nuns in an orphanage in, then, Calcutta. They would put us in touch with her if we wanted. Kathy lived in Washington, DC, and travelled back and forth to India as an adoption facilitator with Mother Teresa's orphanages. We could have a daughter. All those little girls with such a grim future! Our friends looked at us, their brown eyes eager. We didn't mind being persuaded one bit. We liked Subhendu and Leela a lot. We'd eaten Leela's samosas, shared a love for lengthy, over-the-top Indian movies, like *Mother India*. They knew someone who worked with Mother Teresa's nuns! Wasn't that a sign, almost a confirmation of our family-making ways?

We finished off the tea and the peanuts. The saffron light of early evening turned blue- black. We swatted at mosquitoes and lit torches. A little girl! Not an infant. There were few infants in Mother Teresa's care; the girls available were toddlers. So a little girl from India. That's what we wanted.

There seemed no *good* reason for the child to resemble Minh. *The kids aren't a pair of shoes*, I thought. And so we began the process of adopting a girl from India. We contacted the social worker, Marilyn, again. We began amassing documents, a statement from our bank, a statement from Ken's boss, verification of our moral soundness from friends, our doctor. We had done a good bit of this before with Minh, we knew the routine.

When people heard that we were adopting from India, they said we had no idea how we were complicating our lives, taking a kid who would look so different from Minh. "Why make it harder?" We ignored them, almost scorned them.

In fact, they were right. It was harder because the children did not match like a pair of shoes, but at the same time—we had a daughter, not a pair of shoes. Still.

Why is it birth parents don't seem to feel as if they need to explain their children? Of course, sex and what often follows sex, birth, are viewed as part of the human condition. Adoption is not *apart* from the human condition, but not the norm, not at all the norm. Only 2 percent of all children in the United States are adopted. Adoption's not regarded as a bad thing, but it's marginal.

Then there's the process itself. I believe in home studies. We have completed three of them. We discussed the details of our marriage and family life. We had background checks for felonies. We wrote a statement that described us and our reasons for adopting and sent it off to the agency, a different one each time we adopted. We did this because we wanted to. No one made us do it. We thought the prize was worth the trouble. And it was. But it isn't what most people do. People will sometimes say to me, "I could never do what you did." That leaves me flustered. It seems to imply that I'm either a saint or a crazy woman. I used to assure them that they could adopt. I don't say that anymore. Maybe they couldn't.

We applied to adopt from India. We wrote the statement we knew how to write by then.

> We are very happy with our son. And we want to adopt again. We have friends from India. We met them here, in the States. We feel a connection to the country and would be thrilled to have a child from India. We understand there are little girls available. We would like a little girl from one to three years old. We are willing to accept a child with problems that we might be able to remedy.

We gathered pictures of the house and the yard. We snapped Minh, the potential sibling, driving his Matchbox cars. We filled in endless forms and sent thick packets off with notary signatures and apostilles. We handed them to the clerk at the post office, told a little of our story, and double-checked rates and time, the best method of mailing. The clerk was excited for us, said he felt like a doctor at a birth. And for years after that, every time I mailed a package or bought stamps, if Anita came along, he leaned over the counter and plied her with sticks of Doublemint gum.

Subhendu and Leela burned incense for us.

The packets made it to India; the incense continued to burn while we waited.

Two months later we got a phone call from Kathy, the person who navigated the complicated adoption process in

India. The phone rang the same way it always rang. It was a could-be-a-friend-calling ring, on a normal night in the fall. Nothing special. "You'd think something would clue you in," Ken said later. "How does it happen that it comes out of the blue like this?" I laughed, glad for the call, excited. What would it be like?

Kathy was sending a sheet of names and descriptions. She wanted us to study the names and descriptions, then pick a child from the list. Just names and descriptions, she said. No pictures and not much description either, only the age and a line or so about the child.

"We pick?" we said. "We pick a child from the list?"

"That's the way I do it," she said. "You'll be fine." The children were girls from one to five years old. Our job was to decide which one. Kathy was leaving for India in two weeks, and if we made a choice quickly and then phoned her with our choice, we could have a daughter in a few months.

My stomach flipped. So fast? I hadn't thought it would happen so fast. I was still in the part of the adoption process that allowed for sending off paperwork but didn't include the idea of an actual child. My daughter was still a vague daughter. I was like a birth woman in the early stages of a pregnancy, somebody who talked about being pregnant, but could still fit into her jeans.

"The rainy season will start soon. The kids get sick then. There are always a few who die. A thing like a simple cold becomes pneumonia and kills them. They don't have the stamina of American kids." She was matter of fact, no fooling around. If we wanted a child, we should pick from the list she was sending us.

"Oh." I bit my lip. Some blood dribbled down. I didn't want to have my child die waiting, maybe die of a cold that would be no more than a day in bed to an American kid. "Oh." I didn't want to upset this woman either, another woman who was giving us yet another child. But picking? How would that be possible?

"Don't take too long about it," she said, clearly ready to end the conversation. I knew she had adopted four children from India herself. Did she pick them? Probably. Probably she was in the orphanage and pointed, *that one!* But I didn't want to do that any more than I wanted to pick from a name on a list. I became paralyzed choosing from a menu in a restaurant.

Anyway, even if I had been able to pick from a roomful of kids, we couldn't go to India. We were crazy to go ahead with the adoption at all. In the time between sending our paperwork to India and the call from Kathy, Ken's boss had lost major grant money, and a good chunk of Ken's salary went with it. There were no other grants in the works at the time. The university would only provide half pay for him. He took on a second job in order to make up the difference. But it never occurred to us to not go ahead. "We're too far in to turn back now," said Ken. "You aren't scared, are you? We'll just tighten our belts and go ahead." He took my hand and rubbed his fingers against my thin wrist. I felt a rush of love and that same old impetuousness that had me by the throat when I'd first met him. Scared? Me?

I knew how to tighten a belt. I knew how to stretch rosemary chicken to last for more than one meal. I knew how to cook potatoes. They could be boiled, steamed, baked, fried, mashed, and grated. "I'm not scared," I said. Maybe I should have been scared. There was no guarantee at all that Ken would have full-time work—if no more grants came through, the university would let him go. The second job would be unlikely to become full time. Then what? But I went to sleep easily that night curled up next to Ken under a red and white quilt, a wedding present from Aunt Loretta in Cleveland. We would manage.

Well it worked out. Ken got a grant. We moved from tightening our belts to having more than enough. But I have great fondness for the young couple, no sure source of cash, who chose to go ahead and adopt a little girl.

It was late October, the nights already cool. Minh played in the garden in the last of the day's light, wearing a brown sweater Ma had knit for him. I watched him from the window driving his Matchbox cars around under bare, low-hanging tomato vines. Ken drank coffee and ate apple crisp in the tiny dining room, just off the kitchen. He sat at the Amish-made table we bought when we got the green house. It's in the basement now. The grandkids play Chutes and Ladders or squash Play-Doh on it.

I sat down beside Ken and leaned my head against his shoulder. He smelled like coffee and apples. He was studying sheets of data. "Oh, honey," I said. "It's never what I think will happen. I didn't expect we would *pick*."

We were going to get a list in the mail. Someone on that list was our soon-to-be little girl. It was more surprising than getting that phone call and saying yes to an unknown Minh. In some ways we probably thought it was divine intervention when we got Minh. How should we think of picking from a list? I had no idea.

I brought more crisp to the table, an extra spoon. We ate from the same bowl. Names say a lot, I said to Ken, and there would be *some* description. It would work. But my voice sounded thin. He squirted a bit of cream onto the last of the crisp before he opened his mouth.

"It'll be fine," he said. Some whipped cream stuck to the stubble on his chin. He always needed a shave by the end of the day. "I mean it," he said. "It'll be fine." How could he be so sure?

When we talk about it now, he says he only meant that he was sure we would pick a name. After that, we would figure it out. He was right, although neither one of us could have imagined how hard the figuring would be.

People shook their heads when I told them about the list. How could we be so—and they were silent for a pause—*trusting?* Take one kid sight unseen, another on the basis of a name and a two-line description? Maybe they didn't mean to say trusting. Maybe they meant blind? Stupid? Naive?

"Why did you do that?" people asked. "Pick from a name! How could you *do* that?"

How? We weren't stupid; we were eager. Maybe we were leapers-of-faith. A person could call that naive. But we never thought so. We knew, that night in October, that we would pick our East Indian daughter from a list of names. The list came less than a week later. It was handwritten, wrinkled, as if someone had put it in their pocket or purse before they sent it to us. We held the 8½" x 11" sheet of thin blue paper carefully, afraid we'd tear it. We read the list hunched over at the kitchen table. We would show that list to Anita for the first time when she was seven. Later, we would give her the list in a special box, along with her coming-home outfit. The year she had her baby boy, she looked at the list for a long time. Then she said very slowly, much older by then, having been to hell and back, "Maybe, maybe, I *was* lucky." She touched her finger to her name, then traced the names of the other girls who were picked, or not.

It was as if those children on that list had taken first breath in the orphanage. There was not one bit of information about parents or circumstances of birth. A single piece of thin, blue paper with ten names, and one of those names belonged to our daughter. Ken read the names out loud: Pua—three years old.

Strong-willed. Healthy. Dark-brown skin. Is walking and toilet-trained. Indrani—two years old. Normal intelligence. Good-tempered. Light-skinned. Ashanti—a year and a half. Is being toilet-trained. Likes attention, clings a bit, has medium-brown skin.

He kept reading: Pavrita, Gita, Anita, Madhu, Sajala, Sai, Namita. Which one? My voice shook. "I don't know how to do this." Which one?

Minh played underneath the table, driving a dump truck around, occasionally bumping our ankles. We looked at the names and waited for something, an idea, a feeling. Maybe a name would float up from the page? I got up and poured coffee. There was a name in the middle of the list—a name we had heard along with the other names, but hadn't focused on. We studied the name and the description, small as it was.

Anita—two years old. Amiable. Obeys the sisters. Eats neatly. Enjoys the company of other children. Medium-to-dark-brown skin. Very small. Loves sweets.

Anita. We had a pocket book of Indian names and looked up the name. *Anita* meant *full of grace*. "Well, full of grace sounds good," said Ken. "We'll need that. Anita is a nice name. Minh and Anita. If she likes kids, she'll be glad for Minh. We'll call her Sweets, sometimes, for fun. She'll be a sweetie pie." Ken always had a plan. He was a guy who made a note on the calendar when he planted his tomatoes. *Planted Early Girl May 30. Expected ripe date July 30.*

I'd remind him that it all depended, the rainfall, the coolness of the nights, the amount of sun. Lots of things would play into that expected ripe date of tomatoes. But every year he did the same thing. Some years it played out. Some years he was crestfallen; the tomatoes didn't ripen or were so late ripening they tasted flat, like store bought.

Actually, we ended up calling our daughter Sweets a lot. I blame Ken because he started it when she was little and she liked it, so he kept it up. "Where's my Sweets?" he called when he biked home from work with a treat in his basket. She ran to him and he picked her up, swung her up and around.

We pulled Minh out from under the table and showed him the name, Anita. The name meant nothing to him.

We phoned Kathy to announce our choice and she said, "You picked a good one. She's a doll. I saw her when I was there last month. She's really small, which might give you some problems, but she'll come around. I'll get a picture in the mail to you as soon as I can. Congratulations."

That was that.

Minh and I bought a globe—on a stand, with all the new countries and their right names. It even lit up, and when Ken came home, we clicked the switch. We put it in the middle of the living room and spun the globe to find India, lit up and glowing. "There! There she is."

And she was there, waiting.

There were eleven million abandoned children in India when we chose Anita. Most of those abandoned children were girls. It was not an historical high. If you check UNICEF records you will find the number was higher in 2013. Anywhere between twelve and, by some counts, twenty million children were abandoned or orphaned. Abandoned or orphaned children end up in orphanages, good, bad, or indifferent. They are taken to work in brothels and textile factories or they sell plastic flowers on the street.

Kathy Sreedhar told us that Anita had likely spent months in a police station, probably in West Bengal. Indian policy was to take abandoned children to the nearest police station and hold them in hopes their parents might claim them. After that, if they were lucky, somebody came by and took them off to an orphanage.

I was not thinking of poverty or abandonment when we chose our daughter, though. I was thinking of Anita.

Her picture came, a black-and-white photo. She was frowning and wearing a dress with a wide ruffle at the neck. We could see skin folds at her neckline—she wasn't in great shape. She had huge round eyes and dark-brown skin.

I made copies and sent them out to the family. Minh went around telling people what I told him: he had a sister in India.

I took her picture to my mothers' group, women with kids from Korea, a few from Vietnam. No one in the group had a child from India. Anita was a rarity. I drove out Zeeb Road to a house with a grapevine wreath on the door. In the middle of the wreath was a blue sign that said, *Welcome.* Inside, there was a plate of caramel brownies in the middle of the coffee table. Decaf brewed in the kitchen. I sat down and pulled out the picture. Everyone said, "Let's see!"

Beth, who owned the grapevine wreath and the blue sign, looked at the huge round eyes, the frown, the dark-brown skin. "She's cute. But no one's ever going to think that this kid and your son are brother and sister." She bit into a brownie and passed the picture to her left.

The group went silent. What were they supposed to say? What was the right attitude?

Should adoptive parents *approximate* a matched family? Do white adoptive parents allow for epicanthic folds, but not dark-brown skin?

The picture made its way back to me and I looked at her.

A little girl. Only a little girl.

Anita: amiable and full of grace. Our little girl.

"They'll know they're brother and sister, all right. They'll know we're a family." I said that. My words were defensive, probably not the right words. If I could go back, have had the right words . . . Oh, I wish I had had the right words! I never came up with them. Surely, a perfectly articulated statement would have made things go more smoothly for the kids. The right words like a perfect test score: 100 percent. A+. The kids could have used them as a shield. But even now, I sometimes find myself searching for the right words.

I held the picture, flushed with anger.

"Of course," they said, "of course." No one sounded convinced.

Because Beth *was* partly right, and maybe those women knew that people would not, never do, perceive Anita and her brothers as siblings. When Anita is out with one of her brothers, people see a dating couple, a married couple, friends, any of those things as a possibility, but not siblings. They are astonished when they find out.

But I was right too because *they do* think of themselves as siblings.

The picture went around one more time and everyone agreed, she had the biggest eyes.

Chapter 8

I AM YOUR MOTHER

Anita came to us in early spring, mid-April, snow still splotched on the ground. She had rarely seen men: the driver for the orphanage, maybe a doctor. The nuns warned us. They sent a note.

> *She has only seen men on rare occasions. Your husband should be slow in approaching her. She eats three bowls of rice a day. Is toilet-trained. She sleeps eight hours without fussing. Do not undo our good work with excessive treats and spoiling.*

The nuns were nervous about Anita being spoiled in America, the land where kids ate big bowls of ice cream—no *gulab jamun*—and watched endless cartoons—no singing-on-the-potty time. Kathy had sent us a picture, a copy of one she used when she went out fundraising. Whole rows of kids sat on what looked like metal bowls, singing and laughing. We didn't see Anita in the picture, but we had a picture. The kids looked happy; two nuns in white saris with blue trim stood nearby laughing.

A note was written across the back of the photo: *The children sing and clap. They enjoy their potty time.* There was nothing like that in the States, for sure. So whenever we sent pictures of our life to the nuns—we were sitting around the table, eating that apple crisp, or reading on the sofa—the nuns wrote back reminding us not to spoil her. As if they were not at all sure she was heading for a life that would do her good. Life in the States was too easy.

The family in Saint Marys loved the idea of one of Mother Teresa's kids. My sister, Rosie, the one who would later cry at Sung's graduation, sent a donation to Anita's orphanage. In return, she got Mother Teresa's biography signed by Mother Teresa herself: *M Teresa*. Rosie gave me the book to keep for Anita.

We got a one-line reply to a letter we sent thanking Mother for our daughter and describing our lives with the little girl she had cared for.

Children are God's miracles. He has blessed you.
M Teresa

Mother, that's what they called her, all those children crammed into the cement-block orphanage in Calcutta, a place where the nuns did laundry by hand, scrubbed off the mold that grew everywhere, and went without when food was short.

Anita, sweet girl, sweet Calcutta babe, came through the doors of Detroit Metro Airport carried in a stranger's arms, a man's! After they had warned us about men! But escorts were never easy to come by. It was a tough job with no pay, maybe a reduction in the fare, I'm not sure, but a hard job every time with a scared-sick kid. The man wore a navy-blue suit—like Ken when I met him all that long time ago. The suit was rumpled from the long flight and from holding Anita. He smelled faintly of sick when he approached us, from Anita we guessed. He was a businessman from Detroit who had agreed to fly back to Michigan with Anita in tow.

Yet again, we needed no identification. We were told a man would be carrying a small girl child off the plane. He was told that a man and a woman with a small Vietnamese son would be waiting. We stood still, barely breathing, we and our Vietnamese son who wore a red sweater that Ann had knit for him. He was three years old. Ken and I held his hands while we watched the man walk toward us carrying Anita, carrying the rest of our lives. The man said almost nothing to us. "Here," was what he said. He handed Anita over like she was a grenade with the pin removed. "Good luck." He took off so fast we never got his name. One child was handed over to us by a woman named Dusty and another by a man whose name we never learned. I didn't care, not then, not now. What mattered was that we got the child.

Anita was blasted from the trip and thin living, a scrap of a kid with big eyes and the bloated belly of malnutrition. Her hair had the red tinge that signaled protein deficiency. She wore a checked brown-and-white top with yellow overalls, the top damp with sweat, her pants soaked. She looked impossibly fragile, our baby grenade. She stared at Minh, who thrust a small bear in her direction. She pulled away from him, from the bear.

People rushed past, glanced over; a few stopped to watch.

Anita didn't *cry*; she *keened*. A high-pitched wail that came from deep inside her, bounced off the walls, and sunk into our bones. We looked at each other. *What now?*

On the ride home, she went silent. And there we were, our new family, Ken and I and Minh riding home with Anita. Grief strapped into a car seat, wearing a new red-knit sweater over the top of her overalls, a welcome-home present from Ann. The match of Minh's.

Back home, we rubbed her with lotion, offered bits of chicken, stuck crackers in her pockets, tried to cover her bones with a little flesh. It felt like her bones cut into my dreams. I didn't deep sleep anymore. I half slept, waiting for her to wake, waiting for a night terror, those awful times when she woke screaming stuck in some fear of her own. We would hold her, talking softly. She looked awake. Her eyes were open, but she didn't see us. She saw something else. "Anita, Anita, honey, we're here. It's okay." When I told the pediatrician what happened at night, he used the words "night terrors" and said we were doing the best we could. That was some comfort, but not much. We held her almost every night for months while she cried, looking past us, frightened, of what?

I had tried to learn some Hindi. "I am your mother. *Mei tumari mata hun.*" She looked at me, no recognition. "*Mei tumari mata hun*, sweetie."

My mother's grief, until that point the largest grief I had known, was nothing like my daughter's. Anita's grief! The night terrors were the only time that Anita would make sound. During the day she was completely silent. And the silence of her grief, those mute tears, terrified me. If I reached for her, a brush of my hand, a blanket wrapped around her, she withdrew and then, as if she couldn't go far enough, she withdrew some more.

That should have been a clue. This child had been hurt somewhere, sometime. I watched her. It's not so easy to observe pain, to comfort and yet not claim that pain as your own. No. Pain intrudes itself; it takes over. Pain, if there's enough of it, becomes all there is.

A month after she came to us, Anita was still silent. We lived from day to day, not because of what we knew. We lived from day to day because we didn't know. We didn't know never talking was a possibility. There are children so damaged they never talk, but we didn't know that, so when the pediatrician shook his head at our girl sitting mute, shook his head at us trying to hold her hand or stroke her head—we refused to take in what he probably meant by that shake of his head: *bad news here.*

And then one day—she reached to take rice from Ken's hands.

It was almost the end of June when she reached for a little bit of rice that Ken held out to her.

Every day, I made rice and she scooped it up from the bowl in front of her. She ate with her right hand, Indian fashion. She would not take even a grain from our outstretched hands. We watched her eat; nothing fell but she picked it up and put it in her mouth, every single grain. She was two years old!

Ken said he'd hold out longer than Anita. He was convinced that at some point, she'd cave and take something he offered her. Mr. Patience whose patience was rewarded. Because one incredible day while Ken talked to Anita about the squirrels in the yard (why was it different on that day?), she held out her hand and took rice from the strange man who offered her rice, a man who was her father, but of course, she didn't know he *was* her father.

She stretched out her right hand and reached for the spoon of rice Ken offered her. She still would not speak, but she ate the rice.

She took food. The simplest of things. A bit of rice, a gesture, the rice going from the spoon in Ken's hand, into her hand, and then her open mouth. I wanted to pick her up and whirl her around. But I stayed quiet and blew a kiss to Ken. Minh was there eating Froot Loops, and he offered her some. She took those too. I knew we'd be okay then. Because it's at the core of family, the giving and accepting of food. *Here*, we say, *have some.* We don't stop to think when we do that. We expect to do that. So when Anita took food, I rejoiced; we'd build on that.

The Year The Trees Didn't Die

Years later, Ken and I would reject the food Anita offered us. We would walk past the table she had set with food and flowers. We would refuse her. We would be silent.

Chapter 9

BAND LA, BAND LA

And then—we never knew why it happened—she sang. We listened, breathless, like we'd waited in line for tickets, slept nights under a tarp in pouring rain to hear her.

She sang in Hindi, the language of the nuns in her orphanage, clapped her hands, rocked her body back and forth. Maybe the kids sang that song during playtime or potty time? She cried after she sang, but there was sound; it was a sound I could wrap my arms around.

I pulled her to my lap, slowly, slowly. "Sing it again," I coaxed. She burrowed into me.

Ken and I can sing that song even now because we sang it every day for years, mixing the Hindi and English. I have no idea if I even have the words right. Maybe we never learned the right words. What we heard, what we learned to sing, was something like this:

Band la, band la, band la, band la.
We made meaning along with sound.
Band la, band la, band la.
It's okay, it's okay, it's okay.

After that day, she stopped retreating; she began to move into life in the green house, and her life in India receded. I was grateful. That sounds appalling, but she had to adjust or how could we manage? But I could still see pain: she fell asleep at night holding her red Indian sandals. She searched out every grain of rice that fell to the tray of her high chair. She could not tolerate any chastisement. One night she went to sleep with her head on Ken's chest, covered up with my red scarf, so small she could do that. I looked at her and was swept with the enormity of her resilience, her ability to live. She would always have that ability.

She rode in Ken's bicycle basket under the pale-blue Michigan sky down the street to home. Late afternoon, early evening, we walked up the street to meet him at the corner, stood there waiting until we saw him biking uphill toward home, riding a garage-sale bike with racing tires and a basket, a bike he loved, a bike he still rides. She called and waved; he braked to a stop and I lifted her in. She fit perfectly. Minh and I raced them downhill to our green house.

* * *

Inoculate often against racism. Make certain your child knows what you believe and make certain you are clear yourself about your beliefs.

We knew about racism. But we didn't have much experience of it and there's a big difference between knowing and experiencing. The experiences with Anita would be different from the experiences with Minh, harsher.

Initially it was easy. We'd say, "We love your dark-brown skin"; she would smile at us or pay no attention. People pointed out her curly hair or big eyes, her diminutive size. I waited and watched and thought about how to manage. She wasn't going to be two years old forever.

What was the best way to inoculate? We didn't know. There was not a lot of public discussion or knowledge. The only discussion going was at the local parent support group. But nobody there had a child with dark-brown skin. I thought I understood some forms of racism. But, I was in need of more education. I needed to understand what Alice Walker later defined as *colorism*, the idea that within or without a racial group, lighter skin is the better skin. But nobody was talking about colorism then. Issues of race and color would be discussed years later. There was no book called *"Why Are All the Black Kids Sitting Together in the Cafeteria?"* I'd find that in 2003. It didn't fit my situation, but it would have been helpful. Chi Muoi Lo's *Catfish in Black Bean Sauce*, a movie that shows two Vietnamese kids being raised by a black couple, would appear in 1999. I wouldn't find it until ten years later, when I Googled "movies showing adoptive interracial families." There was no Cheerios commercial with a curly-haired, brown-skinned kid talking to her Caucasian mom and African-American father. That happened in the spring of 2013. In the Ann Arbor that Anita arrived in, there was one Indian restaurant, Raja Rani, on the corner of Glen and Huron; the owners were astonished when we came in with Anita—not unkind, they were very nice, but it was hard to appear normal when she caused a sensation. How could we affirm her, make her realize that she was, perhaps unusual in the town at the time, but she *was* normal? In the seventies, the UofM had not yet begun to reach out to a diverse student population. There was one African American professor in Ken's department, no Asian Indians. The seventies were a time after the civil rights movement, but before the implementation of education about diversity and the outreach in universities that would result in the heterogeneous mix I see on UofM's campus today. I can find almost anything I want to know about issues of race and color now, in a bookstore, at the library, online. But not back then. I don't think we did a bad job affirming Anita, helping her to understand her worth. Still, we never knew enough. We blundered. I thought that if Anita understood we saw her as beautiful, she would absorb our belief as truth. That would be the best affirmation. That's what I thought. "You are beautiful," I told her. "Exactly right."

"Honey," Ken said, "you are a pretty girl from India." He said that he'd choose her all over again, and how could you not? She was wonderful and funny: she would chase sparrows away before she went out to play. She'd open the screen door a little, stick her hand out and wave it back and forth. "Shoo!" she scolded. "Shoo!" She insisted on taking her bath in a bucket. We'd set it in the tub; she'd climb in and sing her *"Band la"* song while she scrubbed. She fit just fine. Ken has the picture. She crawled through an old milk chute. We used to have milk delivered for a while, a small kind of box, with a ledge and a door that opened to the outside for the milk to be shoved through. In and out, in and out. Nobody else could do that. We would choose her every time.

The year she turned four, she sat on the bathroom floor with a balled-up blue washcloth dripping water. She rubbed at her arm. "I'm trying to get the dark off," she said to me—like you'd say you're trying to get a stain out—the same way I rubbed at my nightgown years ago, leaning over the bathtub, rubbing the blood away.

I lifted her to my lap. Water dripped all over us while I showed her our arms together, the white and brown of them. I pointed to places where my skin was darker, where the sun hit. "Do you know that people pay money to have brown skin? To get a tan?" Of course she didn't know, and what did it matter? I feared my inoculation was all wrong, like a flu shot that misses the season's newest strain.

Years and years later, she walked a beach in Hawaii with her husband. Someone stopped her to ask her how she got her tan. When she returned home, she told me that. She was amazed. "They thought I had a tan. Wanted one just like it."

"Told you so," I said. We laughed because, by then, we *could* laugh. It felt good, easy breathing after a long, hard uphill run.

She was smart, quick to sense what people thought, to pick up on looks and tones. We told her that we loved her dark-brown skin. Fine. She believed us, but we didn't live in her skin. When she was six, the two of us walked through Ann Arbor's art fair and stopped to watch a street juggler on Liberty Street near Sam's, the store where everyone in Ann Arbor goes to buy their Converse. A group of black teen girls stood next to us, watching the juggler. One of them pointed to Anita: "She's darker than I am." Anita shrank against me. I had thought our troubles would come from people like me, pink-toned whites. I had so much to learn! I ran my hand over Anita's head in a motion that claimed her, and remained quiet. When I think about my silence now, I am swept by shame. I want a redo. Because I didn't have the words back then.

I didn't have the right words, so I held my silence and walked away with my daughter in search of cotton candy. We pulled blue sugar from a white cone. She was happy enough eating blue sweet, but I was upset, a loser mom. We finished the candy and she asked for more. "Sure, sweetie." I bought more candy because I wanted to make it better. Our mouths smeared pink and blue, sick of sugar, we headed home. I've played the scene out many times since then. I am ready. I see those girls in a scene I imagine, and I say, so cool, competent, and wise, "Yes. She's gorgeous."

Six, seven, going on eight, she asked, "Will I get lighter?" As if I withheld something from her. I said her brown skin would

The Year The Trees Didn't Die

not come off, and we didn't want it to. *She was beautiful.* And, Lord knows, she was! Strangers stopped to look at her and asked to hold her when she was still a toddler. Hair all thick and curly, eyes like two brown moons. Features so regular, so chiseled, that a person could hardly believe it—no one could be that beautiful. So, how hard was it to say what was true? All our friends, Indian, Vietnamese, Caucasian, said it was true.

But beautiful or not, she lived with skin that often elicited comment when she was out with us. Skin is the largest organ. It's what people notice. She was beautiful, okay, but lighter skin would probably be better. Only one person ever said that, but I think Anita knew that lighter was the preferred skin shade almost everywhere. In the United States, India, Korea, Southeast Asia, the Philippines. Where was it not the preferred shade? Every Indian movie we rented had light-skinned heroines. Every Indian fairy tale talked about the golden-skinned princess. She did not miss that. Then there was the fact that people found Anita hard to slot. She was not black, although people always thought so, at a quick glance. "Black," they said to themselves, looked again, were unsure, and asked, "What is she?"

What is she? They meant where was she from. They did not mean she was another species of being. But I always wanted to say, "A girl. She's a girl, a little girl." What I said was, "Our daughter was born in India."

People knew so little about India. They know more now than they did in the years Anita was a kid. India? Back then, India was more exotic than the moon. People starved in India, didn't they? They worshipped cows in India. People lived on the streets in India, actually slept there! How—and people were honestly puzzled—how did we ever get a kid from India?

I wanted to clap my hands over Anita's ears. Apologize to

her. What would I have apologized for? Adopting her? People who said stupid things? Maybe so. Maybe I felt responsible, like I had brought her to a place where she was seen as out of place.

Anita pays attention to color even now. But she, herself, a grown-up Anita, has a family like the family she grew up with. A family that *does not match*—her family is a color palette of skin tones that range from pink to dark brown. Still, she thinks about color in a way that I don't or can't. When we go shopping, she picks out clothes for her son, her husband, even her brothers. She knows style and they're glad to have her do it. But here's the thing. She matches colors: a light-blue shirt and dark-blue pants, khakis with a dark-brown sweater. "I like things to match," she says to me. She would never pair dark-blue pants with a lime-green shirt. She comes home to visit and stares at a room that I have painted. The walls are lime green and I've hung purple curtains. She looks at me, appalled. "Leave it to you," she says and shakes her head, puzzled. She forgives what she sees as my quirk. Some part of her probably feels that I don't have a clue.

* * *

Most times, parenting the kids in the early years, it seemed as if we all shared the same skin. It wasn't that we didn't recognize differences, we could see as well as the next person, but the differences didn't take up much space. I didn't think: *I am putting my adopted brown-skinned daughter to bed. I am making my tan son, who has eyes with an epicanthic fold, put away his toys.* We lived those days bumping up against each other for the fun of it. The years were ours. We shoved the larger world aside. Perhaps, we shouldn't have. Perhaps, we should have been more vigilant. Still, the everyday was our reality and it was good.

Ken went off to work on his bike, wholly engaged with computed emission tomography. He had his own research grant by then; he'd left his part-time job; he was writing a book chapter. His world, like the world of most of his colleagues, held two things: work and family. Research is cutthroat competitive. Part of the competition is to see who can spend the most hours in the lab. Sleeping there would be best. The pressure sometimes led to fights. I'd complain that we never went out, never saw a movie, never did *anythingatall*. And I still had not gone back to school. How could I manage with Ken's work hours? And what about money? There wasn't enough to pay for child care.

I started running in those years for something that was mine. I ran with another mom, Cheryl, who lived around the corner. We met at six every morning. Ken got the kids ready for the day while I ran out on Pontiac Trail, three miles out, three miles back. I managed ten-minute miles, no great feat, but it felt good all the same. I craved that run every morning. I'd go on my own if my friend didn't show. I ran in rain, snow, ice. It didn't matter. Running was a high, a clear accomplishment.

The kids and I moved through our days slow time, picking tomatoes from the garden, making stick roads between the garden rows where the kids drove their expanded collection of Matchbox cars. (Those cars are still around. The little girl in the swishy purple dress at Sung's graduation, and that little boy of Anita's played with them. They drove them on the dining room floor and left very small scratch marks on the wood.)

Ann had three kids by then, like me, and they'd come to play in the afternoon while Ann and I talked. Her kids and mine would go crazy with the hose on hot days, squirting each other, making enormous mud puddles, jumping in them until they were coated with muck and Ann and I called a halt. We'd wash the kids off and wrap towels around them. Then we'd all head to the picnic table for red popsicles.

Come evening, on a really good day, Ken came up the driveway with chocolate in his bike basket. "Treats," he said, waving the candy bars. The kids jumped at him, almost knocking him off the bike. "Hey, hey," he said, but they knew he loved it. We sat on the front lawn and ate chocolate before dinner. I was in love with his fervor for science, his clear commitment to family.

The days of chocolate, Matchbox cars, and popsicles were not slam-bang. They were easy days. Everybody got to have chocolate, and it was fine. Then those days were gone.

Chapter 10
JUST ONE MORE

Anita left a note on the kitchen counter for me in the years our family was submerged in a slag heap of trouble, years of days that left no room for anything but survival and no idea how to do it. Anita was probably fifteen when she left the note, no longer the little girl who rode in a bicycle basket and ate the chocolate her dad brought home. She was a teen and her grief and anger, at that point, were so fierce we struggled to breathe when she was in the same room with us. She took up all the air. She hissed at us, snapped. Or, she went back to silence, so quiet that I wanted to yell just to startle her into speech. She put words to paper though: ruled paper, Post-it notes, my stationery, her old Strawberry Shortcake notepad. She wrote what she wouldn't say.

> *When Sung came, it was like I was left out. You kept telling Minh and me that we'd be fine. You said we would be fine as a family. But it didn't work because I wasn't fine anymore. I was the odd one out when Sung came.*

She signed it: *The Odd One Out.* I put the note in my pocket and called to Sung to hurry it up; he was going to be late for school. Anita was out the door already, headed off to school with her older brother who drove a rusted heap we had passed along to him.

    I remembered that woman, Marge? No, Beth. Beth at the adoption group, the time I passed around the picture of Anita. I hadn't seen her in a long time, didn't know if I'd recognize her, didn't know if I'd recognize anyone from the group because I hadn't been to a meeting in forever, hadn't been anywhere for a long time. I still ran with Cheryl, but by the time I read Anita's note, I was moving toward isolation. Had Beth been right when she warned me that it was a dicey idea mixing skin tones? I did not want to believe that.

I pulled the note out of my pocket and read it again. Sung, now in third grade, was taking his sweet time getting ready for school; he'd be late. I thought back to the decision to adopt him: How did I come to be nagging a ten-year-old Korean-born kid to hurry up? Why did I feel scared when I read Anita's note—as if we were, all of us, in the arms of that bear back in Saint Marys?

How was it we adopted Sung? We had two kids, a boy and a girl. That was supposed to be the right combination, the right number.

Maybe I was like my mother, crying for more babies, although I would never have said so. Instead, I told both myself and Ken that we could handle one more child. Life with Minh, Anita, and Ken was basically sweet. Even with little money, even with Ken's long work hours, and my complaints, I loved our life and wanted more. *More. One more child. Let's adopt one more time.*

The kids and I sang/yelled, off key, loud and raucous, in the living room. I pounded an old upright while we sang "The Green Grass Grows All Around." I was a mom, face up, exactly the way I had planned. We had nuoc mam sauce and rice and tandoori chicken. We had chocolate. We had plenty. I was giving the kids the mother they wanted. Or, more accurately, I gave them the mother *I* wanted. And most of the time back then, it seemed fine.

And *that's* why Sung came. Life was good. Why not add

more good? Ken suggested a boy: "Maybe a little boy?"

It was summer, late July. We had a new social worker. We had met her in her office for the preliminaries. Then she came to do our home study. Small and earnest. Jean. She reminded me a little of Dusty, the woman who'd carried Minh off the plane. We sat at the picnic table Ken had made with a kit he'd bought from Fingerle Lumber, varnish coming off in spots, the table a little wobbly because the kids used it to jump off of so much. The worker asked Minh and Anita, who were going into first and second grade, to draw pictures about life with another child in the family. She asked Ken why he wanted a boy. Another boy would be fun, he said. Besides, Anita liked being the only daughter. I raised my eyebrows at his frankness and picked off a wide spot of varnish—what would the worker think? Was that a bad reason for wanting a boy? But Jean smiled and said it made sense to her. She put us down for a little boy from Korea, no older than three. There were no little boys in India. Boys were not abandoned there. But little boys were available in Korea. They often waited a long time because most people wanted to adopt girls. Girls were seen as cuter, easier. We were unlikely to get an infant since we had children. Childless couples had first dibs on infants. We didn't mind.

The kids drew a picture of a girl, and then a boy. They wrote *Welcome* in huge letters across the pictures and handed them over for Jean to see. "You have amazing children," the worker said. "They're so loving." I turned a glowing face to Ken. Jean drove off in her gray van, honked as she turned the corner. So simple in some ways. So easy, straightforward. It seemed like that. *You want a little boy? Okay.*

And here's the part I returned to when I read Anita's note to me: Did we even think that Anita might feel like the odd one out? Ken and I shared color. Few people could distinguish one Asian ethnicity from another, so Minh and Sung were viewed as one ethnicity, whatever people thought that was. Anita was the one people pointed at, the odd one. Should we have weighted that when we adopted Sung? And if so, how much weight should we have given it? Is family like a math problem? *This father + this mother + these children = family.*

Ken reasoned that Anita, who even as a small child could be thorny and emotionally volatile, would be more confident if she could be *the only daughter*. And he was right. She loves it. She still signs her father's birthday cards that way all the time: *Your Only Daughter.*

I'm the only one, she says. It still matters to her, even as a grown woman.

Why revisit the decision about Sung? Could we have prevented what happened if we had chosen differently? If I had never asked for just one more? If we had tried to match the kids? I wonder about it still, but it's impossible to know, and Korea was where our son to be lived. We wanted him, although we didn't know him.

Chapter 11

THE YEAR THE TREES DIDN'T DIE

I remember Ken standing near the phone in the kitchen, the same phone that rang the time we learned that we were to pick our daughter from a list of names. The same phone that would ring not too many years later, letting us know about her again, but then it would be bad news. When Ken answered this time, though, it was Jean, the social worker who'd visited that summer day. There was a little boy who was waiting. He had been in the orphanage for a year. Which probably meant other adoptive parents had said no to his referral, afraid that he would fail to develop. He was about two years old, they couldn't be sure of his age. He had developmental delays. Plus he cried a lot. Were we interested? So fast! Not even a full month.

"Well," Ken said to Jean, "if he makes noise, he's vocal. That's a good thing." He was not eager to repeat the long silence we'd had with Anita.

"I'll send you a picture," the worker said. "Have a look and decide."

We knew even without the picture. The little boy was meant to be with us. Contemporary adoption research does not encourage the idea of the child *meant to be*. It's too much like a fantasy, Santa or the Tooth Fairy. I know that any number of other children might have been referred to us. I also believe Sung was always ours. I've never had trouble reconciling opposites.

We waited for the picture.

The kids and I were at the pool for the last swim of summer. We were eating soft serve when Ken found us there, and we offered him a lick. His brown eyes shone, words fell before him.

"I have a picture." A picture! The child! So fast again! It had only been a few days since the phone call.

There he was. A picture of a little boy standing in a walker, one of those things with wheels and a row of colored beads across the front. The walkers aren't around anymore because kids got hurt in them, but he was in one, in some kind of yard. There was grass but no trees. The sky was blue, cloudless. He had his arms out, palms up, as if he were trying to catch something falling from that blue sky. The photo was taken at his orphanage outside Seoul.

He was frowning into the sun (a little like Anita's first picture, that frown), wearing only a diaper. He was the size of a good roasting chicken, and he looked—almost like a puppet, not a real little boy. Was he sick? Hard to tell. He hadn't been fancied up for the picture, that was for sure.

"He doesn't look happy," said Anita. She sounded anxious, circling the last of her cone with her tongue.

"He looks mad," said Minh.

I looked at the picture and thought, *Two boys and a girl.*

"There is some information on him," Ken said. "It will be coming in the mail." The frown and size of the child didn't seem to worry him.

When the information came, it was, like the information about Minh and Anita, bare minimum. Sung's height and weight and approximate age were noted on a sheet of paper. There was information about him eating rice, learning to say *ba* and *ma*, receiving inoculations. In a note at the end of the sheet, someone had written: *He fusses much. Will grow to be a much nicer boy in nice adoptive home. His name is Moses. We call him Moses.*

A failure-to-thrive baby.

That's what we know *now*, but we didn't back then. It wasn't a term I had heard. But now I know that he was so slack in tone, so wretched looking because he was ready to give up. If kids don't get what they need, food and cuddling and someone to encourage them, they might give up.

Sung, like Anita, spent time in a police station waiting, in case someone came to claim him. He had been found on a bus in Seoul. Jean got that information for us. He was just learning to walk and talk when he was assigned to us. He'd spent way too many hours in a crib; the back of his head was flat. The social worker joke for this was to call it Korean bed head. We knew only that much. Anyway, Sung was ours.

All our kids live with the long-term effects of their early lives. It's clear to us now that Minh and Sung cope with some form of attention deficit disorder that leaves them struggling to process what you and I might not give a second thought to. They are competent adults, but they can rarely remember where their keys are or what they're supposed to get at the grocery store. It's difficult for them to relate things in sequential order. They drift off and lose track. They are whip smart. But every day requires effort just to make it through.

Anita's early life left her with emotional vulnerability, which led to trauma as an adolescent and a lingering general uneasiness in the world. She tends to wait for the sky to fall in on her.

It would have been good if we had known more in those years. We needed to be educated about failure to thrive, about emotional trauma, malnutrition, and their ramifications. But who knew? The pediatrician said nothing. The social worker said nothing. It was early days on the international adoption scene.

Everyone needed education. So although Sung's bit of information was daunting, no one said *failure to thrive*, not once.

I asked Ken one time—the kids were grown and we talked about the past like veteran warriors; licked ice cream all on our own in front of the Washtenaw Dairy, the same place we had taken the kids on hot summer days—why he wasn't concerned when he saw the picture of Sung. He put his tongue between his teeth as if he were testing his words before he released them.

"It never occurred to me," he said. "I figured we'd be able to manage."

I took a lick of my cone, bear claw, and snorted. Although, if I had thought for a second, I would have remembered my urgings to go ahead. Why shouldn't he have been confident? We usually assumed we would manage.

* * *

Even if I didn't know the words *failure to thrive* back then, I asked Ken daily if he was sure it would be all right. I felt the same exact way I had felt one time when we hiked to the bottom of the Grand Canyon on those skinny little trails. I had wanted to go, but one wrong step . . .

Still, I had *seen* him . . . in that picture. I had said *yes*.

What would have kept me from going ahead? Information that the child had blindness, deafness, paralysis, spina bifida. I am pretty sure I would not have gone ahead if any of those things had been the case. But they were not the case, so I closed my eyes and jumped, convinced that the water was deep enough. *Yes*, I said, and we had a son in Korea.

* * *

I imagine how Sung was found. The driver finished his route and walked to the back because he heard a whimpering sound, and there was a baby boy wearing a diaper tied Korean fashion, a stained shirt, and red-and-white-striped rubber shoes too big for him. He was taken to the nearest police station in case somebody came to claim him. He stayed at the police station for six months, and was then sent to Green Meadows Baby Home outside Seoul. They called him Moses there, the found baby, and, sometimes, when we were goofing around, we called him Moses too. "I'm the discovered kid," he said. "You guys are lucky the bus driver found me." But he said that only when he was feeling great.

Anita and Sung bonded over their time in police stations. "Police station!" they yelled when they heard their stories as they grew and realized what that meant. "We weren't criminals!"

"No, of course not," we said. "But that's sometimes where they took babies who were left in India or Korea before they took them to an orphanage." They looked distressed, sad for the babies. It made me sad too, no way to imagine anyone singing them to sleep, covering them with a blanket, offering a drink of water when they cried.

When it was time for Sung to go, somebody dressed him, put on his red-and-white-striped shoes, packed some extra diapers, and waved good-bye. "Bye, bye, Moses. Have a good time in America."

Jean came to the airport with us. It was July, so almost a year after we had seen Sung's picture. The adoption process had met snags. Papers had been lost; there had been long waits for a visa. But there we were. "I love this part," said Jean. We were standing there waiting, early again. "This is the best part. I get to go on the plane and bring him out to you." I smiled. Why begrudge her? I preferred being alone; no one had gone with us before this, so the moment had been all ours, but I smiled at her again, and then she drifted from my sight line. Because right then, someone shouted, "The plane's in!" The kids let out a whoop. We peered through glass and saw the wings of a Northwest plane. Somewhere inside that plane was our little boy.

Sung. *Sung*, we sort of slur the *u* in pronouncing his name. Sung means wisdom. And, again, the name seems to be the right one. We picked the name from a list a Korean-born colleague of Ken's had. Sung was called Moses in Korea, *the* name given to children who were found abandoned. We had no plans to call him that. So, we went to visit Min-jun in his apartment. He made us bulgogi and we ate two helpings each, stopped ourselves from licking the plates. I got the recipe and we found a Korean name for our youngest son on that list.

Sung looked like he had hardly *ever* eaten. His stomach was distended, his legs so limp they seemed to be an afterthought. Maybe they had just put him in that walker for the picture. Maybe the reality was that he spent all his time in a crib? His hair had that same reddish cast we had seen with Anita. Kwashiorkor. I caught my breath. Ken squeezed my shoulder, murmured: "Hey there, hey there. It's going to be all right. We're going to be fine."

A lovely child. Will do best in a nice adoptive home with loving parents. Cries loudly and frequently until he is held. Is not yet on target developmentally. Will need patience.

Again the words. They were handwritten on a piece of paper that came along with Sung, on a piece of paper that listed his medications and his feeding schedule. Did the same person write both notes, the referral note that came to us and the note I held? Somebody who liked Sung but knew he had troubles?

I sat on the floor in the airport lounge holding him. Jean took a picture. The picture shows a child splayed on my lap face-forward. I have one arm around the child and the other around Anita. Ken and Minh are holding a small stuffed giraffe they offer to Sung. He refuses it. (He learned to love it and cried all the way back to Ann Arbor two years later when he left it behind in the Chicago Field Museum.) He looks catatonic. Ken, Minh, and Anita look concerned. I look scared.

"Well," Ken said. "Well, let's go home with the new family." We headed out the door into the hot summer night. He seemed so calm, but I never knew if his calm was real or something he shrugged on for the occasion.

Riding home with our new son in the dark of the car, I remembered how Ma cried so much. Did she ever cry because she thought she had too many babies? I didn't think so. Ma was always in love with the idea of the newest one. I felt like crying, though. I wasn't at all sure I could manage three. I was afraid for my new child. Maybe I was afraid *of* him, afraid of his slack skin, his limpness, the lack of weight. He hadn't gained much weight it seemed, and he was two years old! He wasn't what anyone would picture as a child, more like a quick job of gray-brown skin over a skeleton. So needy, he was almost toxic.

I carried him to the room I hoped he'd sleep in eventually and sat down on the floor with him. He crawled from my lap to a high old dresser up against one wall, slid under it, and stayed there. I could see him, like a starved raccoon. I pushed a baby bottle of rice milk toward him. He grabbed it and sucked so fiercely the nipple popped with the sound of a small explosion when he released it from his mouth.

I stroked the hand holding the bottle. I felt him shake, heard him gulping sobs and milk.

"*Omonoi, omonoi,* I am your mother. I will love you." I would love him. Right then we were strangers, but I would love him.

I offered a rice cracker.

I tried just touching my lips to his arm. "Here, little boy, have some love . . ." but *no, no.* He did not want my American love. He wanted Korean love.

"*Wa,*" I said. "*Wa,* welcome." I tried, "*Bae go pa?* Did you eat?" Or more correctly, "Have you had rice?" There was no phrase in my *Easy Korean* book for, *Are you afraid?*

He was not silent like Anita. He made noise, angry sounds, animal like, as if he were caught in a trap and snarling. He didn't seem to be using any of the Korean words they said he knew.

Just survive. I had to survive. He had to survive. Everybody had to survive.

Kenzaburo Oe wrote a book after the birth of his son who was born brain damaged, a version of Oe's life written as fiction, *A Personal Matter.* I read the book lying on the floor next to Sung. The main character, called Bird, talks to his in-laws while his newborn brain-damaged baby lies in a bassinette. The baby's father acknowledges he had wished to have the baby die. Now, although he has no hope for the future he imagined, he wants to learn about forbearance.

I gulped words and phrases from the book the way Sung gulped his milk, looking for something to offer relief, solace. I wanted that little boy to be okay. I wanted to comfort him, stroke him, teach him how to trust. I wanted to be okay myself. I wanted all of us to be easy and happy.

Take a break was what I really wanted. Sung was so intense! He stayed under that dresser most times, shoved everybody away and growled at us. My back ached from lying on the floor next to him. I knew staying next to him was the right thing to do, knew to continue offering whatever he was willing to take, crackers, milk, a little rice, but I wanted that break. I was not so different from my mother and her wanting. Lying on the floor next to Sung, sticky in the July heat, I thought of my mother again, how she yearned for a pool, something she could sink into on hot summer days. "It would feel so good," she said, "and it's not as if your father couldn't make one."

I rolled over searching for a cool spot on the floor and remembered what my mother got.

* * *

We all watched while Dad pounded together a swimming pool with scrap wood he'd lugged home from work. He nailed together a 9' x 4' rectangle, lined it with tar paper, and painted it green. There was nothing else like it in the neighborhood. Maybe anywhere. "Here you are," he said to Ma. She looked surprised, tentative, but not unhappy. It was not what she'd imagined, but it did hold water. If she got in and swam around, it served as a pool, so that's what she did.

Ma crouched in the water holding a baby. The skirt of Ma's swimsuit flared out around the two of them like a blue ruffled sun. She looked up to a sky plain as her kitchen counter. "Well," she said, "it's not what I pictured, but I'm in water; I guess you could say I have a pool." The sun and the water sparked light, and I reached across to touch my mother and the baby.

We made a circle, the three of us in the pool.

* * *

Sung was not what I imagined. There was so much anger, the shoving away, the almost snarl, the fear, the endless sobbing. No. He wasn't what I had imagined. I couldn't even remember, lying next to him, if I *had* imagined what he'd be like. It didn't matter. There he was under the dresser, crying and snarling, gulping rice milk; it was my job to claim him. I had another son, a Korean-born son.

Minh and Anita were suspicious of Sung, angry with Ken and me. What had we done to them? Where were the singing and dancing? The ice cream?

There was no family leave for adoptive parents, so Ken went back to work, two days after Sung came home. He got the older two over to the Leslie Science Center for nature classes in the morning. I collected them at lunchtime. I walked the mile over there with Sung on my back. It seemed to soothe him and it helped me feel as if I were out in the world. When he fell asleep, exhausted from crying, I read a story to the older two. They liked that. Or I'd let them make mud sundaes: ice cream, chocolate sauce, crushed Oreo cookies, and gummy worms.

There was never enough of me. Ken came home, most nights, to find me beleaguered, the older kids sullen. He'd put Sung on his back in the orange pack and we'd all walk around the block. We'd stop to visit with the neighbors, Ann, Cheryl, elderly Mr. Ryan who looked at us and said, "You guys look like you could use a little time off." When I went running with Cheryl and she asked me how it was going, I told her the truth. That it was hard. "I might just keep running," I joked. "I might keep on going." She came around later in the day with a bouquet from her garden. I was in the basement doing laundry and didn't hear her knock. She left the bouquet in the milk chute.

Ann took Minh and Anita to play with her kids whenever she could. September came. Anita and Minh went off to school. There was no one I could leave Sung with. He demanded too much. But one day Ann insisted that she could watch him for an hour or two. "Even if he cries the whole time," she said, "it's just for an hour or two." Ken and I went out for lunch—tuna fish sandwiches at the Flim Flam. I felt airborne. This was how people in a normal life lived!

It was a long time before Sung crawled out from under the dresser and allowed me to hold him, months before he stood in the kitchen eating crackers and drinking rice milk. If there was a moment I counted as a turn, it was the moment we found Sung dumping crackers into a tub full of water. He'd made his way into the bathroom where somebody had not drained the tub. Sung always carried crackers around, took comfort from them. That day he had a stack of them in their sleeve, and he dumped them into the tub. We found him leaning over the tub, watching crackers float, become a soggy mess. It was ordinary, the kind of thing a parent might complain about, and I had no thought of complaining because it *was* ordinary. I laughed and went to get a long-handled spoon. We stood around and watched Sung lean over the tub and stir. Everybody took a turn. Bathtub soup.

Oe wrote truth of how a family survives.

Forbearance, the virtue I wanted to dismiss in favor of ease, got us from one day to the next until we made a family, the five of us.

He played under the wild black cherry trees in our yard, green through the summer and early fall. Come October, he watched as the leaves colored up, then mass dropped. He scooped up the leaves and put them into boxes, stuffing boxes full until the leaves started dropping faster than he could scoop. He crawled back under the dresser, crying. What was he afraid of? How could I know? He didn't have much language yet. All that winter, he kept his distance from the trees. Almost no one believes this. People think it preposterous. Sung himself has no memory of it, finds it hard to believe, like you reject that awful picture of yourself, even though it's clearly *you* in the picture. He doesn't recognize the boy under the dresser, has no memory of him, and doesn't seem to want to know him.

But we know him; we remember him.

Come spring, when the leaves came out, he pulled me out of the house to look at the trees. Ken took a picture of us under the newly green leaves and labeled it: *Sung and his first Ann Arbor spring—the year the leaves came back.* We sighed. The way you do if you just miss having your car impounded or falling through ice into deep water.

We watched Anita and Minh pulling him around the yard in the old red Radio Flyer wagon. Sung's first Ann Arbor spring.

"Here we gooooooo," they yelled. "Here we gooooooo . . ."

He held on to his pack of crackers. He wore the red sweater too small for him by then, and he laughed; everyone laughed. I loved them.

Chapter 12

A BUBBLE OF A PLACE

"Ann Arbor must have been a great place to raise your family, no problems; I mean a college town and all, it must have been great." People who live in Ann Arbor, people who don't live in Ann Arbor, who have only heard of it, say the same thing. Sometimes, people who don't live in Ann Arbor give a little chant when I tell them where I live. "Go Blue!" they say. "Go Blue!"

Rita is an old mom friend, a person I hung out with when Sung was at Northside Elementary. Her son was in the same grade and we'd wait out soccer games together. I ran into her at the People's Food Co-op during the summer of 2013. We caught up with our news while I dumped my tamari almonds into a paper sack. "You're lucky your family grew up in this town." She gave a nod toward the Asian-Caucasian couple buying soy milk, another nod to an older black man with gray dreads moving down the aisle. "There's no place like Ann Arbor."

A place free from racial tension. An inclusive place. A lucky place to be. That's the image of Ann Arbor. You can buy shirts that say so: *Ann Arbor and the rest of the world. I'd rather be in Ann Arbor.* People who do not live an interracial life, like Rita, look around and point to what they see as an iridescent bubble. And they aren't wrong, but they aren't completely right either.

There are great things about Ann Arbor. Right now, I can walk downhill from my house on Broadway, over the bridge to Zingerman's Delicatessen, the farmer's market, and three coffee shops. The Dalai Lama has been here. The Blind Boys of Alabama played at the Ark. We took Mookie, our Afro-Amer-Asian granddaughter, to hear them. We whooped it up and danced in the aisles. The guy across the street shares his snow blower with us. Two kids in the neighborhood are adopted, both interracially. So isn't Ann Arbor a bubble? Wasn't it a great place to raise our family? I love Ann Arbor. But it isn't a bubble now, and it wasn't when the kids were growing up. People like to say there are no bad places in Ann Arbor, which implies that everyplace in Ann Arbor is green (we're a tree town) and safe, but that's not true. There are places that have a good share of drugs and guns and trouble: South Maple, Hikone. People who live in those places know the risks and take measures. They are aware. People who live in green and safe neighborhoods, like Broadway or the Old Westside, walk beneath their trees, mostly risk free and unaware. But from time to time somebody gets jumped. Cars are broken into. A bank is held up. A student is raped. Then people get nervous and pay attention. They call for more police protection. They want to walk underneath their trees without worry.

Still Ann Arbor has always had the cachet of imperviousness, as if the town were free from all harm. The people and the place intersect to produce an image of a perfect place to live. For example:

In the fall of 1986 Sung and I boarded the bus and headed off to the Y. He had been with us for about two years by then. Minh and Anita were in elementary school. Sometimes, I asked myself whether it was the kids' needs or mine that made me drag my feet about getting on with my MA and landing a job. I didn't know, and I wasn't doing very much about it. Sung was going to take a gym class at the Y while I learned to throw a pot. We got off the bus and walked down 5th Avenue past Afternoon Delight, a restaurant that makes giant muffins. People sat on stools, drinking coffee, eating their giant muffins, looking out the wall of windows at the street. Sung had new green shoes with frog faces. He walked along, holding my hand, then he pulled away and stuck his foot up next to the window. "New shoes," he called. "New shoes." People smiled and clapped. One guy, he introduced himself as Tony, came out to admire the frog shoes. And every time after that, when he saw Sung, Tony would wave. Once he came out with a muffin for Sung. He looked at me to make sure it was okay to offer it. I was charmed and agreed. What harm could there be? A blueberry muffin from Afternoon Delight. Sung and I broke it in half and ate it while we walked the last block to the Y.

A bubble of a place that floated easily in a deep blue sky. That's how Ann Arbor felt just then.

But not always. That same fall the kids and I took the bus into town to eat gyros at the Parthenon, now glitzed up and called Lena. On the bus, an older white guy pointed us out to a woman sitting next to him, who might have been his wife, or not, who knows? Our stop came up, the same stop that Sung and I had used. On 5th Avenue, just before Afternoon Delight. The man grabbed my arm as I moved past him. "You should be ashamed of yourself," he said. "Ashamed. How many men did you sleep with, anyway?" Why was it often men accosting me, telling me to be ashamed? First that kid on a bike back on the Broadway bridge, then the guy on the bus.

The kids looked straight ahead. The other passengers looked straight ahead. The driver looked straight ahead. I thought about smacking the guy, but I shrugged, and got us off the bus. My older two knew what the guy was talking about. Not Sung though, who at four only sensed that something went wrong. I really didn't care that the guy accused me of sleeping around. He was nobody. But I was furious that my kids were exhibit A. I told them the guy was a jerk who knew nothing about adoption or biology. "He thinks I'm your birth mom. But if I were your birth mom, you'd be a mix of me and your Asian dad. You'd be biracial." They nodded—they didn't want a lesson. They ran on ahead down 5th, around the corner to Liberty and Main—eager to eat gyros, and maybe flaming cheese, at the Parthenon.

I told the bus story to Josie the next week. She had kids who had been adopted too. We met each other at Seva on Liberty for a Saturday lunch from time to time. She stopped forking up her nachos. "Oh God," she said. "What did you do? What a wacko." The waitress who came by to pour more iced tea heard me tell the story. "That guy couldn't be an Ann Arbor person," she said. She almost wrapped me in her arms.

That was a nice thing to say, an indication that Ann Arbor had diversity, inclusiveness.

But the doctor I had met in the emergency room a few years earlier was a person who lived in Ann Arbor. I had taken Minh, who was five then, in for an acute asthma attack. The doctor commiserated with me on the middle-of-the-night visit. Did I have a far drive? I didn't. We bonded a little. He assured me that he'd take care of Minh, who would need a shot of epinephrine. It was a little bit of a nasty shot, he said. Then he added, with complete sincerity, that Minh would not feel the pain, though. "They don't feel pain the way you and I do." A believer in the myth of Asian stoicism, who gave Minh a red sucker after he poked him.

"Blow it off. Why do you take it so much to heart? People don't mean to be rude. They just don't know." Well-meaning people said this to me when I complained, and they had a point. It was unreasonable to expect adoptive heaven in any town. There weren't even that many adoptive interracial families around—they were just coming on the scene in the seventies and eighties. Think about the numbers for a minute. About twenty-five thousand kids came to the States from Korea in that time period. Vietnamese adoptions had peaked at a thousand children in 1975, then almost stopped. Indian adoptions were minuscule, way below five hundred in any year of the seventies and eighties. We knew some families in Ann Arbor who had kids from Colombia and Ecuador. But there were never so many adoptive families around town in those years that you wouldn't notice another family on the street, smile, maybe talk with each other to connect. So even in Ann Arbor our family wasn't the norm.

Interracial international adoptions are common now. Once movie stars began adopting internationally/interracially, the pictures of their families were all over the place, so even that guy on the bus might understand my family, if he had read the issue of *People* magazine with Angelina's family on the cover.

Tony left Ann Arbor for Boston. I never saw the guy on the bus again. Over the years, I learned to cope with doctors, teachers, strangers, friends. I could be angry. I could resent that news articles always referred to "the adopted child of . . ." but never referred to "the birth child of . . ." I could point out dated attitudes in supposedly on-top-of-things Ann Arbor. People might be surprised, might not like it, but I could do it.

I need to aim for balance though.

"Mary. Chill!" We were out in the yard grilling—half the grill for meat burgers, half for the veggie burger crowd. I had pointed out yet another reference to "adopted child" in a newspaper article. Like adoption was the equivalent of a scarlet letter. Cheryl heard my grumbling and told me to chill. She gave me a Sam Adams and a hug. I took a swig and hugged her back.

"Think if you had tried to raise us in Saint Marys," the kids say to me now that they're grown. "We had enough trouble in Ann Arbor. What would have happened to us there?" They go back to Saint Marys for my father's birthday, sometimes Easter. They love my family, but they don't blend into the place for sure.

Sometimes, we considered moving to a place where there would be more job assurance, no endless applying for NIH grants. If Ken had worked at, say, Cleveland Clinic, we could have lived in Cleveland Heights. We had family in Cleveland. We imagined ourselves in the grocery store, walking around Coventry, going to Little Italy for cannoli. It could have worked.

We never moved, though. We had made a life for ourselves; acquired favorite places without knowing it: Afternoon Delight, Zingerman's, the Huron River, the Washtenaw Dairy. How could we leave the People's Food Co-op and their tamari roasted almonds? What about Cheryl and Ann? What about the river? Ann Arbor was a great place for yoga. What about yoga? We had become attached. Which is exactly what people said would happen when we arrived. "There's no place like it. You won't want to leave." It seemed that they were right. There were and are problems in the town we love. There are places as good or better to live, no matter what the T-shirts proclaim. Ann Arbor is not a bubble. But it is the place we call home, the place our children return to when they want to come back home.

Chapter 13

FINDERS KEEPERS

So we didn't live in a bubble. But it was a nice place, and most days when the kids were young, we made it up to the corner with everyone happy. We had three children, a family knotted together with industrial-strength rope, no umbilical cords. We, the parents, made certain the knots were tight.

But, after a while, Anita and Minh didn't want to go up to the corner. They were big kids by then, nine and ten. I unfastened a knot, allowed for some slack. Sung was still little and glad to walk to the corner with me. He pointed out a plane overhead coming into Detroit. He asked if there were kids on the plane, kids coming to America from Korea; he was curious, waving to those maybe kids coming to new homes.

I plopped Sung into the bike basket when Ken pulled up; his legs hung out over the edge. It could not have been comfortable, but he *wanted* to be squashed in the basket. Sometimes, Ken gave him a basket ride *up* to the corner, where Sung dropped letters in the blue mailbox. The letters went to Korea marked: *please forward.*

Sung dictated the letters, which I wrote in my best script. We sent the letters to Green Meadows Baby Home.

Dear Korean Mother,
It is nice here. I like Butterfinger Bars. I go to school.
I have a brother and sister and live in a green house.
What do you look like? I don't know if you will get this, but if you do, write back.
Your son,

Sung
PS I would like to see you but just for a little bit.
PPS They called me Moses when I lived in Korea.

I imagined her. I imagined a small woman in a black plastic raincoat getting onto a bus in Seoul. The bus was crowded; she had to stand. She carried a bag of flyers in a red tote that kept slipping down her arm. The flyers said she was looking for her baby, although he would no longer be a baby; he'd be a little boy. She had left the baby on the back seat of the bus and she was sorry; she wanted him back.

What if, somehow, she read Sung's letter, wrote back and asked for him? Always, one part of me was saying to the kids, "Yes, you can miss your birth mom and want to see her," while the other part of me was saying, "I am your mother. I am the real mother."

Of course, she was real too.

There's a legend in Korea. We often read the story to Sung because it seemed a good way for him to understand the place he came from, the culture he owned and missed—the legend of Chindo Island:

A fisherman was stranded on an island offshore and prayed for a way back home. He wanted nothing more than to get home. He begged and pleaded to the gods. Every day, the same prayers and pleas. Eventually, the gods heard his prayers and rewarded such fervor. A low tide opened up a land bridge that allowed the man to return home. So now, every year visitors go to the bridge to Chindo Island and pay homage to this legend by crossing the bridge.

There is always some kind of need for us to go back and move around in the space we come from. There would be a need for the kids to return, psychologically if not physically. We understood that. After all, I was the woman who kept returning to Saint Marys; sometimes packing all of us into the car, slip sliding our way on snowy roads up over those hills. But, there was also the nagging voice inside my head that kept asking, *which place is home*?

Did Sung's birth mother believe that Sung was home, or did she think he was lost? Surely, she thought he was lost: to her and Korea. The same with Anita and Minh and their birth moms.

And what about the bridge in the Chindo Island story?

I still believe it's my job to be a bridge between countries for the kids. I need to allow them to cross that bridge, but I hope they always return.

* * *

I listened when they talked to each other, the three of them curled on my bed. They liked the big bed, liked sprawling all over, and I didn't care. There were piles of pillows and they made a fort with them. They talked a lot in those years. Minh and Anita preteens by then. Sung about five. They talked about big stuff, compared notes, and it did not seem to bother them that I was curled up in the old orange chair of Ken's that he'd shoved into the bedroom. I think they wanted me to hear. It was their way of telling me things. I kept quiet and listened.

"If a war broke out," Minh asked Anita and Sung one time, "which side would you fight for? I mean if there was a war between Korea and the US. Or India and the US? I mean supposing somebody asked you to choose sides?" After a long minute, Anita said she'd choose home. She did not say, "I would fight for the US." That wasn't immediate enough. What she said was, "I wouldn't let anybody take our house." Sung agreed; he understood that. They would fight for their home. But their voices held uneasiness. They were not comfortable with Minh's question. Other kids didn't have to choose. Why couldn't they be the same as everybody else?

Sometimes every one of them shoved their birth countries away. They rejected the multicultural mix we fed them, snapped at us that they'd had enough of Korea, Vietnam, and India. No art, stories, music, flags, dolls with brown skin, or posters that showed multiracial kids scattered over the globe of the world. They satisfied themselves with Power Rangers, Cabbage Patch Dolls, cans of Pringles potato chips, bologna sandwiches, Tommy Hilfiger.

Minh had another question for Sung and Anita, probably the one he really wanted to ask, but was afraid to. Did they want to go back, just for a little while, just to see what she looked like? Meaning, of course, the birth mother. Anita almost never talked about India willingly. She loved the food, but she wasn't big on anything else to do with India. Definitely would not wear a sari, no matter that Leela and Subhendu sent her gorgeous ones. But, she heaved a sigh and said, yes, she'd go back and take a look. Sung said yes. He was curious.

Yes, they would like a look. No, they did not want to stay. I admit I breathed satisfaction, validation. Biological mothers don't question their status. But my children have other mothers; my mothering hinges on choice. Still, I don't want to have the children choose. It's cruel, unfair—like a bad divorce. However, when I heard my children pick me, I was glad. The need to be *the mom* trumped my wish for the kids to be free.

In one of those talk sessions, Minh told Anita and Sung that he often dreamed his Vietnamese mother was living in a village near the Mekong River. She was alone. In the dream he was afraid that she was hurt or lost. But he couldn't get to her to help her. Anita said she never dreamed of her Indian mother, not once. She dreamed of animals: tigers and elephants appeared in her dreams. They came up to her bedroom window, reached in, and carried her away. Sung said he dreamed of bodies hauled off in garbage trucks while he watched. These were real dreams. I knew that. I had comforted the kids when they woke from them. They were the kinds of dreams kids can have as they come to terms with the issues of loss and separation. The dream of the lost birth mom needing help, the dream of being taken away, those are common. But Sung's garbage trucks! We never figured them out. What had happened to him, to give him dreams like that? He says, even now, that he still goes back to that dream when he's stressed. I fuss and urge him to find someone to talk to and he tells me he has had plenty enough of that. He's a big guy now.

Sometimes—I thought, it's not anything the kids ever said—sometimes, it seemed that being adopted was like being halfway home, as if they walked in a place they sort of knew, but the grass was the wrong shade of green and there were no signs in their language; it was a nice place, but a place that left them just a bit anxious.

People often asked the children, *Do you remember?* People asked if they could speak Vietnamese, Korean, Hindi. *Can you speak your language? Do you remember it?* "They were very young," I said. "They don't remember." The answer wasn't that simple, but my voice was brisk, a broom sweeping litter away. The kids looked uneasy, as if they should be able to remember.

Maybe they tried to remember. Maybe they heard the faintest sound of another language. But it was a language they no longer understood.

Chapter 14
WHAT'S MISSING?

My mother never believed that kids could have actual troubles; they could have nothing more than trifling grief. "Children can't have troubles," she said to me when I was a kid, and again when I was a new mom. "What do children have to worry about?" She sipped coffee from her pink Melmac cup and the women in her kitchen nodded in agreement. The women were like my mother, hard-working, women who rubbed their bad backs and grumbled about the bushel baskets of ironing growing moldy in their kitchens. Whenever my mother was not lying facedown, she drank coffee from pink Melmac with those women who said over and over: "Oh to be a kid again. Not a worry in the world."

They were wrong though. My kids had troubles. Like poppies, their troubles shot up and out in what seemed like a single day, made Ken and me catch astonished breaths. So quickly I heard things from the children they had never said before. I listened to them say: *I don't fit. This isn't the right place. Why did you adopt me anyway?* I knew those words meant more than a skinned knee. They were trying to comprehend what makes family, trying to understand how our family fit into the concept of family. The questions began around the third grade for each of them and worked their way out from there. Back and forth. Up and down. Easy and hard, terrible then okay.

I looked at the kids and when I saw them I thought, *my children*. I knew they counted me as their mother, no matter that they said they didn't fit. They yelled at us and hugged us at the same time. Some days I wished it were easier, but I loved the kids—*forever.* That was the promise. It felt good to say that, the words melted in my mouth.

The kids smiled when I said *forever* and told them they were caught like a fish on my hook, an animal in my sight line. They laughed and shoved their spoons deep into bowls of ice cream. They wanted that ice cream. They begged for more every time I headed off to the grocery store: chocolate chip mint, peppermint stick, fudge ripple, marshmallow. They loved what they had, but they wanted other things too. They wanted their story. They wanted to know who they were before I caught them on my hook. Their story! Like in a baby book, between covers, fastened with wide French ribbon, their newborn picture in the lead spot. Where were they born? How much did they weigh? Was it snowing or raining, cold or sunny, the day they were born?

Most of us consider birth weight and place as markers in the bigger story of our lives, nothing we pay much attention to. But without those markers, it's possible to feel there is no story at all. Which might make you listen to any story you hear, good or bad. Which might make you question your family.

Well, we had that picture of Sung. We had the potty time picture for Anita. No pictures for Minh, the get-out-of-Vietnam baby. Mostly we had nothing but a blank in place of their stories. We kept the clothes they wore on the flight to the States. We filled albums with cards and drawings. We kept mementos: the bear John and Mary Ann gave to Minh, the white dress with pockets Ma gave Anita, Sung's red-and-white Korean shoes. We took pictures of them and their birthday cakes every year. But none of that was the story they wanted. Who were they before they were Minh, Anita, and Sung? They didn't even know their real birthday! How weird was that?

* * *

In Ann Arbor on the edge of Tornado Alley, residents are expected to listen for trouble. Every Tuesday once a month, from April to October, sirens shriek a practice test. We're encouraged to have a predetermined shelter, a battery-operated radio, a flashlight, and medical necessities at the ready. But most of the time, when the sirens shriek, people pay no mind. Most people think, *It's going to be okay.* The worst that happens, a few tree limbs come down. Ann Arbor is fine.

But what if, sometime, it isn't? What if we are caught in a mean rain, shivering, bone cold, the roof torn off our house? We are baffled—as if a bullet lodged in our chest cavity while we were giving change to a homeless person. The story is all wrong.

But why should we be surprised?

You will never know. You have to be prepared for surprises. Every time we filled out an adoption form, we were reminded of that. I thought I was prepared, but the truth is, I wanted, even expected, a story I would control, start to finish. My kids yearned for their stories. I wanted mine.

The moments when our stories merged were what I lived for.

* * *

One summer day, when the kids were still young, we took a day trip out to Independence Lake. We ate tomato-lettuce sandwiches, spit pits from Royal Ann cherries until it was dark and the park ranger sent us home.

Ken drove down North Territorial, past Saint Patrick's Church with its red steeple poking up into a navy-blue sky. Anita, in the back seat, made up a goofy song:

Hot, hot, hotter than a pot. Hot, hot, hotter than a pot.

She stuck her bare foot up toward me; "Hold it," she commanded. I grabbed her foot, held on, and turned to Ken. "You can drive off the edge of the world now," I told him.

He smiled his patient smile, always more laid back than I was. Always the one who expected things to work out. He believed the kids would find their way, lost stories or no. Things would work out. He listened to my concerns about the kids, but he didn't share them. He had grown up assured. No one in his family did anything that deviated from a confident, successful life. They were expected to do well, and they did. No fuss. At sixteen, Ken drove from Cleveland to Washington, DC. Alone. He did not mess up, did not wreck the car or even get a speeding ticket. Did not party wild. He spent the summer at Georgetown University taking a course that would qualify for college credit. Then he drove back home. No drama. And, of course, he drove to Olean, New York, where he met me at seventeen. Easy as pie. He found it hard to believe that our children would not behave the same way. Why not? So he smiled that patient smile of his and continued to drive, past the stone lions in front of the big house on Barton Drive, around the corner, and up our driveway.

Inside the house, I turned on the attic fan and cool slipped over us. We put blankets on the kids, already half asleep, then curled next to each other under our own.

The Amtrak train whistled as it rounded the bend of the Huron River. The sound came with me into sleep.

That day was the story I wanted, a story both the kids and I were glad to have. Everything about it was right, beginning, middle, and end. It would be lost. Gone before I heard a single warning siren.

Chapter 15
KISSES

A kiss is such a little thing. You can shrug it off if you want to or take it and ask for more.

There were plenty of kisses between Ken and me.

There were kisses I gave the kids. Smooches all over when they were little, quick pecks as they grew older. Minh gave kisses by blowing them into the air. Sung planted his kisses on my cheek. Anita gave them or demanded them, like so many sticks of gum. "Kiss," she urged when she was four. "Kiss!" She pulled at my leg. I leaned down, and she covered me with kisses. I kissed back, her neck, her hair, all ten of her fingers, one by one. "Kiss," she yelled when she spotted Ken coming home on his bike.

The year she turned thirteen, Anita's kisses became a problem. The kind of people she gave kisses to didn't want just a kiss. They waited and eyed her, planning for the time they could make a move. We grabbed hold of her and tried to pull her back to safety, a place where her kiss was plenty enough. But she eluded our grasp.

We talked and encouraged and counseled. We kept her close. We worked so hard. And it didn't matter. The things she had cared about, sleepovers and friends, even her track team, didn't get a glance anymore. It was as if someone had turned our girl inside out. We didn't know her, just that fast. As if a timer had gone off inside her. We knew her, and then, *poof*, the girl we knew was gone. Without a trace. How can you hold on to someone who has left?

She was way too young to be giving out kisses like that.

I hounded Ken. "You have to stop her," I said. "Do something! What if she ends up pregnant at thirteen?" It was unfair to say that and I didn't care, so terrified for my girl. He listened to me, still pretty calm. Or maybe he was unable to believe his daughter had such a big problem. He tried. "Sweets," he said. "Let me be your guy a little while longer. We only want what's best for you in the long run." He sounded like every parent. He didn't judge her or yell. He offered help. She sucked Pepsi through a blue plastic straw, gave him no answer, gone back to the silence she kept when she came off the plane.

What else did we do? We talked to her school counselor who said she was perfectly obedient in school. She never gave anybody any trouble. She was a quiet kid in school. Although, it did look as if the guys were coming on to her, but nothing totally out of line, not that he saw. She was a nice kid though, not one of the troublemakers.

I didn't think she was shoving people on the stairs or mouthing off to teachers. That wasn't her style. Her style was to pull inside herself. She'd never say anything. She'd act from someplace inside herself. I knew that from the early days of the long silence she held. What do you do then? How do you manage silence?

This past year, I read David Sheff's *Beautiful Boy*, the story of his relationship with his meth-addicted son, and I recognized his frustration when he talked about the people who gave him advice. *Take control.* That's what people told David to do. But a parent isn't a warden or a therapist. Can you be with a person every minute of the day? Can you be a person's mind? Anticipate the next move? You do the best you can. Which might be effective or might not. Sometimes, I was sure that we were doing a good job no matter that there were problems. Then I was unsure, and felt that I knew nothing. But one thing I knew for certain: it does not take long to move from a good story to a bad story. It can happen so fast you don't even know when the page was turned.

By spring of the year Anita was thirteen, a time we imagined as a time she would have crushes and be agitating for makeup, I could make out just enough, from the shrug of her shoulders, the way she hooded her eyes, that she had way more than crushes on her mind.

"I'm not like you guys at all!" She screamed that at us. She opened her mouth wide and moved from silent withdrawal to screaming. And then she tried to do everything she could think of that was not like us. When I talk to adoption specialists now, some of them suggest it's possible that Anita was acting out her worst fear: that she didn't belong in the family. She could keep the fear at bay if she told herself she didn't care, tried to be as different from us as possible. You don't mourn what you don't want. Maybe that was part of what happened. I don't dismiss the idea.

I began to feel we did not live in our green house by the river anymore. It felt as if we lived in a haunted house with false doors, blind turns, and mirrors that gave twisted reflections. I shrieked danger like the tornado sirens, but I couldn't get anyone to head for the basement.

Ken's upbringing, that mix of assuredness and confident expectation on the part of both Ken and his parents, left him little room to imagine a daughter who tossed kisses like confetti, a daughter who began to lie as easily as if she were reading a grocery list. He tried bringing her roses and stood baffled and hurt when she tossed them aside, left them to go dead in a heap on the floor. "She is still a kid," he said to me, pained and puzzled. "We need to be loving, but firm. We're her parents." We were her parents all right, but she had moved to a place where there was no room for parents, biological or adoptive, as if she thought she lived alone and would make her own way. No more conversations with her brothers, no foot stuck out for me to hold. She cordoned off an area and it was No Man's Land.

Should we have expected behavior like that? We were told no guarantees, but I never thought that meant *real* trouble. I thought that meant we would need patience. I thought there might be school issues, maybe some health issues, adjustment issues. I thought of those things, and I have to be truthful, always in the context of being able to deal with the issues. I would fix whatever was wrong. I did not think about a daughter who seemed to transform overnight, who split between crazy street-wild and a girl who would, even at thirteen, still hurl herself into my lap, demanding hugs. Perhaps, I might have imagined such a situation if I had known more. But I know more now, and still I can't see how I could have imagined it. All kinds of things can be anticipated: floods, tornadoes, hailstorms. But you can't look at a six-year-old girl laughing like crazy as her dad bikes her down the street in his bike basket and think: *She might hang out with gang members. She might know drug dealers. She might end up pregnant way too young.* And what if I *had* expected real trouble? What might I have done differently? Would I have given her more ice cream, or less? I've never been able to answer that.

The year she turned thirteen, I had nothing my daughter wanted, at least nothing that I was able to give her. Like weather, for instance. My daughter wanted a perpetually clear blue sky with sun directly in the middle. "I want full sun and nothing coming down from the sky." She looked at me when she said that like she thought I should pull strings. She couldn't be serious!

But, first thing when she got up mornings, she checked the sky. If it was gray, which it mostly was in Michigan, she looked at me as if I had failed, even though she knew I could do nothing. Maybe that was the message she intended. *I could do nothing.* She sat on her bed, knees up to her chest. I looked at the gray sky with her and rubbed her back. She seemed smaller than ever, as if she were going backward to the girl she was when she first came. I offered her some toast, orange juice, maybe an egg?

She said no, no, no.

"Anita, I wish I could make the days sunny for you."

"You can't. There's nothing you can do about it."

"That's true. I can't." We were talking code.

We surprised her with a greenhouse window for her birthday the November she was thirteen. We had it installed in her bedroom so she could create her own small garden in a miniature climate system, the next best thing to a perpetually sunny sky.

She landed full kisses on both of us when she saw the window and made a little summer with pots of cilantro and thyme and a miniature yellow rosebush. Minh and Sung wandered in. "Pretty cool," they said. All that winter she tended her plants and us cut sprigs of thyme, cilantro, mint. We admired the small yellow roses that bloomed. She seemed happy with her greenhouse window. But come summer, she stretched out on the grass and took in sun like a woman hungry for touch, a girl who had decided to be a woman. The plants in her greenhouse window turned brown and died.

So easily we left the good days behind, like a jacket lost on a day that starts out cold, then turns warm. Like the leather jacket Anita begged for. It was a brown leather jacket, too pricey, but Anita begged and wheedled. Ken finally agreed to get her the jacket. She had it a month and came home from school, no jacket. It was gone, lost or stolen or exchanged—for what? She didn't offer much in the way of details. The next morning she went off to school wearing jeans and a hooded sweatshirt. "Look for that jacket," I called after her. "Check lost and found."

"Yeah, I will," she said and waved. But I knew better.

The days of going out to the lake, fooling around, search as hard as I might, they were gone too, and, after a while, I couldn't remember the last time I saw them. I only *thought* I could trace the end of the good days, only thought I knew when things began to turn bad, the point of tilt from good to trouble.

* * *

I remember one day in particular when I try to put this story together, a day that, in retrospect, should have been marked as a divide, the start of my story gone wrong, pages ripped and torn. It happened before Anita got her greenhouse window, so before she was thirteen, before she gave out kisses.

It was a Thursday in the long slog from January to spring. Things were okay, not great, but okay. I had learned a lot by then. I already knew that Minh, for instance, was never going to *buckle down*. He always had unfinished homework, lost papers, a mass of ignored assignments at the bottom of his backpack. Anita was pushing for pierced ears and makeup . . . the clothes she wanted to buy were nothing I would agree to, a bit too edgy for someone who was still just a kid. Both Minh and Anita were not what educators call school compliant. They wanted the social life of school, not the subjects. Still, things seemed manageable.

So the Thursday I remember happened before we were seriously worried, maybe just a bit uncertain, knowing that we were headed into the teen years. Anita and Minh came home from school and stood inside the back door. Minh's coat was ripped, and his lip was bleeding. Anita had no coat. She cried that she had dropped it somewhere on Barton Drive. They had run from kids chasing after them.

I pieced the story together. There were a bunch of white kids who snatched their backpacks, shoved them, taunted them. The taunts had been going on for months. Kids called them names, *banana* and *oreo*, *chink*, *nigger*, *gook* . . . Only words. No actual physical assault. They ignored the words. Isn't that what we parents preached back then? Don't engage? Ignore taunts and the taunts will eventually stop? But they hadn't stopped.

On the Thursday they stood messed up inside the back door, Minh had taunted in return, *Honky! Honky!* Then there was physical stuff and my kids lost the fight.

Anita went to her room.

Minh sat on the couch and looked at the place on the floor where they had drawn outlines of themselves with markers one early morning while I slept. There were still faint outlines when light hit the floor the right way, like cave markings.

You prepare your children. You say that most people are kind; some people are not. You counsel caution. Don't be the one to punch somebody, but don't be a punching bag either. It's like the tornado sirens though. You expect things to work out because, mostly, they do. When you discover that things haven't worked out, you are shocked—the tornado really did touch down. The fight upset me, but the months of taunts I hadn't known about made for real distress. Why wouldn't they tell us?

I taped up his scrapes. "Oh, Minh . . ." He shrugged, a minute lifting of his shoulders meant to convey coping, to suggest it was what it was.

I went in search of Anita's things, found them, and knocked on her bedroom door. "I found your pack in the bushes. I got your coat too."

"I hate India," she yelled, from behind the door. "I hate my birth mother. I hate adoption. I hate this family. I hate everybody."

"These kids are not the whole world, honey."

But Anita flamed up and out, like she was covered in oil and someone had lit the torch. "I hate the whole world," she shrieked, loud, loud, loud. "Hate it. Hate it. Hate it."

That's the time I remember when I go back and try to figure why we began to lose the good story. It was only some bullying. Lots of kids get bullied. Everyone has to learn how to stand up to it. Bullies aren't, I told the kids, the whole world. Still, that day is what I remember, the day my world began to change.

Chapter 16

HUSBAND AND FATHER

Ken had known bullying. The smart kid who got the grades had been called names, had his jacket torn, his books stolen. He didn't dismiss the problem when he heard about it, but he thought the kids should have told us they had a problem. It would have been smarter to tell us rather than end up bloodied. They would survive though. After all, he had survived and he'd been a skinny nerdy guy. We fought—in low angry tones. I was emotional. Ken was reasonable. So reasonable I got angry at that, too. "How can you be mad at me for being reasonable?" I could be. I knew it wasn't the end of the world, what I'd said to Anita. I even allowed that Ken might be right. Still, I wanted Ken to be unreasonable, like me. In the end, we called a truce and sat in front of the fire drinking mugs of hot cider. I still thought he was more wrong than right.

In the years when we lived in the green house, when money was tight and the kids were little, we fought over Ken's work hours. I'd complain that he spent every minute he could in the lab. He'd point out that he needed to work those hours or he wouldn't have a job. I argued that I had no free time. "You get to think," I said. "I don't get to think." He'd look sad or guilty then and he'd take over for a night or a Saturday while I went to a yoga class or a full-day workshop and tried to master *Chaturanga Dandasana*. I loved the feeling of alignment that is Iyengar yoga. Alignment led to balance. Balance was the key. After a while I lured Ken into yoga and when the kids got older, the two of us went off to yoga class together. Ken did a great *Chaturanga Dandasana* from the get go, all that male upper-body strength.

I could hold downward-facing dog for ten minutes. Yoga was serenity. But I still got angry. No serenity then. My go-to argument was that Ken was just like my father. "I'm not like your father," he would protest. "How can you even say that?"

My father loved to tell me that he grew up in the woods. He said that he was off in the woods alone when he was seven. He came home when it got dark. This seems a stretch to me, but it's true that my father loved the woods. "Nothing will hurt you in the woods." He still says this to me. "You don't need to worry in the woods. It's people, towns, and cities you should be afraid of." He called Ken "city guy" the first time he met him, and it wasn't a compliment.

Ken had no woods experience, unless you count hiking marked trails at Independence Lake Park. But he asked to go out doe hunting with my father one fall, the Monday after Thanksgiving when we were back home to visit. It didn't seem like a good idea to me. "Don't count on him," I said to Ken. "Once he gets out there, he'll forget about you. You're nothing beside the deer he wants."

"It'll be fine," Ken replied.

"Why do it?"

"It's an experience; maybe I'll get to know your dad."

It was still dark when they left. I saw the headlights of the car hit the bedroom window, heard the wind rattle the plastic that was tacked over the inside of the window as insulation. I slipped deeper under the covers. A thin snow started up around midafternoon. Rosie came to see me. She lived about ten miles from Saint Marys, married to a guy who had no inclination to go out in the woods. "Poor you," she said, then laughing, "poor Ken." We drank tea and made turkey sandwiches with the last of the bird.

They all came back around six, long after it had grown dark. Ken told this story: They had gone into the woods around Clear Fork. My father left him under a tree as soon as they got there, around seven. Ken was supposed to drive any deer he saw toward my father, who walked away with his rifle and a promise to be back.

Ken usually did what he said he would do, so he looked for deer to drive toward my father and waited. Around noon he ate his turkey sandwich and drank from a thermos of coffee, hunkered down, and waited some more. He stayed under the tree the whole day, never once seeing a deer. It grew dark around four and still my father did not come back.

Ken, my cautious city guy, had a compass and a sense of direction. He made his way out to the car, cold and angry. My father showed up an hour later, yelling that Ken should have waited, he'd have come for him. He might have had a deer if Ken had waited. He wouldn't have left Ken there much longer. Just long enough to get a deer.

My father still complains about that time. But I tell him Ken should have driven off. I say it would have been no more than fair.

So it would seem that Ken is not like my father. He follows the rules, unlike my father who has little use for rules. Ken is cautious. He carries a compass, not a gun. He spends hours studying equations, lines, data, on computer screens. He's spent twenty years looking for the one result that will allow for a precise dosage of radiation that will erase the tumor with no trauma to the surrounding area. That's his work and he does it well. He does not fudge results, does not forget that people are the endgame.

Which is not what a person could say about my father.

He has always done careful work. The houses he built are solid. There is no skimping of detail, nothing slipshod. People are glad to buy a house my father built. The thing is, my father sees them as *his* houses. Only incidentally do other people live in them. When we drive past one of his houses, he will point out what he claims are flaws. "But, it's what they wanted, Dad. They wanted a bay window there." He'll tell me a version of what he said to Ken when he met him at the car: "If they had done what I said, they would have had a really nice house."

My father is brash. He's fallen off a roof and broken his leg, nearly lost an eye when a nail went flying. Because he scorned safety measures. "A man should be able to stay alive without babying. I've been busted up," he says. "Busted up good, but I've always come back better than before." But that's not true. He can hardly walk now. His leg never healed right, so he doesn't have a usable knee. He has to use a walker. He's hunching over, becoming smaller.

He'll tell stories long past the time a person can listen. When my mother was living he told her stories until she cried for mercy. "Red!" People called him that because of his fire-red hair. "Red! Let somebody else talk." But he rarely did.

That is not how it is with Ken. He will listen. Although, sometimes he does not hear, so deep into the data or the corrections he's making in an article for the *Journal of Nuclear Medicine* that I have to tap him on the shoulder. "I focus," he says when I complain that he hasn't heard me. He's like every other nerdy type in Ann Arbor. Involved in ideas. "What do you talk about with him?" somebody once asked me. "What can you say to him?" The question seemed strange. I had not considered it. Ken would be glad to talk about physics with me, but we don't.

We talk the day to day, not nuclear medical research. The same as we did when we first met.

Once I asked Ken if knew he was going to die soon, what he might do differently. "Nothing," he said. "I'd keep things the same. I like my life." He wouldn't go off on a phenomenal trip. He wouldn't dedicate every minute of his life to me and the kids. He'd keep things the same, grateful for the day to day. He has always been steady.

I grew up thinking my father was steady and my mother unreliable. An idea based mostly on who came in the back door and who was facedown on the bed. But I learned over the years that my father was not so much steady as reluctant to engage. "Why make a fuss?" My father said that all the time, still says it. He has congestive heart disease. He needs to make choices, but he won't. He claims it's making a fuss. Still, how many times does he want to be taken to the emergency room? "I'll go when the good Lord crooks his finger," he tells us, his daughters. But how can we tell when that happens?

When I was a kid, my father warned me not to be a fool. Fools get between a bear and her cubs. Fools step over a rock or a log without checking for snakes. Pay attention! I did not get mauled by a bear or bitten by a snake. I went off to the city with Ken. The advice my father gave me would seem not to fit this place. Still, I hear him. "It's not the fault of the bear," said my father. "It's never the fault of the bear."

Never?

I look at Ken out in the garden now, staking the spiderwort, something I nearly pulled out of the ground this spring. I thought it was a weed. He's wearing a blue sun shirt and his Indiana Jones hat, bent over, intent on the job.

I go out to bring Ken tea. He looks up and smiles with

satisfaction. "That's good," he says. "Look," he gestures to the garden. "Look how nice the spiderwort is. Aren't you glad you stopped to ask me if it was a weed before you pulled it up?" I am.

Chapter 17
TEEN QUEEN

Sometimes, even as I write this, I think I could have changed things.

Even when my daughter says, when the two of us talk about those days now, "No you couldn't have," or Ken protests, "We tried; we tried," I still rework events. What if I had not returned to graduate school the year Anita was twelve? Minh was headed to high school. Sung was in second grade. I had to get busy if I wanted that degree, and I wanted it.

I had been a member of a writing group a few years by then. There were five of us women meeting Sunday mornings at the Espresso Royale on Main Street in Ann Arbor. The Sunday Morning Writers' Group. That's what we called ourselves.

Laura was a member of the group. She had long, thick hair gone prematurely white; she was a practicing Buddhist and a writer who intended to publish a great short story. Flannery O'Connor and Katherine Mansfield were her role models. She'd quote lines from their stories. I thought she had her life exactly the way she wanted it. She seemed so wholly confident. Then, the phone rang one night. "You won't believe this, Mary. Laura died. Her heart just stopped." Laura? She was young! She knew what she wanted to do. It wasn't possible. I sat up all night reading her stories, searching for some line that would help me understand how she could go like that. But there was nothing in those stories that gave even a hint that she would leave.

I went to Muehlig Funeral Chapel with the remaining Sunday Morning Writers. There were pictures of Laura in the room. There she was. Up north in Michigan. Hugging her daughter. Planting trees. Only the pictures, no more Laura. My grief had no comparison to the grief of her family, a young daughter, her husband, and yet I wanted to yell at the body lying in the casket, "Get up! Get up! It can't be the same without you!"

It wasn't the same. We held together as a group, but we mourned the woman who ordered lemongrass tea and a chocolate-chip cookie. We missed Laura, with her white hair, bent over writing comments on our manuscripts. I still miss her. And, we were scared. For a long time, it felt as if we were stumbling through our editing sessions. We had lost the ease of believing that we had time on our side. We had thought that we were living in a safety zone, too young for death. But after Laura died, I took heed and forced myself to move on with my life.

I entered the MA program in creative writing at Eastern Michigan University. I wrote and I read. Ken came home from work early three nights a week to make baked squash or spaghetti for the kids while I went off to school in Ypsilanti, about ten miles away.

Did that unmoor things? I always had the personality of a diplomat; Ken was more of a disciplinarian. Maybe I had made life too easy for the kids? Maybe they resented Ken's rules: eat your squash, clear the table, bedtime at nine. Nothing severe, but delivered in a no-nonsense tone. Probably they did resent his rules, but I don't think Ken's firmness hurt the kids, and even when they fussed, I wasn't tempted to drop out of the program. I didn't feel the way I felt when I drifted away from the world after Minh came. I'd learned some things about balance in my yoga classes, and I felt the sting of Laura's death.

Leela, the friend who encouraged us to adopt from India, once told me the story of a devoted East Indian mother who, waking to find a tiger in her bedroom, tells the tiger to eat her quietly, not to wake the children.

Such a sacrifice is glorified in East Indian folk tales as the standard of motherhood. I don't think Leela expected me to do that. She was helping me understand East Indian culture. Nevertheless, I didn't want to be eaten.

About two years after I started the program, I had my degree and Eastern hired me as a lecturer. Anita hated that. No matter that she might run wild, she wanted everything else fixed: pictures on the wall, the same place for vacation every year, the identical menu for holidays. She hadn't liked my going to school, and now, even worse, I was teaching. I wasn't just her mom anymore. She said that as if she thought I had broken off a great chunk of myself and taken it away from her. But I was teaching part time, a couple of courses, not a career fast track. Yet she still cried out for that mythical East Indian mother, the mother who asked the tiger to eat her and not wake the children. But in Anita's version of the story, the mother allowed the tiger to eat her and then, because she was magic, reappeared whole to care for the children. Anita wanted magic, a perpetually sunny sky, perpetually sunny mother.

* * *

This summer, we went to the house where we gather every summer on the shore of Lake Erie, the whole clan of us from Cleveland and Ann Arbor: John and Mary Ann, Phyl, Ken and I and our children. Our children are grown now, of course. The only kids are our children's kids. We jumped waves, lay on the sand and watched old family movies at night. Everybody crowded on the sofa, the floor, watching in the dark, the lake outside dark too, only an occasional boat going by with running lights. Somebody made popcorn and exclaimed over the strangeness of the past: hair too short or too long, funny-looking clothes. "Oh, my God," someone said, "tell me that's not me. I look like a cow!" And then someone else said, "No, that's not true. It's just a bad picture."

But this summer, I saw a saw a beautiful picture in one of the movies, a picture that made me want to leave the room.

There was my daughter. She was so young. How old was she? Thirteen? Fourteen? She was spinning around in a white sundress, long, dark hair spinning too. She danced with a small child, her cousin, in the very room where we watched the movie. I recognized the wrought-iron table, the one with blue tiles and ships sailing across those tiles. It stood next to the yellow sofa that we crowded on. She leaned over in the movie and gave the child a kiss on his forehead, then left the picture.

"Oh look," the family said, "look how young they were. Look how sweet!"

Somebody took that movie. Somebody thought, *good moment*. I shut my eyes against it. *Not this movie*, I wanted to say, *not this one*. She was lovely; she danced so smoothly. And I knew what came after that part. The picture hurt to look at.

She was still a girl—all angel child. A quick glance and you might have thought she was eleven, so fine-boned you wanted to touch her gently, as if she'd break under a tight grip. My daughter. But she had this *need. Tell me I fit somewhere. Make me feel good.* A regular person could not know that, but I knew. I knew that the very day she danced with her cousin and gave him a kiss, she took off down the beach that night. I chased her down, pulled her back. She refused to say where she was headed, lips shut, eyes looking off across dark water. She didn't need to say. I knew. She went in search of guys. Guys who were probably too old. Guys who had seen her and eyed her, a cabin full of them, just down the beach. Ready to tell her what she wanted to hear: *You'll fit with me, honey. I have the map. I can make you feel good. I know what you need.*

Those guys, or other guys like them, seemed always to be lurking around when we went out together.

They were everywhere. In every color, shape, and size, and they never imagined we were mother and daughter. They always walked right past me, headed for my daughter. We could be in Kroger, grocery shopping, and if I moved a little bit away from her, say to find biscuit mix in the baking aisle, they hit. They moved right up to the lovely needy girl-woman who was in the next aisle over from me, checking out Cheez Curls.

I heard them.

They always began in the easiest possible way. "Hello, pretty girl." Like they were friendly puppies, playing. It never took much before they had her in their mouths, like a toy. She flipped around dizzy, gasped for air, but always wanted more. She never wanted to be reclaimed by me, dragged off with my hand over hers. She hated the look of surprise it always got. *You're her mother?*

She didn't want me to say yes. She wanted to be without a mother, alone in the wilds, in the arms of the bear.

It seemed to me that it took no time to lose my daughter. Things were hard when she turned thirteen, but in the space of one short year, from thirteen to fourteen, Anita exploded, like she was a landmine I'd stepped on. Pieces of her were all over the place. Pieces of me too.

There were scenes at the mall where Anita screamed at me that I was not her mother, yelled at me that she'd buy anything she wanted to buy, skimpy or not. "What do you have to say about it, anyway? You aren't my mother, the boss of me." She thrust her small hips forward to show me that, yes, she had it, the body. She could wear skimpy. I couldn't, could I?

There were unsanctioned parties with alcohol and everything that meant. She went to the sketchy parts of Ann Arbor, out South Maple maybe, the place where angry kids got high while they listened to Public Enemy.

She pushed all her old friends away, pushed her brothers away. Plus, she never brought her books home from school. Never did her homework. And then one awful time, in that same year, when she walked our dog, Sugar, she came back and told me, told me!

"I could have gone off with a guy; maybe he was thirty. Older, that's for sure. I could have gone with him, if I didn't have the dog. The stupid dog wouldn't let me go. The dog snapped at the guy. I should have left the dog and gone. He drove a great car."

She used a sharp, flip tone that implied: *She didn't care. What did I know?* But, she always made sure that I did know. She dropped hints or left her diary open on the table like she wanted me to know. Or she wanted me to say, *Yes, Anita. Thirty years old. Forty years old, who cares?* Did she think I would? She did. She said she was running her life, she was taking charge. She wanted us to agree that it was fine, like we were all on Team Anita. I couldn't figure out how this girl, the one who wanted a blue sky, full sun dead center, was running into the eye of a tornado, dragging all of us along with her.

"Go to your room," I yelled at her. She was home late from school again, insouciant, defiant. "Do your homework. Stay there until I come to get you." She looked at me as if I were a stranger. Not anybody to pay any mind to. I grabbed her and pulled her down the hallway to her room. I shoved her on the bed and slammed the door. I phoned Ken and cried. "She doesn't seem to care at all anymore."

"We'll use the big guns," Ken said. "I'll see if anybody around here knows someone." He worked with MDs, at the university hospital, so he'd find someone to recommend the best person for the job and we'd get help. We would seek out the best help Ann Arbor had to offer, psychologists, psychiatrists.

What had happened to her though? Because at the same time she used that snarly tone with me, the one that held scorn—*And who's asking you to go off in a car, Mom?*—she asked me to rub her back or get her a drink, like she wanted to keep me close when she could hardly stand me. Like she was not sure whether I was the enemy or the Red Cross nurse. Sometimes she cuddled up with her breath toothpaste-sweet and slept. Other times, many, many times, she waited until *we* slept and went out of the house before we caught her. When she came back, she snarled, nothing toothpaste sweet about her then.

When people say that parents need to be responsible, I agree. *Yes*. I listen intently, wait to see if they can show me what we might have done. Show me! I bet there are lots of parents, adoptive and biological, who would like to have someone say, *See? Right here? This is what you should have done*. Given that information, the parents might say, *Oh*. Their pain might make sense then. They could see what they should have done, what they did not do. They would still feel pain, but they could identify the reason for it. It would be defined with precision—*this and this and this*.

So much of the time what happened made no sense. I was not the glorified East Indian mother, but I would have done anything to keep my daughter from harm. Like the mothers in Holocaust films who hurl themselves in front of guards about to kill their children, I would have hurled myself in front of those guys. When I went for a run, I fantasized about shooting them, shoving them off a bridge or in front of a car, poisoning whatever they were drinking. But they paid me no mind at all, knew they were safe from the likes of me.

That year, we called the police because it was two in the morning and our daughter had not come home. I don't know what we thought would happen when we called. Did we think they'd find her and bring her home, in some fantastical way? I don't think we had any clear idea. We had never called the police before, had never expected to need to call them. They came to the house, gruff and practical. "Do you know these guys you say your daughter's off with? Do you have proof of their ages? Do you have any reason to suspect abduction?"

I did not know who they were and I thought Anita had gone off willingly. I had a surly, lost teen girl and odd bits of information: pages in a diary, voicemail in a strange voice, a glimpse of a car that turned the corner when I pulled up. The police left, nothing they could do, no need for them to stay with us, the sad quiet guy, the disheveled weeping woman. Why should they have taken on more grief than their job demanded?

Chapter 18

DRIVING PAST THE LIONS

We called in Ken's big guns. He found a University of Michigan psychiatrist through his connections at work. That doctor urged us to allow him to put Anita on antidepressants, which we did, but it was still too soon to tell if that would help. (Anita claims it never helped.) He also recommended a psychologist. Said she was good with teen girls.

We drove out to the south end of town and turned down a road marked with two massive stone lions. I thought of the lions outside the big house on Barton Drive, the time we drove home from Independence Lake. When I held Anita's foot and told Ken to keep on driving. She was fourteen though, and I was not holding her foot. We drove past the lions and pulled into one of those office park places. Ken made a growling sound as we passed the lions. Anita ignored him. I laughed, for old time's sake, but I wasn't good at laughing anymore.

Anita sat in the back, slouched and silent. I sat in the front seat and pulled the strap of my purse through my hands like it was a rosary. Our daughter had to be walked-dragged inside and upstairs to the office. She looked as bad as she could. A year of trouble had left her skin ashy, her hair almost crisp to the touch. The skirt she wore was black and very short. She had black stiletto boots on her small feet. My mean teen, my beloved dog-walking daughter who was ready to go off with a stranger. Or had she just been taunting me? I didn't know. Maybe the psychologist would know. Mean teen stood just inside the door, and held her silence as if that were the last thing she had.

"Please sit down," said the psychologist, pointing to the couch. "Sit down, all of you."

She seemed nice. She wore a loose, purple, ankle-length dress and big hoop earrings. Dressed in of-a-certain-age, Ann Arbor chic. I was sure Anita gave the purple dress minus points, too baggy, too old looking, but she probably liked the earrings. The psychologist smiled at us and asked Anita to begin. "How about if you go first?" was what she said.

My daughter's voice was tangled and rough, like her hair.

We were too possessive, too strict, too fussy. We thought she was our property. Just because we adopted her didn't mean we owned her. Why couldn't she bring boys over and have them in her room? Why didn't we recognize that we had messed up her life by bringing her here? She didn't want to call us Mom and Dad. She wanted to call us Mary and Ken. She finished in a gulp of anger and lit up a cigarette.

I flashed Ken a look. I *knew* she was smoking, smelled the smoke on her clothes. He wanted to think her smoking was erratic, experimental, but there it was, another issue. The psychologist pointed to the sign above her desk, NO SMOKING. Anita said she'd go outside. I reached to grab her, no telling if she'd take off.

The psychologist kept her cool, suggested that Anita put the cigarette away and we try to agree on one point. "You have a lot to say. Let's see if we can agree on one single thing. Let's give it a go." Her voice was like cream spilling into coffee. It made me uneasy; it felt too assured, like she thought she understood the situation. I didn't see how she could. Still, she came recommended. But before half the session was over, my uneasiness increased. I hated that she talked to us about her own teenagers in the school band, off on some school trip. "They're about your age," she had said to Anita. "You know how teen boys are." She probably intended to reassure us she had personal experience living with teens, not just counseling them. She probably wanted to find some common ground with Anita. Maybe she wanted to suggest to Anita that she could have a version of that life. But no matter, the minute she talked about her kids off on a school trip, I resented it. It was a mean, spiteful, jealous, ugly, wholly unfounded, completely unreasonable resentment, and it slid right over me like my best sweater. *Oh sure your kids are in band and on a school trip, bitch.*

I choked on every good feeling she offered because— school trips were a foreign concept just then. My daughter had in mind trips way more complicated. The woman kept her tone upbeat, as if we were just in a bad patch. I wanted to shout that we were not in her office because Anita didn't do homework. We were not there because she broke curfew, although that was true. We were there because we had a girl who seemed intent on getting hurt. We needed help!

And there was this: Anita half told me things. Or gave me clues to things. Things that made me want to grab hold of her and run with her a long way. The way she allowed me bits of information scared me, a scribbled note on the dining room table, a sentence she started, then left unfinished. Was she asking for help or taunting me? But when I repeated what she had told me, the psychologist frowned at me. "No, no. Do not repeat what you have been told. Let Anita tell it in her own time." Okay. I understood the value of privacy, of letting my daughter tell her own story. But. This was big stuff I was worried about. The woman looked at my daughter and said she seemed like a pretty normal girl, maybe a little rebellious. Was it possible that I exaggerated things? Perhaps my fears were unreasonable? Maybe I did not feel confident as Anita's mother? Maybe I let the issue of adoption assume too much importance? It was, she said, important that I allow my daughter to separate. We needed to allow her to make mistakes. She smiled at Anita, told her that the teen years were rough, said she bet lots of boys wanted to take her out.

Well, she was right that I wasn't oozing confidence. But. Boys? I'd be grateful for boys!

She fingered an earring. Could we agree that Anita and a boy could be together in the living room? She waited for our answer, wanting good things for us. She was not stupid or incompetent. But she did not know our life. She seemed to find our life hard to imagine, seemed to think that I was overly anxious. She had no knowledge of young girls who were willing to go off with thirty-year-old strangers. How could she? It was probably not a story she had heard before. Most people in the middle-class university-type circles of Ann Arbor didn't have that kind of story to tell her. I knew then that we were alone.

There were no adoption specialists in Ann Arbor in those years. The psychologist whom we saw was nice and concerned. But she had no clue. Maybe my frustrations with her were the frustrations of a scared mother who wanted more than was possible? I wanted someone who had depth of knowledge about core adoption-related issues. I wanted someone who understood what the spillover might be from Anita's hard first two years. Who knew what might have happened to her before she got to Mother Teresa? I wanted someone to understand the possibilities and help me deal with them. I called Jean, the social worker who had helped with Sung's adoption, and talked to her. I hoped she might know something that we didn't. She commiserated with me, but she could say only that we should keep doing what we were doing. She urged me to hang on. Said I could call her anytime, which was good because I wasn't able to talk to many people. I hinted about our troubles to my Saint Marys family, to the Cleveland family, but not much. I had not yet hinted to my friends. How could I tell my friends how hard it was when it seemed as if their kids earned good grades, had normal kinds of hassles? When I finally was able to talk about our struggles, I wondered why I had been unable to for such a long time. How could I have become so isolated? I have a theory about that now. I think my silence was something like the silence of women diagnosed with breast cancer, before women talked about breast cancer. Pink ribbons and Walk for the Cure are everywhere now, but there was a time when no one said the words *breast cancer*. Saying those words would invite pity or horror. Not so long ago, women with breast cancer kept silent and wore wigs, not lovely scarves around their bald heads, no pink ribbons in sight.

That's what it was like for me. Maybe for Ken too. We did not want to invite pity or horror, didn't want our daughter shamed.

We wanted to believe in the power of psychologists and psychiatrists, school counselors. But we felt as if they were dismissing us as overly attached, overly concerned, uptight. Certainly we presented as concerned people. We didn't dismiss Anita's behavior as normal teen rebellion. I knew she wasn't just streaking her lips with red carnelian after I told her no lipstick until fifteen.

So, the psychologist sitting across from us came recommended, but she seemed too ready to believe our daughter's complaints, too unwilling to validate our concern.

We agreed to the boy in the living room. We would be happy to allow Anita to have a boy in the living room. A *boy*; I emphasized *boy*.

How old a boy? Nineteen, twenty, even eighteen, that was too old for a girl just turning fourteen. I hoped the psychologist would make that clear.

"Anita, your mom and dad are right about the age thing. Stay away from older boys. They aren't good for you. You want to take care of yourself."

But Anita said *she* should get to decide; my daughter who would run headfirst into steel walls, no idea of the possible brain death that might await her.

"I get to decide who comes over. You just open the door and let us alone. I know what I'm doing. I can handle myself." She tossed those words out into the room, and got up from the sofa, ready to end the session. The psychologist stopped writing, her pen hung midair. For sure, she had not come across anyone like our girl with her no-holds-barred attitude, no one quite like Anita at all. Ken tried to calm his daughter. "Whoa, whoa, take it easy," said Ken. "Take it easy, honey."

The psychologist murmured protest. "That isn't a profitable attitude. Let's try cooperation." I shot purple-dress woman a look to let her know I was not a crazy mama. *See? I think my fears are not so crazy, lucky lady with the kids in band.*

We proposed fifteen as the age for a boy for Anita to date, seventeen at the most. Seventeen felt like caving, but we were willing to cave a bit if we could avert disaster, typical for stressed-out, overwhelmed parents. Anita frowned and picked at her skirt; she pulled at a thread and the hem unraveled, part of it hung loose, less than a quarter inch of black fabric, a skinny little hem. I took it as a sign of our skinny little hopes. She went to work on the rest and before we left her skirt had a ragged edge all the way around, a lot like the three of us.

Who does my daughter know? Who does she want to have

come over? Please, please, not any of the guys in the grocery store. Not the guy she talked to walking the dog.

Ken growled again as we pulled out, headed home, while Anita sank into the backseat, small and mad, saying the whole idea of therapy was stupid.

Who does she know? No teen boys, that's for sure. I'd bet on that.

Ken still believed progress could be made one step at a time. He ignored his daughter's sullenness, my silence, and suggested Indian food.

Later that night, I lay in bed and counted the years until she would be grown. Fourteen, fifteen, sixteen, seventeen, eighteen.

Can I keep her safe for that long? How would it be if she went back to India? Maybe the two of us could volunteer in her old orphanage. We could stay for years. Maybe we could all go, the whole family?

I pictured myself writing a letter to Mother Teresa, telling her that Anita was in trouble. I would have to say that it seemed as if we had ruined her good work. She would be surprised at the way Anita looked, the skirt, the boots, defiance shellacked all over her. India and Mother were so far away and, although we had written, we never hinted that their good work was endangered, their amiable Anita in trouble. I got up from bed and went to the window. The traffic light on the corner switched to blink, a steady pulsing red, like the blood in my veins. I wondered if, in the end, my blood would prove to be all wrong for our daughter.

Chapter 19

WHAT ELSE THERE WAS

She kept shouting at us. "I'm the most different!" she shouted. "I'm way different! Nothing at all like you guys." Sometimes we let her shout, convinced that she must trust us or she wouldn't yell like that, a screaming, shrieking thing waving her fists in the air. Sometimes we shouted back, turned away. Sometimes I wanted to shake her. Could it even matter if I caused brain damage?

And we had two other children. Both of them shell shocked. They wanted to know where their sister had gone. Minh and Anita had been a tight pair and, for a long time, Minh tried to keep it that way. He never told on her and he got her out of what trouble he could. But, after a while, he plugged his ears and let her shout. Sung kept out of her sight.

Also, Minh and Sung had their own troubles. Anita's anger seemed to increase Minh's reserve. He never, ever said, "I'm sad," or, "I'm scared." He must have felt both those things with Anita's problems taking over our lives. But he didn't say so. He always had, still has, the personality of someone who gets along. He doesn't rock the boat, not Minh. Which can lead to passive-aggressive behavior. He'll joke about that with me. "I don't yell," he says, "but I'm great with the passive-aggressive routine." I laugh because he's a good guy, a good father, a Vietnamese-American male who has, after years, come to peace with the issue of his lost Vietnamese mother.

Back then, Minh's yearning for his lost Vietnamese mother seemed to be constant. Maybe he could save up and go to Vietnam and look for her? Maybe she had made it out and was somewhere in the States? But he didn't want to hurt our feelings, so he didn't say, actually say, any of this. He just hinted at it. He sort of daydreamed aloud. And he studied Asian women. I saw him looking when we were out. Of course, his Viet mom was not walking around Ann Arbor; he knew that, but he studied Asian women anyway.

He looked out the window, lay on his bed, eyes roaming around the room, scanning, scanning . . . looking for a face, but not my face, not Ken's face, even though he said he loved our faces. That was the thing about Minh: he *always* said he loved us and he meant it. I knew that he meant it. But sometimes his love felt slippery, as if he still had a coat of vernix on him, as if he had not quite made it from his birth mom to us. It was hard some days to believe he planned to stay for a minute longer than he had to. I tugged at his shirtsleeve. "Minh, Minh." He turned and looked at me. Perhaps, he was surprised to be in his room, with me for his mother.

And his grades were terrible! Right before every marking period, I got calls from teachers who began their complaints by saying that he was so polite and easygoing, but he never seemed to understand that he *needed to do the work*. He drew on the pages of his textbooks—and those books were school property. His homeroom desk—the teacher could hardly describe it—was a mess. Moldy lunches, notes he was supposed to have taken home and have me sign, homework he never bothered to hand in.

He was—here the teachers stopped and took a breath—not defiant, never that; he would clean up the mess readily enough, if someone stood over him. But—they let out breath in a collective sigh. He was way too *dreamy*. What was he thinking about? They always wanted to know that. Me too. I wanted to know too. He had always been the kid who was school averse. Once he got past kindergarten and the hands-on material, school was not for him. Too much sitting and working, all of it boring. Once in third grade, he was found reading a book on spaceships during a math test. "Minh," said his frustrated teacher, "don't you want to do well on the test?" It didn't seem to matter to him whether he did well on the test or not. He wasn't interested in the test. He could take things apart and put them back together, a car engine, a toaster, my dad's old pocket watch, whatever he found. That was interesting, what he could manage with no problem at all. So he was smart. But dreamy. I understood what his teachers meant. For Minh, school was just a place he had landed in without his say-so.

He studied Vietnamese language tapes when he should have been doing schoolwork. Truthfully, I did not mind that so much. I bought him the tapes and thought—I remember that I thought—*Good. Good. Good for him. Good for us. This is nothing to worry about.* It felt as if that should have been happening, a long way from what should not have been happening with our daughter.

He began by trying to learn a phrase that he might use if he happened to find his mother or anyone else in his Vietnamese family.

Ong co khoe khong (How are you)?

He practiced the Vietnamese greeting—anticipating the moment. When he talked about his other life, he said his mom must have left him because she could not feed him. She did not want to let him go; she had to let him go. It *could have* been so. He always said he bore his Vietnamese mom no ill will. He bore us no ill will. I wondered if so much amiability kept him from saying what he really thought.

Then there was Sung. Sung spent too many years as a kind of punctuation mark, a comma—Anita, Minh, and Sung. I said it that way. *Anita, Minh, and Sung*, with a little pause after the first two names. Their lives were in my head that way: Anita the scariest problem, then Minh and his need for a birth mother, then Sung. Sung got the tag end. He had problems, but they did not seem insistent, so I put his problems on the bottom shelf of my mind. It felt as if the older two were tossing knives, and Sung was off in the living room playing with his Power Rangers, so what we did was make sure he had a good supply of Power Rangers. We loved him, but his life back then was a Band-Aid kind of life. We kept applying the Band-Aids to anyplace that might hurt, but he didn't need Band-Aids. He needed parents who were not eaten alive with worry.

Sung was only in third grade when Anita was busy kissing strangers and Minh was listening to Vietnamese language tapes. When he talks about that time, Sung tells us he felt like a walk-on in the family. I hate that. We tried to come up with good things for him: movies, take-out Korean food from a place called Kana, sleepovers with his friends. But we did not manage very well. We tried; we did try, but here's the thing: worry spread around us as if somebody had spray painted it all over the place. Everything was coated with it: rice bowls with rabbits on a blue background, our books, the special chopsticks. Worry everywhere. I didn't pound on the upright or laugh anymore.

We continued to see the creamy-voiced psychologist. At times, the whole family scrunched on the neutral-colored sofa, three on the cushions, one on each arm. She patiently went over the family ramifications of various life stages and suppositions about how adoption impacted child growth: separation, socialization, a sense of self-individualization. She wondered aloud if children like ours didn't require more time to negotiate the stages. That made sense. But what were we supposed to do about that?

"Does adoption affect how a kid learns math?" Ken asked. There were still a few minutes left on the clock. Ken usually listened more than he talked, but he said before we left to meet with the psychologist that he wanted to get a question in.

She looked startled. "Hmm. I don't have any data on that. But, I suppose if we're conjecturing malnutrition, of course math skills could be affected."

Sung could not learn math. Right then, his third-grade year, he *could not* manage his times tables. We lured him with extra chocolate: a sheet of problems done correctly equaled a piece of chocolate. We used flash cards and marched around the house chanting, "Four times four is sixteen; five times five is twenty-five . . ." and still the teacher sent home notes complaining.

Sung only *sort of* learned, for a minute or so. We held our breath while he recited the two's table, finishing up with, "Two times twelve . . . twenty-four." *Ah, he has it. Two times twelve is twenty-four.* Then, about fifteen minutes later, Minh walked by and asked him, "Sung, what's two times twelve?" Nothing.

Twenty-four, I coached him mentally, *twenty-four, Sung!*

He stomped off, worksheets left on the table. He huddled in his orange room, the color he had picked out with Ken. "You think he can sleep in this?" I asked when the two of them began to brush paint.

"Why not?"

Sung loved his bright orange room, like it was a flare he could use if things got too dark. He lay on his bed, in his orange room, listening to Ken or me, even Minh and Anita sometimes, chant to him in made-up rhymes: "Two times twelve is twenty-four, shut the door."

The chants helped, but never enough, because the *minute* he turned his back, the answers left—gone as if he had never known them.

One morning in his third-grade year, he curled up in the closet of his orange room with a blanket and pillow. School was stupid; he was stupid. *Stupid, stupid, stupid.* Pulling him out of the closet took both of us, and he landed a kick at Ken that connected hard. Ken jerked him around and returned a smack to his bottom. Sung went completely berserk. Screamed and cried, pounded and kicked. I could not imagine that any teacher would want to deal with him. He sobbed in the orange room while Ken and I pretended to drink the last of the breakfast coffee. The dog went in to him. When I checked later, the dog lay next to him on the bed. Sung was quiet. "You have to go to school, Sung. It's not a choice. You have to go. This afternoon, right after lunch."

The dog and I walked him partway. I felt my throat catch as I watched him cross the street, a hunched figure in a fake-leather jacket with three patches he had chosen and I had sewn on: a small Korean flag, a small US flag, and his level-two swim patch which meant he could enter deep water.

Why put up with such nonsense? I had described the school temper tantrum to Cheryl and that's what she asked me—why did I put up with such nonsense? Her two kids were about the ages of my kids. But her kids did not have school problems. Cheryl planned her life carefully. Two kids were her limit. It was clear she thought I should have done more to cut Sung's tantrum short. I thought about asking her just what she might have done, but she changed the subject and asked if I wanted to exchange childcare some night soon so that we could each have a night out. That sounded good. Maybe a bit unfair to her since she'd have three of mine to watch, but the idea was appealing. We'd take each other's kids for the evening—supper and a movie. Back by eleven or so. Great. Ken and I didn't get out all that often. We could go to a movie. We could see *The Crying Game*. Sure we'd do it.

In the end I said nothing to her about why I put up with Sung's tantrum, but I wondered if I had missed some essential information about parenting. What else could I have done? What didn't I know?

If I could have made that boy learn third-grade math, I would have. I would have made every one of the kids learn whatever they needed to learn in order to be safe and happy.

* * *

"I can't make you happy or make you choose wisely."

Even the psychologist said "can't make you" when we dragged Anita in to talk with her. "That's a choice you have to make. Your parents can take care of you, but they can't make you be happy."

My daughter was fourteen! What do we choose at fourteen? What was Minh choosing? Sung? And how could we have made sure that they chose the hand with the Hershey's Kiss, not the hand with the baby grenade?

And no matter that I said I would not behave like my mother, often enough, when I sat in the psychologist's office, I wanted to. I wanted to lie facedown, put a pillow over my head, shove my hands under it, and shut my children out.

Chapter 20
I HAVE TO SAVE HER

It became very clear Anita believed skin was no friend to her, not her brown skin, not our white skin. She talked incessantly about living in a different family—at a minimum she wanted a family with skin that matched. I hated it when she said that. It felt as if a wall made of skin separated us. Ken and I shoved at it, pushed it, stretched and pulled, but Anita remained on the other side.

She told my mother that she wanted a different family, and Ma didn't act shocked. She put her arms around Anita and told her to hang on to all of us, skin or no. In time, things would get better. "Honey," Ma said, "you are good, a good girl. You have good stuff in you, like those jars," and she pointed to jars of plums that she had finished canning. Fourteen jars of plums, picked from the tree in the backyard, luscious dark ovals swimming in sugar syrup, cooling on my mother's kitchen counter. Anita laughed at that, a sound I remember liking. She begged for some plums and Ma was happy to oblige.

I loved Ma for loving my girl! Ma's aching back, her moodiness, the warnings she sent after me, her comment about blood, none of that mattered compared to the way she kept hope for my daughter when I could not. And I loved that Anita and Ma understood each other's need for a dependable sky, something not to be found in Ann Arbor or Saint Marys. Ma adored going out in the sun with Anita when we went back home in the summer—the two of them oiled each other's back to a slick, then stretched out on an old white sheet. Anita joked about Ma trying to turn a shade or two darker. "You should have planned it out better," she said, "like me. I don't have to cook myself to get a little color." Ma love-smacked her and they sipped iced tea with quarters of lemon and special sugar dots from a yellow box. I watched the two of them sipping, turning over from time to time. Ma never even complained about Anita's swimsuit, two very small strips of blue-and-white checks. Ma, herself, wore shorts and an old white blouse. She slipped the blouse off once she lay down, pulled down her bra straps. "When you get as old as I am," she said to Anita, "then you get to do what you want. You'll see," she said. Anita said she didn't want to wait until she grew old. Ma sighed and said she would if she knew what was good for her. I was sure that Anita did not know what was good for her.

Ma sent mail addressed to: *Anita, My Lovely Granddaughter.* When Anita opened the envelopes, she found cards with suns on them that said:

> I can't shine without you.
> Love you honey,
> Grandma

She let the cards fall on the floor like they were too heavy to hold, or the suns burned too hot. I picked them up, put them away.

* * *

Later there was a box in the attic in the house we moved to or ran away to, a person could describe it either way, a white house on a hill. One time, we went up to the attic together, Anita and I, a good while after she was done with trouble guys and their ways. Anita pulled the cards from the box. Ma was dead and

Anita was a mother with her baby napping in a room just below the stairs. It was a hot summer day. The attic smelled like heat, dry boards, and dust. We bent to look at the signature:

> Love you honey,
> Grandma

Anita cried as if she'd just found out Ma had died.

* * *

Each time she came home from wherever she went to—no place we agreed to, maybe somebody's basement with no parents around, maybe someplace worse than that—Ken and I stood with our arms held out to catch what pieces we could. We lay out in the summer sun, no sunblock, aiming for a tan and some pain relief. But Ken ended up with basal-cell carcinoma and my hands grew speckles like a sparrow egg. He had to wear protective clothing after that, a sky-blue sun-blocking shirt and a wide-brimmed hat that people pointed to when they saw him. "Some hat," they said. Ken smiled. I used a cream advertised to undo sun damage.

We were in therapy for a year. Anita was fifteen. Ken and I talked while Anita went through the motions. After a session, she would tell us that she'd said what the psychologist wanted to hear. I believed her. She wasn't going to tell anything she didn't want to, not a word. One time she came home bruised, a stain of purple here and there on the brown of her skin. "What are you doing to yourself?" I screamed. She wouldn't say and I couldn't pull the words out of her, a perfect secret agent, someone who would never divulge information under pressure.

She was failing school. Just like her older brother that way. I'd manage, sometimes, to talk her through a paper that was due, a project that needed to be done, but she wouldn't buy the idea that school was worth her while. She scorned school. Minh didn't scorn it, he ignored it. But Anita saw school as a place for snobs, brains, people wholly unlike the person she claimed to be. She hung out with other kids who felt the same way. A whole crowd of disenfranchised youth who looked scary, but mostly hurt themselves. For all the trouble Anita courted, she never hurt another person. Just herself.

If we talked about this, in therapy, or alone with our daughter, she turned away. She became distant, like she was a museum display we were not supposed to touch. We cut what privileges she had left. We continued with the psychologist. She seemed not one bit affected or helped. We watched for signs: Did she laugh with Sung? Help mow the lawn? Sometimes she did those things. Were those signs that things were better? They never proved to be.

But somebody had hurt our girl, the same girl Mother Teresa had taken care of, the girl who'd slept under my red scarf, the daughter we loved. A girl we did not hit. Somebody had hit her.

I found out using careful listening and watching, detective work. The counselor warned me that I would lose my daughter's trust—I thought the counselor was crazy; it felt like life and death. I found out that Anita had made the mistake of telling someone off. She had told someone *no*, and that person had given her a good clip. She seemed to think her bruises were what she had to expect if she did something stupid with a guy like that. She said (talking on the phone to one of the crowd who wore black) she had to learn the ropes before she went out with him again. Her tone was rueful, as if she were behind in a skill set.

She had always been an insistent personality. Ken and I joked that the nuns had tricked us. But, at the same time, she *was* the amiable girl described on that sheet of paper. She made Play-Doh figures for Sung; she cooked stir-fry with squash and tomatoes from the garden. She did these things happily at one time. It was only later that she opened her mouth wide and told Ken and me to: *Fuck off. Get lost. Take a hike.*

Mad at us for living, I think, or mad that she was living.

Still, she took the rest of the world in and shut her mouth about it.

Except once she opened her mouth and told someone *no*. "No," was what she said. And then, "Stupid jerk."

By then, I knew enough to imagine the situation: *she said those words to him and he didn't like it, so he slapped her, hard.*

She came home with her face marked up and refused to talk about it. She did write about it in her daybook, which she left in plain view on the dining room table. Which I read.

I knew the psychologist would raise her eyebrows at me; my daughter would slam around, but I wanted to have *a daughter*, a live daughter, even if she was mad at me. Even if I read her daybook.

I read her daybook and my heart leapt to my mouth. It sat there, beating on my tongue.

5/16/90: I was mouthy. I should have kept my mouth shut. Then it wouldn't hurt. Ha. Ha. Ha. But he warned me, so it's my fault really. Next time, I'll know better.

Sometimes she wrote in her book while I rubbed cream on her back, on the places she could not reach where it itched if her skin went dry and ashy. Sometimes I saw things that looked like welts. What were they? Why were they there? But I was quiet and careful, like I was dealing with the bear back in Saint Marys. I had to be. If I moved the wrong way, said the wrong thing, my daughter could be gone in a second. Maybe forever. I couldn't stop her. She was smaller than I was, true. But anger, maybe desperation, gave her power. She could get away from me, so fast. That lovely, lovely girl was nobody I could hold on to.

But she did like back rubs sometimes, so I'd rub her back quietly, grateful for the contact, the small moment of keeping her safe, a laying on of hands; Ken brought us tea. He was quiet too, like he was visiting a sick room. Is it hard to understand why we behaved that way? So cautious with our daughter, so— almost timid.

I know that seems hard to understand. But we already had the big guns and it wasn't helping. We mostly kept at it. That's the right phrase. We kept holding on. The police were not an option, unless Anita named the guy, which she wouldn't do. And maybe she was right. That sounds shocking. But what if her silence kept her alive?

The only thing we could do was try to keep her near us, try to stay sane, try to keep us all alive.

I knew he took her to Wendy's after he slapped her. She wrote about that:

He took me to Wendy's. Offered to buy me a burger.
But it hurt to eat.

I imagined the scene:

She sat at Wendy's but she could not open her mouth far enough to eat, so she sipped a chocolate Frosty, and watched him eat.

He had a second burger with bacon, lettuce, and tomato.

She was cheerful enough. She didn't make a scene, watching him lift the burger between his two hands—like a body he could eat whole.

Maybe she wiped a dribble of ketchup from his chin and swallowed the last of her Frosty, the taste too cold, too sweet, slipping over her tongue. There was another entry in the book right after her entry:

No, it is not right to be slapped and you ought to be able to open your mouth. Honey this ain't good.

Somebody wrote that in her book.

Was it me? Ken? Minh? Anita herself?

I should have been able to recognize the handwriting but I couldn't. It could have been me in some sleepwalking state. We can get to places where, when we hear our voice, see our own handwriting, we don't know it anymore. I had always insisted that adoption had nothing to do with saving a child, but I came close to crazy, trying to do just that.

* * *

Rosie came and brought Ma with her one time. It was the year Anita was fourteen and we first went to see the psychologist.

When they pulled into the driveway, everyone, even Anita, greeted them as if they came with fresh bread and we had not eaten for weeks, as if they came from someplace nice that we only heard of, never saw anymore.

Ma pulled Anita's hair, a friendly yank, and stuck fake violets into a small green bottle. There were all kinds of things cluttering her greenhouse window. One bottle looked like a vodka bottle, but she said she'd never had vodka, had found the bottle on the sidewalk and picked it up. I hadn't smelled alcohol on her. Later, it became apparent that she was drinking when she was out. Much later, Anita told me that she had been so good at lying that she believed the lies herself. She couldn't distinguish anymore. "It was scary," she said. "I didn't know what was true anymore." It is scary. The only practical measure is to believe nothing your beloved liar says. Which is much harder than you might think. We want to believe the people we love.

Ma warned her to *stick around*. Rosie took Sung to school every morning. She had a thermos of hot chocolate waiting for him in the car and he went off, no problem. It was nice, like having disaster relief. And then they left.

* * *

Minh sat at his desk the whole evening.

Ma and Rosie had left that morning. "It will be all right, Mary," my sister said while I stood outside the car, leaning in the open window. "You have to believe it."

But I didn't.

He sat at his desk and kept hitting the repeat button on the soundtrack from *Les Mis*. I sniffed sandalwood (from burning incense) and talked to him—about the problems his sister had, how those problems affected all of us.

"Minh, we have to believe she will get better." Those were Rosie's words, which I had dismissed, but I had nothing better to offer him.

"Why?" he asked, turning the volume higher as the barricades formed in Paris.

That was an easy question to answer. We had to believe because there was no letting go.

"So, what would be the worst thing?" he asked. I leaned in to hear him over the soundtrack. "The thing that would make you let go?"

"Nothing," I replied. "Death, I guess."

He looked doubtful. He shook his head. Why would a person choose grief? I never thought I was choosing grief though. I chose family. Grief came along for the ride.

Ma always said it was a good thing we don't know what's coming. She said it to me when she left to go back home. She held me for a minute, like she was sorry, like she wished I hadn't found out.

Chapter 21

THE PUNCH

Anita loved watching Oprah when Oprah still had her daytime show. She curled up on the couch under the afghan Ma had knit for her in the pink and white stripes she'd asked for back when she wasn't wearing glitter knit and shoving into leather jackets; she paid attention to the show as if she were in school and serious about it. It was like Oprah was her personal tutor, leaning forward and looking into my kid's eyes to make sure she understood. Like Oprah cared. Oprah had had her own trouble and survived, plus she was powerful, so Anita listened.

There is never a reason for a woman to be slapped silly. Hitting and slapping is no good at all.

Oprah talked about slapping and hitting and bad situations that girls and women got into. Anita seemed to consider what she had to say, one brown woman to another. A daytime talk show! But Oprah said what Anita, my girl, needed to hear. All the same things we said, but when *we* said the words, Anita heard garble. If she listened to Oprah, though, it might be good. Maybe our words would resonate, untangle. *Let her listen. I want her to listen.*

There were words painted on the sides of Ann Arbor buses, taped to the walls of bathrooms in places where Anita could see them, if she looked. Every one of those words sent the same message: *There is never a reason to hurt. No means no. You deserve better.*

We said that to her every day. Ma and Rosie said that to her when they were in town. Her brothers, even Sung, pretty young at the time, but nobody's fool, said that.

"Anita, the guy's a jerk. No way!"

But what *he* would say was that *she* was no good. She was no good at all, the wrong girl in the wrong place. He knew where she should be, what she should do. And she believed him. She believed: she was the exception to good. She didn't have the right family, couldn't have happiness, she was all wrong.

Why did she think that?

Sometimes, Ken blamed himself. I was surprised when he did because mostly he argued that blame did no one good. Action was where a person could do some good. And God knows, he tried action, but when we were saddest, he'd say Anita's grief was his fault—because he never knew how to say the right things, didn't know how to give word strokes, things those guys must be doing; otherwise, why would she go off with them?

I knew Ken was the guy who taught her how to play touch football, gave her the greenhouse window, and bought her the leather jacket. He would hug her, if she'd let him. Still, sometimes, I blamed him too. I used mean words. "If you had told her more often that . . ." I laid blame on him. Stacked it there in great heaps. Grief demands too much. Sometimes anger and blaming can be relief, even when they're wrong.

What might he have said? He was a father, not a miracle worker, and our kid was intent on living a non-miracle life. The Bloods and the Crips had made their way to Detroit from LA. Drove down I-94 to places like West Willow, the south side of Ypsilanti, places Anita knew. Places we didn't know. Ken drove to those places searching for her, his small brown-skinned daughter with a blue handkerchief knotted around her head. He must have been a sight in those places, the worried pink-toned whitey, driving a Sable, searching for his daughter on porches and in parking lots.

* * *

The guy who slapped her around came to the house, hunting for her after that trip to Wendy's, mad about something. He crashed through the honeysuckle on the side of the house, crashed through the dark, crashed into our lives. The whole sky crashed down on a dark summer night. He came into the house.

Did she let him in? Maybe she saw him standing outside her window, unlocked the door, and let him in. It was all too likely. She would have done that. Kept it quiet, not let us know.

Caught between his anger and our knowing, not just guessing but knowing she was in huge trouble, she chose what she thought she could deal with. She thought she could deal with him, but he rammed his fist into her mouth, no slap that time. He let her know who was boss. A part of her tooth broke off. She must have taken the punch, no sound at all. We never heard a cry.

We were upstairs in our bedroom with the fan on. It was Ken who woke and went downstairs. I watched him push the sheet back and pull on his robe. Something seemed not right to him. Maybe the echo of the punch? The dog whimpering? He found her sitting on the kitchen floor, the back door open and her tooth hanging loose. She held her pocketknife, a tiny Swiss Army knife, a smaller version of the knife I kept in my dresser drawer. Her knife had tiny scissors and a tiny can opener. She made very small cuts on her arms, just enough to break the surface of her skin. Nothing much, really. "I need to do something," she said to her father. Things were out of hand, she said; she needed to take charge.

He called out to me in a low voice, not wanting to scare the two boys who still slept, their own fans humming away. "Mary, come here." I don't know if I heard his words, but I knew the sound he made, fear.

I got down on the floor next to her. The cuts looked like red seeds.

It was not at all the way most people lived. Most people found it hard to understand, *very surprising*, but even more surprising was that we told her it would be okay, as if we knew how to fix such things, and we explained the situation to Sung and Minh very calmly when they heard us and woke and came into the kitchen. *It will be okay.*

We did not call the police that night. We practiced containment. We tried to contain the damage to our girl and our family. We let out a cry, "What happened? What happened?" but we did not ask, "Who hurt you? How did the person get into the house?" I know what she would have said, though. "It's better if you don't know," she would have said.

We cared nothing about the guy. We wanted to take care of our daughter. Maybe we were wrong. Maybe inept. But we counted on each other, Ken and I. We were independent by nature and protective. What should we have done? I go back to that night and study the scene again. I can't come up with anything that would have changed things. Nothing. Anita was a chameleon. She took on the coloration of her surroundings. No psychologist, no teacher, no counselor, nobody ever saw the girl we knew: so conflicted, so angry, so quick to change. The same girl who could let the guy into the house thinking she could manage him could burrow into my lap, the way she way she did that night, burrowed there and butted her head against me, like she was trying to move on in.

And then Ken got her up from the floor and told her he was taking her to the emergency room to make sure nothing was broken. She cried and begged him not to leave her, to stay with her the whole time; she wanted her father—the man who couldn't give word strokes. They drove off while I stayed behind and talked to the boys, keeping it calm, talking through the dark coming down on us.

Ken returned with our girl just as the sky was lightening up, both of them drained. It couldn't have been an easy go. Anita fell asleep on the sofa. Nothing else other than the tooth was broken. The doctor was convinced that Ken was not the one who'd hit Anita and did not press the issue of a police report. I could hear Ken turning from grief to anger and back again as he told me the story. How he pulled out his University of Michigan ID, how he sat quietly while Anita said what she was willing to say: she was involved with a guy who could be trouble, but she wasn't going to let him hit her again and she wasn't going to name him, so don't ask. How the doctor looked astounded. Like how was this situation even possible? How could a guy who did medical research have a daughter who was involved with an abuser? "The worst part," Ken said to me, "is that I don't know how this happened. I never expected this to happen. I would never hit her. I barely smacked her bottom when she was a kid. Why is she doing this?"

I had no answer for him then, but I think I understand more now. When people ask me now, and they still do—it wasn't just the skin thing, was it? I say part of it was the skin thing. But not the way we think of skin, just an easy racial marker. It was never that. It was all the things skin suggests: who belongs, who is pretty or not, who is targeted or not. Anita told me that until she went to school she thought we were the same. "I didn't think there was any difference between us." She told me that after the worst of things eased. What did she mean?

We called her our pretty daughter with dark-brown skin. We didn't back off discussing skin shade. I never expected Anita, any of the kids, to be honorary white. There were differences between us. We all knew that. But she told me that before she went to school, the differences were just color. And when she was small that didn't matter. Once she was in school though, her skin became a marker. Whether or not people thought she was pretty didn't matter to her. All kinds of people thought she was pretty. What mattered was that she had no ready community with which she was identified. If she couldn't be the same as us, where did she fit? She hated being asked, "What are you?" She hated the black kids in school lining up to decide where she fit on the color line.

She sat in the dentist's chair the next day, a guy she had known forever. He looked at her and said the damage could be repaired, all that was needed was a little dental cement to put things back together. So that was good.

The smell of antiseptic, white-gloved hands, the dentist's pink skin showing through the gloves. Hand coming at her mouth again. She pressed her lips tight.

"You'll have to open up," he said. He knew the situation was not good, but he would not hurt her, or me, by so much as a lift of his eyebrows. I wanted to thank him, but I could not open my mouth either. I would wail if I did.

She groaned, opened her swollen mouth, and shut her eyes. What did she see underneath her lowered lids? Did she see him, the guy who punched her? Or me? The distraught mother who held her hand and listened carefully to the dentist who gave careful instructions about keeping the area clean and refraining from solids for twenty-four hours. "Jell-O," he said. "Give her Jell-O."

She slept when we got home; she still had that same striped afghan.

She had burrowed into my lap the night of the punch, and then she didn't. She went back to the Anita who claimed she could manage her own life. Back to anger. Back to resentment so intense that, when we came close to her, giving her a quick pat on the back maybe, we felt heat. She was burning up.

She had a white box full of odd bits of clothing, with FRESH CALIFORNIA ORANGES printed on the side of the box. I had never seen the box before, but there it was, on the floor of her bedroom. She tried maroon. Put a maroon knit cap on her dark hair. Put maroon gloves on her ashy hands, thin edgy fingers, and floated away before I could make a grab.

When she was able to open her mouth again, her teeth showed a milky blue-white like pieces of Styrofoam boxes.

She was three when she bit me and broke skin. I was surprised seeing my blood edge out over my skin. Why did she, so small and seemingly amiable, do that?

"No!" I yelled. She widened her eyes, ready to cry, then licked my blood like a cat, her tongue dainty and precise.

She was often fighting mad, but the thing was, her mad needed *us*. We gave her anger shape, a certain edge. Ken, me, Sung, Minh, her anger found all of us; we were like those receptacles in front of public buildings, the ones filled with sand that a person can plunge burning cigarettes into. We took the burn.

Chapter 22
RESIDUAL COLOR MOLECULES

I was crazy-wild with fear. Every time the phone rang, every time someone pulled into the driveway, I imagined the worst. Even so, I had to bring in the mail, arrange smiles for Minh and Sung, appear normal; I brushed my hair, flossed my teeth, put my shoes on. I could not inhabit my daughter. Ma and Rosie said that to me all the time. *Breathe, even when it hurts. There is life beyond Anita.* I didn't believe them.

Shortly after the incident with the guy in the house, I went back to Saint Marys. I wanted to be in a place where there was little or no trace of my daughter, any one of the kids, actually. Ken wasn't eager to take care of the kids on his own, given the situation, but he could see that I was rattled and agreed I needed some down time. He was, impossible as it sounds, still hopeful. "Go on," he said. So I did. I wanted to be someplace where ordinary seemed possible. Where when a guy came into the house he had been invited and was offered coffee, not a face he could smack at will.

Pammie always did my hair when I was back home. I'd walk into her place, Heads Up; she'd pour me coffee, and we'd get down to business. She took care of me. She did my sister's hair too. She was famous in our family for saving Barb the time she cut her own hair and ended up looking like a bad Mia Farrow. Pammie was not a Mother Teresa, not even a dentist who could bond a tooth in a kid's mouth. She was just an old friend, somebody I'd known in school. She went to beauty college, then set up shop on Erie Avenue, across from the railroad tracks, a little way down from a meat market that used to be there, but isn't anymore. Two doors up from the local volunteer fire department. She understood that I needed to look as if I were alive. She took what she had in front of her and made it work, best she could.

Right before I left for Saint Marys, Ken and I fought. It was pick and rub raw. "You might look up from your computer now and then," was what I said to him. "You might discipline a little more," he said back. "You never . . ." But I was always faster and meaner than Ken. "You think science has the answers? What about entering the human world?" I was like Anita that way. Ken was my receptacle. I stubbed out the flame of my anger and fear in him. He pulled at the skin on his arm, a nervous habit. "Don't," I said. "You'll hurt yourself." He looked surprised when I said that, as if he wasn't sure that mattered to me anymore.

"We have to be friends," he said, "or we won't make it through this. It's hard enough without hurting each other." He sounded tired, as if remaining hopeful was harder than he'd bargained for. We were two people who had lowered ourselves into that red porcelain heart after we drove out of Saint Marys and then, surprise, there we were, wet and shivering in the cold.

People liked to tell us we'd get our reward in heaven. We were angels, they said. So good, so kind, saving kids by adopting them. They'd never be able to do something like that. When they said that, they looked at us as if we *were* angels, wings emerging from our backs, hair all golden and down to our shoulders, feet not even touching the ground. They meant well, but who could imagine angels or saviors anymore? Were there such things?

If there were, wouldn't Anita come to breakfast smiling with her hair brushed, long and down to her shoulders, not all frizzed, sprayed stiff, and angry looking? Wouldn't Minh get his homework done? Maybe Sung would be able to recite some math facts? We would eat toast with butter and honey. We would sit around the table, a mismatched group of bed heads, crumbs down our fronts, honey on our lips, sticky and happy, if there were angels, if we were saviors.

* * *

The minute Pammie saw me walk through the door, she whipped up a paste and put it on the counter in a clear glass dish. "This mix is resurrection," she said. "And, honey, you need some of that."

"Sit down." She gestured to a chair and handed me my coffee. She began to paint strands of my hair. Strawberry—a bit of blonde, a bit of red, light and bright, a color that would distract from my tired face.

I drank the coffee and remembered the time Ma went from gray to bright red, the year that Ken got Anita her leather jacket. I had gone back home and stood in the bathroom, watching my mother lean over the sink and color her hair. "I'm a redhead now," she said to me, "no more gray. I've always wanted a red head. None of you kids turned out that way, so I'm making myself into one." *Cinnamon red*, my cinnamon-red-haired mother. When she was done, she looked in the mirror and smiled, like she'd discovered somebody she wanted and could delight in.

I thought about hair and what it meant for my family, all that hair, from all over the place.

Anita could never stand to have her hair touched. When she was a little kid, I approached her hair with a bottle of spray detangler, a super-fine brush, and a wide-toothed comb. Her hair knotted so easily; it needed constant care. Some days I wasn't up to it. She pitched a fit and I let it go. Other days, I bribed her with sky-blue jawbreakers. Anita sucked, and I slowly, slowly, eased the comb through her tangles. I knew my daughter's hair. I knew it when she was a kid, wearing red yarn ties, and I knew it later in the designs she piled on top of her head, the lacquer she used to lock the whole thing in place. Her hair stood stiff in arranged sections. Sometimes, she offered me a touch, like I was a visitor she was showing around. "Feel," she said. I was careful, a light touch, a quick resting of my hand on the top of her head.

"Was it hard to do?"

She said, "Yeah."

I saw empty cans on the bathroom counter, white nozzles pointing nowhere. I reminded her to keep the window open when she sprayed, warned her about the fumes mixing with her cigarettes. There were warnings printed on those cans. She looked at me and laughed. "Blown up while I'm doing my hair," she said. "Can you imagine?"

I could. But I'd risk a blowup to be able to touch her hair.

Sung's hair was thick and wiry. So thick and wiry, almost, a person could use it to tie things down. He had horsehair. That's what our Korean friends said; it meant he was stubborn. All Koreans knew about the horsehair people, fiery tempered, quick, insistent, smart, and loyal. We didn't disagree with that description. Our youngest, the Korean firebrand.

Nobody in our family had hair half so thick. He spent an afternoon coaxing me to help him streak his black hair blond. He was only nine, but he was so cheerful at the prospect, so needful of some fun, that I agreed. What harm could it do? We put a plastic cap on his head, pulled his horsehair through, coated it, and set the timer and waited. What he got was the merest glint of, maybe, pale brown? He wanted to look punky-Asian blond, like somebody who got the second look on the street but no questions. Like the college kids he saw in downtown Ann Arbor.

I bought another box of highlights and smeared them on, kept at it until something happened. It wasn't what he was after, still no punk Asian blond, but it wasn't black anymore. Whole sections of his hair were an off color, not brown or blond or black, nothing featured on the cover of a box. "Oh, Sung," I said trying for glad, "I love your hair."

"Even now?" he asked, eyeing it, unsure. "I look weird. Like parts of my hair belong to a ghost."

But I did love his hair. It wasn't hard to love, my son's hair.

Minh grew his hair so long he had a past-his-shoulders ponytail held together with a black elastic band. He wore a red beret right in front of the tail. Then, one day, just after he came home from school, he combed his ponytail out over the sink, leaned down and forward, took my scissors, and cut it off. There was a sink full of something dark, like animal fur. He took the hair clippers and buzzed until it was all there in the sink, and he called to me to come in and see his head, a knob of fuzz. "Look."

Anita was in the bathroom with him and she ran her hand over the top of his head like it was new carpeting. "Why so short?" she asked. He said he was tired of combing his hair and the girl he liked was going out with a guy who wore camouflage and had stubble instead of hair. "You'll never get her," Anita said. "She only goes for the big dudes, the wrestler types. You are a skinny Viet guy. You should have kept your tail. It looked good on you. Grow it back."

I told him to get the hair out of the sink—it would clog the drain—and said he could wear any style; he had good cheekbones.

Ken's hair was graying, always too long, a bit curly at the

ends. He had scientist's hair, no glamour, just a covering for his head. He gave his hair almost no thought or time. I'd bring home shampoos and conditioners that Pammie suggested would be good for him. He mostly ignored them, fine with whatever the kids left in the shower. So easy with himself that sometimes he emerged with his hair smelling like apples from Anita's shampoo.

While Pammie wrapped my strands in foil, I thought about losing my husband and his hair. We were fighting so much! We fought before, who didn't? But we had never had stress like this before. I was a person who couldn't let go of stress. So if Ken went off for a swim, maybe to Fuller Pool, Ann Arbor's premier pool for serious swimmers, I'd yell. Unreasonable. *Go! Go!* I said that to him, just before I'd left to go to Saint Marys. All he wanted was some time to do laps in the pool. It made no sense to yell at him, but I did. Sometimes, I thought I wanted Ken and his graying hair gone. He could go for a swim and stay in the pool forever. If he was not around to insist otherwise, I'd let the kids do whatever they wanted to do: eat when they wanted, sleep till all hours, pass classes or not, with their hair any which way. Then they would *have* to be happy. But that was the idea of a crazy woman. I loved Ken. I didn't want him gone. Besides, I could never have managed to handle those kids alone. I knew that. When I yelled, *Go*, I was really yelling, *Fix it, fix it.*

I behaved like the women who came into Pammie's shop, set themselves down, and said, "Do something." Like they thought there was some power that Pammie had, some way for her to make miracles. But, there wasn't. There were only those women with the hair they had, and Pammie who could cut and color what they put before her. That's all there was.

When I was ready to leave, Pammie looked at me sad-like; she knew how bad it was. "You look good, Mary," she said, "but take it easy. The color isn't completely set yet. There are things called residual color molecules. They don't emerge right away; they need time. After a while, maybe a few days, they will activate, and the color will set. Then it's yours."

Residual color molecules. I'd never heard of them. They sounded a little something like my kids, like something that manifested in its own time and place, if a person could wait it out.

I wondered if Ken would like the way I looked. I had a week in Saint Marys. The residual color molecules would have emerged by the time I went back to Ann Arbor. Would I even have the energy to find out if Ken liked the way I looked? I loved him, but hardly said that to him anymore, all my words used up on the kids. What if he stayed in that cement-block place where he went to work, fiddling around with numbers and charts, waiting for his own kind of molecules to manifest themselves? If he stayed in his office and I had no more Ken to stroke my hair and counsel a little calm, I would not be happy. I would look for him to come in the door, look for his head, a mix of gray and brown under his protective sun hat, and there would be only empty space.

Pammie had done a good job; I looked fine. I didn't know that I would be any better at being my children's mother or my husband's wife, but I'd learned about the color molecules, about hair as protective coloration, camouflage, something with a life of its own.

Whatever hair those people of mine had, black or brown-gray or stiff with spray, shaved to a nub, feeling like straw from a bad dye job, I didn't care. What mattered was that I got to *touch* it: the stiffness of Anita's hair, the fuzz of Minh's, the straw-like texture of Sung's. I wanted that. And I wanted to be able to roll over in bed and touch Ken's hair, to stroke the gray-brown and tell him, grief or no, my color molecules were his, if he wanted them.

Chapter 23

CRY UNCLE

For the moment Anita didn't have to watch her back, for which we were profoundly grateful. For the moment, the thug who had punched her was in Washtenaw County Jail.

Ken had whistled when I returned home from Saint Marys and he saw the strawberry red in my hair. He gave me a bear hug, the first in a while, and that's when he told me the guy who broke into the house was in jail, caught breaking and entering a minimart on the south side of Ann Arbor. Anita had told him so. She'd heard it in school and came home with the news. Ken said she looked relieved, no matter that she claimed she could handle the situation. She looked, he said, as if somebody had just given her good news. Well it was good news, for sure.

Ken and I headed to that coffee shop on Main Street and raised our cups in a salute, "To us," like we'd made it past a land mine. It felt so good, that bit of reprieve. Maybe it went to our heads because Ken planned to start an anti-smoking campaign aimed at Anita and Minh.

They'd started smoking in high school. We certainly hadn't given our blessing. But they smoked anyway. They puffed in the parking lot at school—hiding behind the Dumpster or a friend's car. In our driveway if we couldn't see them. They smoked in front of the old Borders on Liberty Street, with friends who smoked too. I drove by and saw them. When I put the window down to call to my kids, smoke drifted into the car, foggy and sweet like insecticide. They spotted me, flicked their smokes away, and jumped into the car.

"Stupid," I said. "It's a stupid thing you're doing." They knew that.

Some ways, the kids' smoking felt worse than the other things, bad company and failing grades. I know that doesn't make sense. But I was afraid that if we managed, by some chance, to get the big problems fixed—the two of them safely graduated from high school, maybe in a two-year college—it would be for nothing. We would still end up walking in front of a coffin. Ken hated it when I said things like that. He'd hustle me out the door in the direction of the gym for some sweat therapy.

There's a thing called the Gravitron machine that works the entire upper body. I used it all the time. I did chin-ups, pull-ups, and vertical dips. I aimed to look like Diane, my trainer, who came by with her belt hanging loose from her shorts, her arms bare in a sleeveless tee, and said, "Good, Mary, good." Diane never smoked. She did not eat junk food or get less than eight hours of sleep a night.

When I told her I stress ate and didn't sleep nights waiting for the car to pull in the driveway, listening to the final track of gangsta rap, waiting for the time it takes for somebody to smoke a last cigarette, she stared in disbelief. "Why do you let them?" she asked. "Why do that to yourself?" "Smoking!" she said. "I wouldn't let any kid of mine do that."

"And how would you stop it?" I asked. "Would you follow them to school? Would you check their breath? Exactly how long would you keep them grounded?" I was furious with her, ready to tell her how it really was. Parenting wasn't like she thought at all. She thought you could control a person intent on no control? I could ground the kids, lay down the law, level consequences. That was doable. But when grounding doesn't work, when taking away the music or refusing the allowance doesn't work, what then? You can strip a room bare. Leave only the bed with its covers, an overhead light, the paint on the wall. Nothing else. But after that, when that doesn't work, then what?

Diane didn't have a clue. That's what I thought. She gave me no answer.

They smoked whenever we turned our backs. They knew how to live in secret, the two of them.

He wanted to smoke Camels. She wanted minty Kools. But they didn't have the cash to buy products with labels. They had to smoke no-names, cigarettes that came in a plain package. Generic.

The day after we went for coffee, Ken came home with pictures of lungs barely visible beneath layers of grunge. They looked like split chicken breasts burnt on the grill, the result of assorted chemical deposits, the same kind of chemicals Minh and Anita inhaled. "Those lungs," said Ken, "are what your lungs will look like."

He had the goods to show them, all right.

"Yeah, well," said Minh, "but those lungs are maybe fifty years old. We're young. We have time."

His sister smiled in agreement. Time was a problem for old people. She took a long deep inhalation meant to illustrate her point.

Did they smoke because it made them feel good? That was probably true.

Like the potato chips I eat, when I swear I won't. They taste so good.

Even now they struggle. They stop smoking and start, stop and start. They've done this for years.

I know this much. It wasn't just us. As the stories unfolded and parents came forward to tell their stories, parents who had adopted in the seventies, and eighties, smoking seemed to be a symbol for all kinds of problems. Like a generic clue.

The kids were already older when the local parent support group ran an ad for an adoption conference, a talk session that brought parents together to share their experiences. The conference covered the standard topics: adjustment, identification, school, adolescence. The session on adolescence had an overflow crowd that spilled out the door into the hallway. Parents told about kids who were in jail, kids who dropped out of school, kids who held on in school by a thread, kids who smoked, kids who were parents, kids who overdosed, kids who shut down, kids who left and never came back. One father stood up and said, "Tell me what to do. Just tell me what to do."

But there is no one thing. It's a stop-and-start road. Sometimes it's a washboard road. Adoption complicates developmental issues. Adopted kids tend to have a harder time making it through the minefield of adolescence. If you add other factors, such as race, to the picture, it's even harder. How can anyone know exactly what to do? I don't think all adopted kids have issues. I don't think that adoption is negative. I believe in adoption. I'm an advocate. But. It isn't an easy road. Great, but not easy. Like those skinny Grand Canyon trails.

By the time Sung hit adolescence, we knew what to look for, how to intervene early on. Sung had contact with psychologists in one guise or another from the time he was in third grade.

In the meantime.

Anita continued to court trouble as though it were her birthright. She said that to me many days. "I must have been trouble. My own mother could not take care of me."

"Anita. Anita," I said to her. "It's true your birth mom could not take care of you, but that doesn't mean there's something wrong with you." Anita said she would not know her own mother if she met her on the street. "Isn't that the limit?" she said. Her words sounded faint, as if she were losing her voice. She was in the kitchen talking to me then, but it was all too likely she would go wild again, take up with somebody else, someone only too ready to oblige her notions of trouble. She'd be smoking when she took off with him.

The same with her brother, the kid from Vietnam. He figured out how to find trouble. He wasn't going to leave it all for his sister; he wanted a share. He took off when we slept to hang with his buds and chug wine coolers in the arboretum while they played Dungeons and Dragons.

All the experts say that adoptive kids test their parents: Will their parents keep them if they smoke, steal, lie, run, get pregnant, get somebody pregnant, land in jail—behave in a way that would make nearly anybody cry, "Uncle!" If I stood near the two of them I inhaled the smoke caught in their shirts and jeans. But I would not cry "Uncle."

* * *

I wanted the kids to believe that love was the deal at the end of their plane ride; there would be no lack of love ever. Love would give them what they needed. But I learned that love was *not* the whole deal. We loved the kids fiercely. But love never made the whole picture.

Like that ad that promised blue water, snowy mountains, no hint of complications from
 smoking, parts of our life were hidden. *Don't look at the parts with bad people, bad times.*

When Sung was in middle school, his class had a project

on family roots. Everybody was watching and reading *Roots*, the Alex Haley story, and teachers loved to assign genealogy projects. For the first time, Sung asked me what I thought about our family, our adoptions. "So what do you think? Are you happy?"

He had sat through some therapy by then, some with the family, some by himself. It gave him the attitude of a reporter interviewing me, a grieving family member, at the airport. He was asking me for my response about the plane crash.

When I answered him, I saw the movie of us that ran under my closed eyelids sometimes: we were picking wild blackberries on Pontiac Trail in front of the old judge's house; we were going into Kroger, filling the cart with Michigan peaches, cherries, sweet corn; we were driving to the Flim Flam, all together, to stuff ourselves with burgers, fries, and handmade milkshakes—*full, full, full.*

In that same movie I watched while Anita snapped at us or took off. I watched Minh take a puff of a cigarette, saw Sung defeated by math.

He tapped his pencil against the kitchen counter, impatient for my answer, waiting for me to tell him if our family worked, if I was happy, if adopting the way we had, no inclination to match or insist on some information, had been the right thing to do. Himself, he said, he never wanted problems like ours, no crazy-making family, no therapy sessions. "You guys are nuts!" He said that as if we were part of a trapeze act, no net. He wanted out of the act as soon as possible.

I tried to be honest. "It's good and it's hard, Sung. But I would never want a different family. Anyway, every family has tough times, even when they all look alike."

When I said that to him, I remembered my mother in the backyard taking her washing off the line the last time I went home to have Pammie highlight my hair. She kept pulling sheets off the line and told me what she believed about life, short and sweet—"Every rose has its thorn, Mary. You have to remember that."

Talking to Sung about his school report, I wondered if, truth was, I hadn't expected our adoptions to be all roses, no thorns, at least nothing that would pierce skin. Maybe most of us are like that. We are aware of bad things that can happen and we try to avoid them, but we don't plan for them, not the way we plan vacations and birthday parties. What we do is, we fill our lives with enough good things so that there won't be room for bad things—we hope.

Of course there were good times. I said that to Sung.

There was a time that I counted as a best time, a perfect rose. I thought of that time while Sung waited, impatient for my answers. I told him about it: Sung was four or five the time I remembered. He was playing in the sandbox while I sat on a green nylon lawn chair, strips of nylon fabric pressing into my thighs, reading *Adam Bede*, in love with nineteenth-century literature, all those repressed emotions, surging love . . .

Ken had come home from work and stretched out on the grass beside me. He was in love with his work: nuclei, neurons, single-photon emission computed tomography. He had taken off his lab coat and folded it under his head like a pillow. I drank lemonade, ice cubes rattling around in the glass. I offered him some. He sat up to drink. The kids came around and piled on top of Ken, two on one leg, one on the other. He groaned and said they squashed him. They laughed and planted themselves a little harder, one skinny scientist and three completely happy kids.

That memory came back to me like the gift of a long-stemmed rose, no thorns at all. "Yeah," Sung said, taking his final notes, "but we were kids then. It was easier then."

I did not dispute that, but I told him that the good times were real. It was important to know that.

Chapter 24

RED ROSE TEA

Ma drank this brand of tea called Red Rose tea when I went back home in those years. She said, every time she finished her tea, "It would be nice to find a rose at the bottom of the cup." I didn't want a rose at the bottom of my cup. What I wanted was a promise that things would work out.

It was getting worse all the time for us.

By the time she was fifteen, Anita moved down the highway way faster than her father and I could; the places she headed to by then were places we didn't know as anyplace at all. She went past Ann Arbor into places that were like countries at war: She moved on past south Ypsi to apartments on Detroit's Six Mile with doors that didn't open unless you had cred. She searched those places out like they were her mother country, the place every internationally adopted kid should return to. What she got in those places was nothing like anything we could give her. When Ken went looking for her, if he was able to find her—in a parking lot or on a street—she was angry the minute she saw his face, the anger and fear in his eyes. If he found her and brought her back, she resented the fear and anger. Sometimes, I had this crazy thought that she was mad we didn't greet her like she had just come off the plane again, that she wanted us to reach out and sweep her up into our arms. *Anita, Anita! You're our sweetie pie.*

No more sweetie pie. We were always caught between relief and fury. We steeled ourselves, prepared for the time she might be gone for good. We gave her fewer of our kisses. I allowed myself to imagine life without her. Sometimes, she looked hurt; she knew. Then I turned away and, the best I could do, offered her the last slice of take-out pizza. "I know it's hard to accept this," said the psychologist, the recommended one we were still seeing, "but you have to remember it's harder for her than it is for you." I couldn't see that my daughter had pleasure in her life, so it made sense. But how much more could we manage?

One Friday we had to leave town for a funeral. Grandma K had died, somebody who, although she was not an actual grandmother, gave the kids dollar bills and bags of strawberry Twizzlers. She was the mother of Mary Ann, my sister-in-law, and she'd been a part of our lives for many family celebrations, had known the kids since they landed.

"I like being your pretend grandma," she said to them. They were glad to call her Grandma, have somebody else to give them treats. Karen and Cathy, John and Mary Ann's daughters, were willing enough to share their grandmother. Grandma K couldn't see in the last years, so, when we visited, the kids would stand in front of her, and she would reach out and touch their heads, tell them they were growing too fast, pretty soon they wouldn't want dollar bills and strawberry Twizzlers. But, they always said, *no, no*, they were glad for her treats, and they meant that. They would sit beside her and let her hold their hands as long as she wanted. They understood that she was reaching out from the dark and they tried to make for a shorter reach. It seemed to me, watching all of them, that they recognized each other's hurt, were clustered together with no words needed.

I got the call that Grandma K had died on a Thursday in early November, a mean kind of day somewhere between sleet and rain. We would need to go to Cleveland for the funeral. I told the kids when they came home from school. The boys let out a cry. Anita put her hands over her ears, slammed the door to her room, and stayed there. Next morning she ate cinnamon toast, then left for school with Minh, her pack slung over her shoulder. I called out to the two of them, "Come home right away. We need to leave as soon as we can." She turned back to give me a hug. We held each other full frontal and I kissed her cheek. Minh slid behind the driver's seat of the rusted Chevy and yelled for her to hurry it up, called out that I shouldn't worry.

Minh came home, on time. But there was no sister in the car with him, no idea where she was.

We waited. Sometimes that's all a person can think of to do. Just to wait and then wait some more. I stared at the last of the Michaelmas daises, sniffed the air as though I could find her scent, but there was nothing. Nothing in the air, nothing in the sky, nothing on the ground.

We were hours late leaving. We needed to go. That's what Ken said. His jaw locked, like it was cemented in place. No grief for him this time. He was not going to listen to me plead for a little more time, one more phone call, a drive round to check on possible places.

How could I leave town without my daughter? Without knowing where she was? "I can't. I can't," I cried. "Let's call the police."

Ken shoved suitcases into the car, shouted at me: "We have to go. Anita won't be back anytime soon; you know that. We can't go looking this time. There are other people besides Anita who matter. The police won't help."

I remembered how we had called the police about our daughter the very first time she had gone missing. I had seen them in our living room with their thick black shoes and holstered guns: sturdy people with I-have-seen-it-all eyes. Sturdy people who said there was nothing much they could do. Did we suspect *foul play*? I shook my head no. I didn't suspect it. I tried not to think about it.

I kept stalling. Ken grew implacable.

"This is Grandma K dead." I needed to realize whom the funeral was for: Grandma K, not Anita. At least, probably not Anita. "We have to go to this funeral. Come on, Mary." His voice softened; he put his arm around me.

We did have to go. So I went. I willed myself to get into the car. I increased the distance between me and my daughter. Even if a person tries to learn nonattachment, lies in the yoga pose called Savasana, corpse pose, meditating every single day, relinquishment can feel like terminal bleeding and you're the person who made the cut.

"Go," I said to Ken. "Go."

Her brothers turned to look back as we pulled out of the driveway like they thought she might be standing in the window or doorway, calling for us to wait, she was coming.

We drove off, the four of us.

I left phone numbers, times, and places pressed to the counter on orange sticky notes. I drew a large red exclamation point on white construction paper and taped the exclamation point to the back door. Underneath the exclamation point, I wrote: *See notes on counter*. She would come in the back door if she came back.

I lied to everyone I talked to at the viewing. I stood near Grandma K's casket and I lied to my sister-in-law, Mary Ann. I lied to cousins and friends of the family who knew us. I said Anita was in a school play, had the lead. It was a big play. People were depending on her. I said she was *so sorry*. If people knew I lied to them, they never said so. But I don't think they knew.

School plays were the norm. What we lived was not the norm, and I had not told anyone in Cleveland the truth about our life. I'd only hinted at a bit of trouble. They were good people; they would not have judged. They would have tried to help. But I held my grief as if it were a private treasure, something nobody else would know how to take care of.

Ken went along with my lie. This surprised me because he was not a guy who lied, not even to be tactful. He went along with that lie though, didn't give a single hint that our daughter was gone, and we had come to the funeral in a town two hundred miles from Ann Arbor, no idea where she was. Maybe he had his own private cache of grief that he didn't want on view.

Do good mothers and fathers do that? I lay awake in Phyl's guest room, the night before the funeral service, and remembered how Anita had looked when she went out the kitchen door. She gave me that hug and hitched her pack over her left shoulder. Then she got into the car with her brother. She had her hair frizzed in front, the bangs a big pouf. She had painted her nails maroon.

Sung came into our room in the middle of the night, crying that we had driven off and left his sister behind. Would we leave him too? "No, no," I said. "We will find her; we will not leave you." He curled up at the bottom of the bed, covered with my coat, whimpering like a dog. I reached down to pat his back until he slept. I searched for Ken's hand in the dark and whispered that we didn't know that we *would* find her. "We will," he said, sounding grim, like he'd abandon the search if that were possible. God. She distributed pain like it was so many sticks of gum.

Soon enough the funeral service was over and Grandma K was wheeled out of the church. We drove to the cemetery where we placed a rose on the casket and then left her to be lowered into the ground.

I wished, as we headed back home, that I had stayed in Cleveland, had lain down beside Grandma K in her beige coffin with the pale peach lining. I would have fit, so skinny with worry. Calm. It would be calm. My troubles would fall away; my skin would fall away, and after a while, only bones would be left, mine next to Grandma K's, gray-white and clean, still as could be on pale peach silk.

But I was not in the coffin. The coffin was in the ground at Holy Cross Cemetery and Grandma K was alone. I was in the car headed home, and it was just past dark on Saturday night when we pulled into the driveway of the green house, dinnertime, about six thirty. Minh and Sung yelled that they saw lights on in the kitchen; *somebody was there.* We got out of the car and went into the house.

Our daughter held up a pan-roasted chicken for us to see, fresh out of the oven. She was smiling. She had set the table in the dining room. There were the Michaelmas daises in my best blue vase in the center of the table. There was salad with the very last of the garden's tiny grape tomatoes rimming the last garden lettuce. Glasses of water with slices of lemon floating at the top.

She wore my green oven mitts, one on each hand, and balanced the pan carefully so as not to spill the juices. The chicken was perfectly browned. Had she gone to Kroger and bought a roasting chicken? Had she walked home with it in her pack? Had whomever she'd taken off with on Friday driven her to the store and waited while she shopped? What had she done for cash?

I never found out. I wanted to scream. Loud.

Anita talked like a hotel receptionist greeting arrivals. "I found your notes. I made supper." Was she saying she was sorry? Did she have any idea? What were we supposed to say: *How was your trip, Anita? We went to a funeral, Anita. Remember Grandma K?*

The smell of roasted chicken hung in the air. It would be years before I could bear that smell again.

When I think about that time, and it's years past, I realize I never talk about that dinner with her. We talk about things from that time now. But that scene's like a bad picture in the family album: something went wrong before the shutter clicked. I shiver when I think of it. I keep that picture in an album on a high shelf in the back room closet, someplace I never dust.

I can put myself back there though, fast. There was the girl-woman holding that roasting pan in my kitchen, offering me food and words: *Eat, eat, take it and eat it. I've made this just for you.* Who *was* that girl?

I wanted to grab hold and shake her, shake her hard. But I did nothing.

Anita grew angry at my silence and banged the pan onto the counter; juice splattered the counter and wall, dotted her red silk shirt. I ignored all of it, the food, the girl, everyone. I went upstairs to bed and pulled the covers over me.

Ken stayed in the kitchen and tried to settle things.

I don't know what happened to that meal. When I came down the next morning, there were no signs, no leftovers in the refrigerator, no chicken, no salad. Even the flowers were gone. The stove and walls were wiped clean. Somebody had opened the windows and a little bit of wind moved through the room. Maybe it moved things a bit because I found one of my sticky notes, lying on the floor in front of the stove. WE ARE NOT

LEAVING YOU! That's what I had written in bold orange marker. In caps. Printed. Just to be clear.

I heard her bedroom door open, her feet move over the wood floor. She came into the kitchen wearing gray sweats with a Pistons logo. I didn't recognize them, but then, she had this tendency to gather souvenirs of her travels, so they could have been from anyone, anywhere.

I put on the kettle, asked her if she wanted some tea. We might be able to manage tea even if we couldn't eat together. We sat at the table and sipped. No pink Melmac, no Red Rose. We poured tea from a brown pot into two lime-green mugs. Darjeeling. For something to say—I would not talk about the weekend—talking about that felt like trying to move a boulder stuck somewhere inside me—I told her about my mom, about the Red Rose tea. She looked at me, her eyes the same dark brown as my mother's. "I wish," she said. "I wish."

And, right then, I knew she *did* wish. Like my mother, like most of us, my daughter wished. I poured more of what I had to give her and let my hand rest with hers on the handle of her cup. The two of us looking, both of us wishing.

Chapter 25

WHAT IT WAS LIKE

After that meal, Anita didn't cook anymore, no surprise meals or arranged flowers, but she still took off any way she could, as often as she could. We'd talk and talk and talk, Ken and I, alone or with the psychologist. We tried variations of ideas, like we were playing duets on the piano. We planned to: *draw the line, love unconditionally, understand the underlying problems, encourage self-esteem, continue to reach out to her, meet her friends, pursue therapy.* I understood two things at the time. One thing was that there were no miracles to be had: no psychologist, no drawing the line, no yelling or crying or threat would effect a miracle and give us a safe and sound Anita. The other thing was that I was not willing to let her go. I didn't think that, in the end, she wanted to go, not forever anyway. If she wanted to go forever, why would she come back the way she did? So, there was a plus. Maybe.

I could add a third thing. We do not want to think that color can matter so much. We want to believe we are past all that, have been past it for a long time. Surely color couldn't have triggered so much pain? But I think it did. There were also two years of her life we knew nothing about. So there is that. There are genetics to consider too. But I still agree, at least partly, with the adoption specialist who suggested that Anita was out to prove how different she could be.

She still broods about differences. She measures fairness and needs to be reassured. She's the one who remembers from one family gathering to the next who took the last brownie in the pan, a grown woman with kids and she remembers that, holds on to that information as if it's important. She is acutely sensitive. Sometimes when she's around, I feel as if I should have been trained to be a firewalker. But she knows I like flowers in the house and she brings flowers from her garden when she comes. She cares more than anyone I know. She cares so much that it came close to killing her.

I didn't think anything would work to lessen her anger and self-destructiveness after Grandma K's funeral. But Ken had found new energy from somewhere and studied the situation like he was applying for a grant. Maybe he was fueled by the same kind of energy that drove him to get those grants, but I was sick at heart. I never knew that sick at heart could be a physical fact. But my heart felt like a hunk of frozen meat. Some days my chest hurt so much I could hardly breathe. Other days I ran for miles and tried not to care.

Minh came home the Monday after the funeral weekend and told us that his sister's travels were the talk of school. She had gone off with some thirty-plus-year-old guy that weekend. Everybody knew and was talking about it. He was ready to crawl under a rock, but there was no comfort I had to offer. Comfort would only rankle, like phone calls from old friends who heard the rumors about my daughter and called to say they were sorry, who suggested therapy like it was a new idea. I knew they wanted to offer me something, anything, by way of help. But silence pulled between me and anyone in a normal life, until I let it snap back, and the line went dead. There was only the place we lived in, only the trouble we had.

We inhabited a place that most people did not recognize. We wished that weren't the case, but it was. So what we did was adaptive. We tried to make the best of things. Ken was pretty good at it and I tried to go along. We bought Minh his favorite videos and more language tapes. Sung got a skateboard. We weren't *buying* Minh and Sung's goodwill, although I worried it seemed like that. For sure, we were trying to assure them ours was a *good home*, that place on the sheet the worker gave a check mark to. Sometimes when I came home with treats for Sung or Minh, I'd look in the bags and realize I had nothing for Anita, like I didn't expect her to be around anymore. I'd go back to the store and grab shampoo or nail polish. Bringing her a treat seemed stupid, even to me, the woman who preferred agreement to argument. But I couldn't bear to have her think I didn't care. It was something I never resolved: Was I supposed to keep reaching out or retreat? Would she see the shampoo and nail polish as a gesture of love or a bribe? I'd stand there in Rite Aid, feeling as if I were trying to solve one of those twisted metal puzzles. Some people are good at unraveling them, not me.

Minh practiced Vietnamese incessantly in those years. He listened to the tonal scale, trying for the perfect rise and fall of his voice. He was failing four out of five school subjects, but was determined to master his native language. He had a book of Vietnamese phrases, mostly sentences that were supposed to help travelers order a meal or get a cab. There was a picture of a smiling businessman, getting a room, buying a meal in a café.

Vietnamese Phrase	English Phrase
Ban co phong trong khong?	Do you have any rooms?
Kin cho ban nam nguoi.	Table for five please.

That was not what my son wanted to say, but there were no sentences for:

I am searching for my mother. I want to find my mother. I need to know if she's okay.

He learned to say *Toi buon* (I'm sad). He was sad about life right then all right, so that sentence was helpful. I practiced my own sentences that I spoke when he came into the kitchen for a drink or food. *I am your mother. I will always love you.* He always agreed it was true. I *was* his mother, but still, he wanted to find the other one.

I thought that any woman who even *resembled* what he thought that lost birth mother of his looked like would be up for grabs with him. It wouldn't matter whether or not she was a dead ringer. He would look, walk up, and grab hold. "Mom!"

I didn't want to mind. After all, he was willing to let us love him, and he said over and over that he loved us too. He said it every time he went out the door with eyes open wide, still searching for the right shape, form, head of hair. "Bye, you guys, I love you."

"This is what he needs to do." That was what the psychologist said whenever we got around to talking about someone other than Anita. "He needs to do this. There is nothing you can do but accept it." I think we tried to do that, even when we angled to hear that he loved us.

There was shock and dismay on the part of people who learned that Minh didn't know who his birth mother was, that none of our kids did. *Not even her name, her age? Nothing? My God! How come? What if the kids carry a gene for some terrible disease? What if*, and when people said *what if*, they seemed to think no one else had said *what if*, but many people had: *What if Minh or Sung end up marrying their sister? What if Anita ends up marrying her brother?* Always the fantasy that somehow one of the kids would come across a *real* sibling and there would be this terrible mix-up, that trouble would arrive wrapped in exoticism. I laughed at those worries. People looked startled. I thought of telling them that trouble seemed way more local, far less exotic.

* * *

That same year of Grandma K's funeral, Ken and I sat in a room on gray metal chairs, eyes straight forward like kids in class. Minh was on stage with a panel of adoptive teens who had been asked to talk about their experience of adoption. The panel had been chosen by a young woman, Mai, a grad student at the University of Michigan, who was studying the outcomes of adoption for male Vietnamese teens. There were six adoptees on the panel, all of them from Michigan. I remember the teen, a wiry, angry seventeen-year-old, who stood up and declared that he was angry. He hadn't asked to be adopted. He was going to find his birth parents, no matter what it took! Another kid said he felt that he'd been robbed of his culture. He couldn't speak Vietnamese, so he wasn't seen as Vietnamese and he didn't feel American. Ken and I gave each other a commiserating look. What would Minh say? He took the proffered mike; we waited—he gripped the mike like it was a winning ticket, and he said—we held each other's hand—he said:

"Well, I'll tell you, I have the best parents. They would go to the wall for me."

Oh, he was right! He was right! We would go to the wall for him. We were his parents, his parents. That was what we wanted him to know. That was what we wanted the world to know. We were not *best*, though. *Best* would have been if we could have loved without the constant voice that said, *love us back, love us back.*

Chapter 26
TOI DEN TU

The truth was, I did not want to go up against a wall if I could help it. I wanted to be best parent, but did not want to smash my brains out. I wasn't sure I had a choice, though, because boy-man Minh had a tendency, at seventeen, to grab things not his own—I never said steal, that was too hard to say. He seemed to want to build a wall for us to crash into, almost as if he were checking to see if he'd get the same amount of angst his sister got. Minh's problem emerged soon after that panel discussion. It expanded like one of those blossoms in a teapot, large and fully open.

After declaring that we were the best parents, Minh began to obsess about old news photos of the Babylift crash. I don't know why he did that then, but probably because he had heard the other people on the panel. It wasn't unreasonable to wonder. He pulled the clippings we had saved from the file cabinet in Ken's study. The same file cabinet held clippings about Korea and India. We'd kept any bit of information we could find. The kids knew where to find anything we had that they wanted to know. Mostly, they chose to ignore it. But Minh started poring over old news articles with the same intensity he gave his language tapes. *What happened? What did you do? Was I on that flight or not?*

We knew nothing more than what we were given. Just those few lines. It wasn't even for sure that he had been on that flight. Nothing was certain. He frowned and looked at the pictures, like the plane had just crashed, and the babies were dying all over again. "All those babies stuffed into the plane and then killed."

"People tried, honey. People cared. They did the best they could in awful circumstances." Did he think we didn't feel his loss? That we had been careless with his past? Maybe we should have been more assertive about locating more information. Maybe we were afraid of seeming to be demanding, afraid the agency would think we weren't happy with the baby with a blank past. Maybe so. But mostly, all we thought about was *the baby on our laps*. Neither past nor future had much impact stacked against that baby boy.

Minh leaned against the upright piano, his feet in black rubber slip-ons that Ken had got for him in an Asian market in Toronto when he was there for a conference. Minh picked up a picture of a dead baby and said some days he thought it would have been better for him to stay put, even though we loved him, even though he loved us. He thought, some ways, he had died. He would never be a real Vietnamese, would never be a real American. He sounded like the kid on the adoption panel! I cried out, "Minh, Minh, you are alive! Be whatever you want."

"Always with the words," he said.

He had learned another sentence from his language lessons, and he tried it out on me. "Listen," he said. "I think I have the intonation down." He planned to use the sentence when people asked where he was from. *Toi den tu Vietnam* (I am from Vietnam).

He was intent, as though he had hardened a bit. As if he had decided the old Minh needed a coat of shellac.

He went to the Nectarine Ballroom, an adults-only dance club, with a false ID and danced with Lexie, who was gorgeous. Her picture had been stuck on his mirror for a long time. Of course, she had long dark hair and dark eyes and nicely browned skin. She was no seventeen though, not if she worked at the club. And I knew she worked at the club because Minh wasn't the only kid going there with a false ID. I heard his friends talking about getting into the Nectarine with fake IDs. I heard them mention the looker, Lexie. Minh probably looked good to Lexie; she believed he was older, or not. It probably didn't matter because he was more than handsome—like the guy in that ad for the Tommy jeans he wore: thin, but with plenty enough for a woman to drown in. I imagined that she danced with him, twisted his long ponytail, grown back, around her wrist and pulled him close. If she did that, he liked that.

It's not that he told me anything. It's not like I knew, not for sure.

After the Nectarine closed, they sat in Minh's Chevy on the top floor of a downtown parking structure, drinking mudslingers. When they ran out of drinks, my son made a run to a nearby parking meter. He did a little fooling around and got what he wanted—always good with his hands. Lexie hardly had time to get restless before Minh was back with more drinks. They had fun in that car, until the police came around. I constructed all of that from bits and pieces, using my storytelling skills.

What is fact is that I was awake when the phone rang at four, a mom used to the night shift. Minh talked fast. "There's some bad news." And before I could ask *what*, he said he was in jail. It wasn't only the drinking. He had nearly $200 in unpaid parking tickets, had received warnings in the mail, intercepted them, and ignored them. Ken was awake by then, pulling on his pants, fumbling for his wallet. We needed to stop at a money machine to make bail. I hadn't thought of that. But of course, we had to pay to get our son back, nothing like waiting for him at Detroit Metro airport when Dusty gave him to us. We listened to two policemen. I recognized one of them. He had been to the house before. He said Minh had a pile of change on him when they took him in. People don't walk around with fifty dollars in change, he said. Minh had probably jimmied a parking meter, but they had no proof, so they couldn't charge him. They looked weary, maybe sorry for us, parents of a probable thief, an underage drinker, parents of troubled kids. *You two have problems.*

I had no idea how we got from that baby coming off the plane to the teen coming out of a holding cell. It was dawn when we got home, the sky graying up a bit.

He stood in the kitchen and drank orange juice, calm and easy, as if he were living the life he should be living and the mess would come out tasting like those long-ago happy pancakes. He claimed that all he did was jiggle the meter and the money came spilling out. No thievery in that. He only picked the money up; just like the time he got change from a pop machine, that time we drove through Findlay, Ohio, when he was a kid. Didn't I remember that time? I did. I remembered how surprised he was. Change came spilling out of a pop machine along with his pop, like he was a winner in Vegas.

I didn't believe him and he was unhappy about that. "I'm your son. You say that all the time. Don't you believe your own son? I'm not a thief." I did not call him a thief, not just then. What I said was we had enough trouble. How could he make more trouble? I used guilt, the parent's worst weapon.

"I have to live too," he said. "I have problems too."

He *did* have to live.

"I'm a good guy," he said. And he was. You might have met him alone on a dark street and not quivered. He persisted in making his point to us: Why should we believe some cop we didn't know? Didn't we trust our own son? His voice rested on the words *own son*, as if he were calling us to task. We should prove ourselves, our devotion.

"Minh," I said, "I don't think the police are framing you." I talked flat voiced, unrelenting. I did not trust my son.

However it comes out our oldest seemed to imply with the lift of his shoulders, the bend of his head. *Whatever.*

Years later, when there was more written about adoption, when there were people who had something to say, I would learn that stealing is overrepresented among adopted kids. So many unpleasant charges on police blotters are full of those kids and their losses—as if they hunt and when they don't find what they're after, they take what they can get. And when you point out to them that what they've taken is stolen, they shrug. They don't see a problem. *It was there, wasn't it? Finders keepers.*

And, sure enough, the next time I went to Sam's Club and reached into my wallet to pay for a stack of things—some Tide, blue flannel sheets, and a couple of bags of mulch, all laid out on the counter with the total rung up—I found blank. There were no green bills in my purple wallet; they had flown away, like that long-ago lucky money. The clerk was nice.

"It happens all the time, honey, don't feel so bad."

She thinks I just forgot the cash or checkbook. She doesn't know. What scared me were the possibilities. If Minh went looking in the wrong wallet or jiggled the wrong meter, then what? Would he be coming into a courtroom while we waited there, unable to change the ending? Our son would no longer be the sexy guy in Tommy jeans, just an Asian-American male wearing orange.

* * *

Every time I rode shotgun and Ken passed a merge on a highway, I anticipated the moment somebody would crash into us. I hated driving on the highway too; I was always checking my mirror and passing ever so carefully. I liked to be sure of things and I didn't feel at all sure with everybody around me going eighty while I drove a cautious seventy. Which suggests a lack of grit or confidence. Ken tried imagery. "Mary," he said. "Pretend. Imagine the traffic's a stream in a nice even flow. Just stay in your lane and it will be fine. See?" he said when a semi merged without crashing into us. "No problem."

He never expected the semi to clip our car and kill us. He had a worldview without *danger* written in all caps. He continued to insist that our life was mostly okay. I thought we were one merge away from a crash and DOA.

Which is a metaphor for the story of a lot of our life.

Like after the night Minh was caught drinking in the parking structure with Lexie, suspected of stealing, charged with ignoring notices to appear in court. About a month after that night, I was sitting in the courtroom, in Ann Arbor, waiting to hear what would happen to my son. "I could give you trouble," said the judge. "But I'm assuming you'll clean up your act. I won't let you off if this happens again, though. You're on our radar now. Better watch it, buddy." An old hand, he glanced at the two of us sitting on the edge of our chairs, Ken in his ancient tweed jacket, me in a gray skirt and white blouse, the parents.

I saw my son; the judge saw a potential felon. I wasn't sure which of us had the better sight line.

When we left the courtroom and were back in our kitchen again, Minh said, "It wasn't so bad." That made me crazy. I pulled out the blender to make smoothies, the only thing appealing just then; I tossed a banana, blueberries, and yogurt into it and pulsed it on high. The blender whirred and then stuck. I hadn't added enough juice; the motor gave off a burning smell. I rammed a knife into the mess. "Hey," yelled Ken. "You'll hurt yourself or break the blender." He came over to me to pull the knife away.

I gave him a shove that sent him off balance. Minh let out a cry. "Mom!"

Ken looked angry and hurt; I didn't care. Right then, I hated my life, hated the kitchen where my son and husband stood, the porch where I waited for Anita to return. I hated all of it, no way I knew to fix it, all my attempts like jamming the knife in the blender.

So I added more grief to the pile. I asked Ken, snide and mean, if he thought we still moved in a nice easy stream. He looked at me, unsure what to make of me. He still wanted us to be friends, but I wasn't even my own friend.

Where had I gone wrong?

"You want to think it's your fault," Ken said. We were in our bedroom, had retreated to privacy to beat each other with words. "You think that if it's your fault, you can control it somehow. But you can't." I noted that his optimism was not so secure; it seemed to be leaving him. His voice didn't hold that same sureness anymore. He wasn't so positive the semi wouldn't clip us, the kids wouldn't end up disasters. I didn't want him to lose confidence, though. I relied on it even when I seemed to reject it, so I tried for a more reasonable tone.

"Minh is stealing. He stole from me. He steals all the time."

"Are you sure?"

I told him about my purse with the empty wallet, showed a bank statement that listed withdrawals we never made—he had used our ATM card. The pin number was in my nightstand drawer—I gave Ken the evidence with a grim kind of satisfaction.

See? I tried to stay in my own lane and we're getting smashed all the same.

Stealing. The nice kid from Vietnam took money from my purse as if it were his to take. Whatever was there, he lifted up and out. Minh maintained that he *wasn't* stealing. If we stood before him with hard evidence, the empty wallet, the change from the parking meter, the bank statement, he denied it or said he intended to pay us back. He seemed grieved by our accusations—like we didn't get the picture or weren't *the best* anymore.

If I went into his room, I looked for evidence, afraid to find it. The change on his dresser. Was it stolen? The new CD, stolen or not? What about the headphones?

"I'm not a thief! I just borrowed some cash. You're paranoid! Things happen."

Was he reassuring us or making a declaration?

"I'm not a kid anymore." He wasn't. We set up a payback schedule.

Ken took to sleeping with his wallet under his pillow. I had pushed him out of his nice easy stream, shoved the truth in his face, but I missed him, the optimist guy.

His senior year, Minh spent most days in the school parking lot with a crew that smoked. Leaning over the hood of his Chevy he drew comics and signed them *Mr. Mischief.* He graduated only because no one wanted to fail a kid who was *so amiable, had so much potential.* "Mr. Mischief," said the principal at graduation, "you are free." Minh raised his arms up and over his head, then waved to us. Anita and Sung cheered, "Yeah, Mr. Mischief. Yeah, Minh!"

"What'll he do now?" I asked Ken. Ken swallowed and shifted in his seat like it was his own lane and I was edging too close.

Chapter 27
KOREAN TIGER

If Minh was reclusive and Anita was wild, Sung was driven. "I'm going to make it," he said to us, as if he thought living with us was a risky business.

"Oh, Sung," people said. They tossed his name in the air like fluff. "He's so easygoing, so friendly. And what a hustler! Most kids never get a job until they're forced to, but Sung, he's out there in the dead of winter, shoveling walks. What a guy!" People could hardly say enough good.

Even the dentist, the same dentist who had poked around Anita's mouth and cemented her tooth back together that night the thug broke into the house, said so. "Mary, that third one of yours knows where he's headed. What a great kid!"

But Sung was *not* the easygoing person people thought he was. It wasn't that he drank or did drugs or took off for places unknown. He never stole. He was a straight arrow, our youngest. So what was the problem? Was I trying to make everything a problem? I considered that, but the fact was there were days, sometimes weeks, with Sung that felt like being stranded on an icy crevasse with no rope.

Kids who have had severe malnourishment catch up physically, pretty quickly in fact. Good food and a stable environment will allow the body to look near normal within about three months. But there are things that don't respond to a quick fix, maybe no fix at all. Things a person can't see, things that are like hard wiring or imprinting. They are somewhere inside a person, in the brain waves, the cells of the body. Sung *was* amazing. But.

But he could never trust, himself or us. A lost book, a bad

test, and he became frantic. He yelled, pounded tables, slammed doors, pulled his hair, swore at himself and us. We have a picture in the upstairs hallway, a copy of an ancient Korean print: a man is in midleap, his mouth open in a shout, his sword pointed, ready to pierce. It's the classic Korean warrior pose. That guy is the picture of Sung, our righteous younger son.

If anything went wrong in the world, Sung entered into the fray if he could, yelling, arms whirling in warrior mode, just like the guy in the print. "I'm fair," Sung yelled. "I get mad when other people aren't fair." He searched for everything that wasn't fair: murders, wars, hurricanes, babies left in cars to roast to death. Those two kids left to suffocate in a locked car while the mom had a massage and her hair curled? He cut that story from the paper and read it every night for two weeks. *The children cooked to death! Do something!*

"What can I do?" I asked him.

He pounded the dining room table, knocked over the vase of asters and zinnias. Water poured across the table and dripped to the floor. "You don't care! You don't care at all!"

Sometimes I shouted back. "I do care. I care, but what can I do? The children are dead. The mother's in prison."

Sometimes I left him, went to my room and shut my door. He'd stand outside the door, yelling and crying, two, three, four hours at a time. "You exaggerate," said a friend. Ken and I timed it. One night he yelled and cried from 11:00 p.m. to 2:00 a.m. Ken went to sleep with a pillow over his head. When Sung calmed down, at 2:00 a.m., I opened the door and we drank cocoa together. "I hate myself," he said. I knew that and it was another worry.

Attention deficit, obsessive compulsive, anxiety disorder. Our pediatrician, the psychologist we found to meet with Sung, his teachers. They all tried one of those labels on him, hoping it would fit, charmed and baffled by the kid driven to excel, so clearly intelligent and easy to get along with. He was friends with the world and still, he had this problem with anger. It could flood him in a heartbeat. He never threatened. I wasn't afraid of him. I just dreaded the yelling. What to do? Sung hated facing us after a yelling session, drained and pale, his voice a croak; he'd look at us, searching our faces for a clue. Did we still love him? We did. We strove to make that clear while trying for reasonable consequences. It was always dicey. The smallest hint of frustration on our part and he would begin all over again. Our Korean tiger. What had happened to him in Korea? "Remain calm," said the psychologist. "You know how to do that. It will be best if you wait to talk until he's calm too." We waited and wondered what had happened to him in Korea, wondered, yet again, what we could do.

"You can't yell like that, Sung. We do love you, but you can't yell." He knew that. He was *sorry, sorry, sorry*, but it never mattered. Once the tiger inside him started growling, it was only a matter of time.

He won that Fulbright and succeeded in Austria. He has friends from everywhere: somebody he met in a hostel in Paris, somebody else from Japan. "Sung," they cry, "hey, man, I've missed you. It's not the same without you." One Saturday, he met me for coffee at Zingerman's, then walked down Main Street with me. I wanted to buy a graphic novel at Vault of Midnight. A middle-aged woman stopped him to exclaim over seeing him again. They talked like old friends while I studied people in line at an ATM.

"How do you know her?" I asked when she went on her way. "She works at the thrift store," he said. "I used to go in there all the time when I was in high school. That's where I got my black fedora." He is the most social person I know. People enthuse about him, his friendliness, his kindness. Shouldn't that be enough? It isn't though. He whips himself. Like those penitents in the Middle Ages who walked over stone roads, lashing themselves with a knotted rope. "Every day," Sung says, "every day, I struggle to make it." There's no self-pity. He's telling me how it is for him. What I handle as normal—lists of things to do, appointments to keep, deadlines, friendships—what I handle without too much fuss is overwhelming for him. He's lost his passport three different times. I don't know how many times he's lost his driver's license. Pieces of his life are scattered everywhere, receipts, instructions, cash, that very important telephone number. He can't stand a wallet in his pocket, too claustrophobic. So he loses cash too.

We bungled along, when Sung was a kid, an uneasy mix of love and exasperation.

And it wasn't as if he didn't have reason to yell, so much of his childhood given to grief, so much of his world a hard place to live in.

* * *

Plus, we had a new situation.

A person he loved, a person we loved, was taken away. We took his sister away. Sung yelled until his voice became a whisper. "You guys are mean. You don't love her. You'll take me away too. Don't do it!"

We had told him we were going to take Anita to a locked residential treatment center just outside Grand Rapids. Sung was ten years old. Anita was fifteen.

Chapter 28

LOCKUP

We discussed the decision with the psychologist the day before we took Anita away. She didn't agree. "This is very extreme," she said. "Are you sure?" No kid she had worked with had ever gone to lockup. The parents of her clients didn't do that kind of thing. She unwrapped a mint and sucked. What had happened to our daughter? She wanted to know. What made her behavior so risky? She dropped her usual careful style and wondered aloud.

"I don't know," I said. "I don't even care. Right now, I'm afraid for her. She knows people who could hurt her." Anita had been seeing the big gun psychologist for almost two years by then. Once, the psychologist suggested that she possibly had an attachment disorder. Which would have meant she had never bonded to us, was incapable of bonding to us. "No. She bonded," I said. I was sure of that much. She had curled up with us mornings, reading Richard Scarry. She had jumped into my arms at Fuller Pool, fallen asleep on Ken's lap, scraped the frosting from the bowl with her brothers. She had bonded.

Anita had never told the psychologist anything other than that she hated her life. She kept the rest of her troubles hidden. So she and the psychologist were stuck in a series of sessions that may have allowed Anita to vent, but didn't do much else. Also, there were many times Anita wasn't there when I went to school to pick her up for her appointment. She blew off therapy. But my girl knew guns, drugs, and the real possibility that she could be taken from the scene in a body bag. Sometimes she intimated as much to me—she knew the real life. I was a wimp.

If I cried out or grabbed at her, she laughed, seemed not to care; maybe she couldn't afford to care.

One night, someone rang the bell, then pounded on the door, mean, angry pounds that woke everyone. Ken kept the light off and we crawled to the window. Strange guys stood on the front lawn. They wore hoods, sweats, and scarves. They called to her, "Baby girl, we know you're in there. We'll find you soon enough." We called the cops. The guys took off before the squad car pulled up. "Get her out of town," said the police. "She needs to leave. Don't listen to anyone who tries to tell you differently. These guys mean business. If you put some distance between them, they're likely to back off. Right now she's easy prey."

I will always be grateful to those officers, people who listened and recognized our fear. At the same time, I felt sick. Planning to take her away, no warning, no clue she could read, was like kidnapping. Was it kidnapping? She was our daughter. We wanted her to live. But I wince even now. Anita never gave the smallest indication that she felt concern, if she felt concern. She had to be scared, but she never showed it. We made her sleep in our room that night. She fell asleep at the foot of our bed. We sat up, awake through the night.

We gave ourselves twenty-four hours to decide. Twenty-four hours wasn't nearly long enough, and at the same time, it was too long. What if she took off or those guys found her before then?

If we took her away, I wanted a place that made big promises and could keep them: complete safety and a happy girl come back to us. And how would we afford that? I would have done anything, would have stolen the gold teeth from my father's mouth to save my daughter. In the end, reality played its hand. In the end the place we took her to was a place with a program of study—she could continue with school—behavior modification, talk therapy, and graduated privileges. Also it was locked. Anita couldn't run and those guys couldn't get in. It was a two-hour drive from Ann Arbor. It had good reviews.

After the Grandma K incident, Ken and I had talked about alternate avenues to try. We had exhausted all the usual things. There was only the last resort. I began to research residential facilities. I read about every place I could find. There was a Michigan facility that was both decent and possible for us to manage financially. They had an empty bed and would wait twenty-four hours for our decision.

At least, my daughter and I would sleep in the same time zone. That's what I thought. We phoned to tell them to save the bed. We'd be bringing our daughter to sleep in that bed.

The psychologist looked mournful; she took both our hands in hers and cried. We left and never saw her again. Sometimes we came across her ad in the paper: *Adolescent Counseling.* She was like the majority of psychologists back then who knew little to nothing about children from nontraditional backgrounds, had no experience with disrupted children, could not comprehend the depth of Anita's grief and self-hatred. It isn't fair or reasonable to place blame, even though I did that. I blamed myself, Ken, doctors, teachers, psychologists. Almost never did I blame Anita.

Would it be different now? I think so. There's better help, much more knowledge. There are people who have years of experience, write articles, and attend international conferences. There's an awareness that didn't exist back then. And that awareness came from those early years, from families like ours.

We told her brothers their sister needed help to be safe. "So you're going to lock her up?" said Minh. "Like a jail?"

"For her own good," we replied.

"Yeah, well," he said. Did I know guys had come into school looking for her? he asked. Guys who were maybe in their twenties, thirties. He couldn't know, but they looked old and hard. They had asked around. He kept quiet and nobody ratted her out. I hadn't known, but wasn't surprised.

We moved swiftly, without compunction. We did what we had to do, no second-guessing, all of it done quickly, kind of like the way we had chosen her from the list of names that time. At dawn the next day, I went into her room and told her to get dressed. "So early?" she said—almost as if she knew. Did she? She could sniff out a scene in no time. "Where are we going? What are you doing?"

I made no answer, just offered her a blue fleece-lined jersey against the morning chill. She took it and left the house with me, a wind-up girl. Eyes straight ahead, walking past her brothers who sat in the kitchen watching.

"Mom? Mom, where are you taking me?"

I stood close while she got into the car, then slid in beside her in the back. Ken took the wheel. We drove off with her brothers standing in the doorway, silent and scared, like they were seeing a horror movie unfold, Sung yelling at the worst parts.

* * *

When the kids were small, we often put them in the car, then told them we were going to a secret destination. We'd end up at the local ice cream place or a park.

We weren't going for ice cream or to the park this time.

It's possible to accuse me of abducting my daughter. It is

possible to say I did an unprincipled thing. I do not think I was ever a baby stealer, but I was a child stealer, an implacable, unrelenting woman who put my daughter into the car without telling her why, a woman who did not tell Ken to stop the car when Anita cried out and turned her face to the window: *Don't, don't, don't. You promised. You said you'd always keep me. Liar.* I was a child stealer. I would do the same thing all over again.

I know it was spring the day that we drove away. Then again, maybe I only think it was. Still, I remember the trees were showing green, so I think it *was* spring.

So much of that day got shoved away.

We talk about almost everything now, Anita and I. We talk about friends, hers and mine, family, money, things we worry about. But two things we never discuss: we do not talk about that meal she made for us when we came home from Grandma K's funeral, and we do not talk about the day we drove off with her.

I wonder what she remembers from the day we put her in the car and drove her to lockup? I know we need to talk about it. She often tells me she does not remember much from that time. She will, sometimes, look at a picture and say, "When was that? Was I with you guys, or was I up in Grand Rapids?" It never fails to make me feel as though I killed her and we are looking at a picture from the time she was dead.

Our daughter looked out the window and I sat thinking, yet again, about whether there was something else that we could have done, might still do. I couldn't think of a thing.

Ken missed the side street we were supposed to turn down and cursed. "Goddamn!" He hit the brake. Anita and I jerked forward. I put out my arms to keep her from hitting her head, but she shoved me away. Ken backed up, made a right turn, and we ended up in front of a row of low brick buildings. There was nothing about them that said *lockup*. The woman who opened the door was friendly. She smiled, ushered us in, told us she would do the intake info. She offered cups of coffee and moved around the room, something like a cheerleader, striving for an upbeat attitude.

We would not be able to talk to our daughter for three weeks. After that, Anita could earn phone privileges. She could have nothing with her but her toothbrush and toothpaste, a pair of pajamas, a change of clothes, a hairbrush, no hair ties. She could earn her personal effects back bit by bit. I felt as if my skin had iced over. What were we doing?

Anita was to see a psychologist every day, the woman explained.

Another psychologist. Would this one help?

The three of us met the psychologist, a nice-looking, calm middle-aged woman. She seemed okay, matter-of-fact, not intimidated by our situation. She told us our daughter would be safe with her. The outside door opened only with a buzzer and an intercom. Inside, there was a special hallway, off the main hallway, which could be reached only through another locked door.

Anita would not be able to run. No one would be able to hurt her. I kept repeating that like a mantra. Anita stayed quiet, stared at her black high tops, the laces hanging loose. The psychologist did not promise a daughter returned to us, smiling and whole.

"Do you want to say good-bye to your parents?" asked the psychologist. "It'll be a while before you talk to them again." Anita did not say good-bye. She walked down the hallway heading to the locked door, the psychologist beside her, making talk. I watched my daughter's dark hair, the slump of her shoulders, until she turned a corner and was gone from view. I called to her as she rounded the corner.

"We will be back. We will come back."

My kid was in a kind of orphanage all over again, a place for kids whose parents said, "I can't do the job." Right then, it would not have mattered to me if one of the guys who had come looking for Anita took me instead.

We drove home listening to NPR, both of us quiet. There was a deer carcass on the side of the highway, the blood-sweet smell of death. Ken glanced at the carcass, and said, "We don't want her dead, do we?" We did not want her to be dead, no.

Later that night, I found him bent over in the bathroom, pale and wiping his mouth. "It feels like a death that we caused."

I knew what he meant. We stayed there on the bathroom floor rocking each other. I never pictured my husband sick with grief when we left Saint Marys so long ago, never could have thought of it.

Still, there was one thing and I offered it to Ken: we could sleep. We had not slept in a long, long time. When we went to bed, we fell unconscious; but always some part was alert, waiting for the phone to ring, a knock on the door, the dog barking to alert us. I could not remember what it would be like to be able to close my eyes and sleep.

Chapter 29

PLAIN COOKING

It was a morning in late summer. Sung had gone off for some Dumpster diving, all the rage in Ann Arbor. Free stuff was to be had, good stuff just by jumping into a Dumpster and checking it out; Dumpsters in front of University of Michigan student housing were the best. Minh had found a new barista job for some extra cash. Anita was doing something, I didn't know what, over in Grand Rapids. She had been in lockup since spring, so about four months. Once a week we drove over to see her. Sometimes Ken and I went alone, sometimes Minh and Sung came along for family therapy. They hated going, though. Hated the click as the door was buzzed open, the way Anita shuffled down the hallway in her high tops, no shoestrings.

I wasn't in love with going either. It was always hard. If I talked about her pattern of running away, possible gang involvement, Anita said I was controlling. If Ken said she had to work on her issues, Anita accused him of being a dictator. We hadn't made a lot of progress. We met with a consulting psychiatrist. "I think," he said while he steepled his fingers, "that she struggles with having a true sense of self. She has a kind of amnesia about herself, sees herself only in relation to others. She's running as far away as she can from you two, and she's getting plenty of help. Which is why it's been hell for you. I'm not saying you haven't been good parents to her. You have. But she's at a point where you can't convince her. It may work out or not. It's a tough problem. You could," he added, "always emancipate her." Emancipate her? Never! He caught our horrified looks. "Well then,"

The Year The Trees Didn't Die

he said, "well then, I assume you will keep working at it." We agreed that we would do that, yes.

Ken left for work that summer morning with a half-dozen zinnias sticking out of the top of his backpack. He wore his blue UV-protection shirt, and he walked off like he believed he would get something from the day.

I did not understand how he did that.

Summer was my favorite season—people walking, stopping to look at Ken's zinnias in the lawn-extension garden, the sound of mowers, somebody calling somebody else to bring out the meat for the grill. Summer was so good I wanted to tie it down.

But not that summer. That summer I walked around the house from the living room to the kitchen, singing an old Beatles tune: *Can't buy me love, can't buy me love*. On really bad days, I chose Patsy Cline. I sang with her full out: *Crazy, I'm so crazy*. Sad Patsy and I sang together, grieving for our troubles. In the late afternoon, I whipped her grief and mine into mashed potatoes. I never cooked ethnic anymore, nothing spicy, no masalas or saffron rice, no fiery garlic shrimp. The nuoc mam sauce sat on the shelf unused. Knobs of ginger softened in the refrigerator. Plain cooking. That was it.

Ken never complained; he sat down to eat when he came home and smiled all around. "Hi kids. How was your day?" I marveled that he could ask.

It made no sense to me. The house felt like a danger zone—walls might collapse at the slightest touch, the ceiling might crash down on us. Nothing was normal anymore, there were few scenes of a regular life. The guy who came home to smile and eat with us seemed like a stranger, his view of life so far from mine. He'd walk in, switch Patsy off, and put on Broadway show tunes. "Something a little more upbeat." I heard *Man of La Mancha*. He loved Broadway tunes, and he sang along in his off-key voice: *I am I, Don Quixote, the man of La Mancha* . . .

The rest of us listened with bad grace, but Ken took what goodwill there was and asked for the potatoes. Sung always finished in a rush, took his plate to the kitchen and left to watch a video on the TV he'd found on one of his Dumpster dives. Every time he left, he came home dragging fish tanks, broken computers, Kmart phones, suitcases that wouldn't close. He defended all of it, hurt or angry if I suggested it should have remained in the trash. At night, he watched endless hours of World War II movies, like he was practicing for combat: crawling through the countryside, hiding out in bunkers. He seemed to find comfort in lugging home Dumpster throwaway and watching war destruction. What did he find in that? He sat riveted as Allied troops moved through the French countryside or bombed Berlin's Gedachtnishkirche. Berlin's people huddled in underground bunkers or died in the streets while Sung watched. The house filled with the sounds of gunfire and explosions coming from his room.

I was upstairs, trying to read, or lying awake trying to sleep, and heard German phrases:

"Schnell! Schnell! Wer bist du? Sprichst du!"

Sometimes, Sung replied, *"Ich bin hier. Ich schlafe nicht."*

I wanted him to sleep, wanted everyone to sleep. When they slept, I counted them. My husband, my oldest son, my youngest son, even my daughter asleep in her locked place. For a time I counted them as safe. That's what I did when they slept. But sometimes Ken did not sleep. He slid under the sheet wearing white pajamas with blue trim. He reached across the bed to me. His arms smelled like cinnamon. I wore a flannel nightgown, faded blue. It smelled like me, a scent of tea gone cold. I was always cold back then, like a very old person. And I constantly read advice books that summer. I read:

Parent Power!
When Good Kids Do Bad Things
I'm Still Your Mother
I Hate You—Don't Leave Me

I read case studies aloud to Ken. I'd almost learned them by heart:

> *Karen: Karen is a sixteen-year-old attractive girl adopted at birth. She became attracted to men who were much older and eventually, to her parents' consternation, she left home for the streets where she became seriously ill. The parents provided medical assistance, but refused to allow her to return home until she severed contact with her former friends. They were able to practice tough love until Karen saw the error of her ways and returned home to finish high school and get a job.*
>
> *Robert: Robert is a biracial male who was adopted by a Midwestern couple as an infant. Robert was generally happy until he reached his mid teens. At that point, he said that he wanted to find his birth mother and left to search. Robert was gone for six months without contacting his adoptive parents. He returned home in distress having found his birth mother who refused to meet with him. His adoptive*

parents assisted him in coming to terms with this crisis. Robert finished school, went to college and now volunteers to counsel troubled adopted teens.

Sarah: Sarah is an Amer-Asian teen who has had a difficult time since she reached her teen years. In the past she rejected her family and experimented with a variety of drugs and runaway behavior. She is now in counseling where she is making good progress.

"Karen and Robert are okay," I said. "Even Sarah's making progress. Maybe we could learn something from these people."

Ken stroked my arm and neck. Slow, like he was learning a new body. "Let go for a little while, Mary. The kids aren't Karen or Robert or Sarah."

I held my book in both hands, felt anger rising in my throat where it pooled and made me cough. Was he telling me there was nothing we could do? No. No. No. I couldn't accept that, not yet. I wasn't willing to play with the guy in white pajamas. Letting my guard down for even a moment might cause the final bit of destruction. I *had* to keep reading.

* * *

We couldn't agree on how sad to be. The more I wailed with Patsy, the more Ken strove to maintain some happiness. He wanted to survive. I wanted to crash and burn.

"Do you care?" I asked Ken. He said he cared, but he would not let it ruin his life, and he didn't think it should ruin mine. There it was. I was willing to live with ruined. Almost, I welcomed ruin, like it was the only sure thing.

One night that summer of the mashed-potato meals, Ken

The Year The Trees Didn't Die

came home and went to bed, no asking about anybody's day, just up the stairs and into bed. The potatoes remained untouched. Minh stayed in the basement working on his computer. Sung microwaved a frozen pizza and watched *The Bridge on the River Kwai*. It was a night Anita was allowed to call home. She was tearful and mostly silent. There were long spaces of quiet on the line.

I hung around the yard after the phone call, then sat on the porch watching yellow coreopsis fade into dark.

Chapter 30

SAVIOR MAN

I should have watched the movie with Sung. I liked that movie, liked the sound of the "Colonel Bogey March," the hawk circling overhead as the movie begins, the tension between Shears and Saito.

"Be happy in your work," Saito tells Shears when he orders him to build the bridge. Maybe, I should have tried to be happy. Instead, I went upstairs after Ken, the guy who wanted me to take what happiness there was. I wanted him dressed in survival gear, tools in hand, unlimited skills at the ready. I wanted him to get out there and make our life okay.

He was in bed with his clothes on, looking nothing like a savior. I saw his white shirt, its ratty collar. He reached an arm up and out to pull me in, but I stayed out of reach.

"Mary, are you ever going to be happy again?"

"I don't know."

He looked grieved; then he rolled over and pulled the covers up to his chin. I heard—nothing. He was able to do that, shut down as if he were a building and it was closing time. It wasn't late, probably only nine o'clock. I thought of the hours ahead, hours in which I would not sleep. I yanked the covers away, shook him, and yelled. "Do something. Maybe if you did something, we wouldn't be where we are right now."

"Where are we?" he asked. "Where do you think we are?"

I didn't know—in a bad place, I guessed.

"I'm a person," he said. "I'm not a savior. We have tried *everythingthereis.*" He ran the words together, his voice cracking, hissing the end sound of the *s*. "Right now, I want some happiness. You want to save the kids; you go ahead and save them, but I'm not willing to die trying, and I don't plan on helping you kill yourself either." He pulled the covers back up, a fully dressed, immovable block.

Even with what he had said, things would have been okay between us if I had made an offer. Something as simple as, "We can maybe go for a walk." But I didn't say that. No matter that Ken had signed off pain, I was still its best friend.

"You want to give up, go ahead. But I promised."

"You made a promise to me too, what about that?"

I hated him just then. I wished every one of his calm genes would self-destruct.

I left the room in search of wine coolers I knew Minh had hidden somewhere. He did that. Used funds, ill-gotten or not, to buy alcohol. I found two six-packs of coolers—lemon/lime and strawberry mist—in the garage behind the lawn mower. I took three strawberry and drank them warm sitting on the floor of the garage, wrapped in beach towels. I spilled some on a white towel with a green alligator dead center—its jaws open and the word *Swim* ballooning out of its mouth. I left the empties for Minh to find and went back upstairs intent on making Ken hear. Maybe that was how the kids felt sometimes, just wanting to make a noise and be noticed on their own terms? Every part of me hurt, my head, my chest, even my teeth.

I went into the bedroom and I hit Ken. It wasn't anything big, not a punch or even a slap. I made a fist that landed on his back, maybe a jab. It felt like hitting something dead. I hit again, and he grabbed my hand. "I'm not going to let you do this," he said. "You're obsessed. Anybody would tell you that. Draw lines, all the psychologists have said that, and what do you do? You keep opening your arms for more. Whatever the kids throw at you, you take. Like you think you'll make sainthood if you keep at it long enough. But you won't. You'll end up ruining your life and mine too."

I said he was a quitter, a failure of a father. He was the cause of all our troubles. It was his fault that Anita ran, his fault that Sung yelled and Minh was stealing. All he cared about was his science. I said terrible things, unfair things, whole sentences I can't write even now. I didn't believe any of it. I wanted to, frantic to find a reason for so much pain. But I knew I was shifting pain, hurting Ken, so I'd hurt less. And I couldn't stop. It was a rockslide rolling out of my mouth, until, like Sung when he yelled nonstop, I was exhausted. Who was I, strange woman who hit her husband with her fist and words?

I'd believed that family was created by willingness, sure that my love would be, if not perfect, enough. I would mother my children with plenty, and they would lap it up. Nobody would be left hungry or alone. I sat down next to Ken shaking and scared. He stayed still and quiet. The air in the room was heavy, hot and humid. I heard our neighbor pull into her driveway. Then silence. I sat in the silence as alone as I had ever been.

Our lives were so far from what I had imagined. I never thought I'd be hitting my husband, drinking my oldest son's illegal wine coolers. I did not imagine a daughter gone to lockup, my youngest son yelling all the time.

I thought regular problems would happen, *problems, normal things*: Minh borrowing the car and running out of gas or getting a D on a test. Anita going on her first date and coming home all huffy because the boy took her to a crummy guy movie and then expected kisses. I had imagined that Sung would struggle with being the youngest, always trying to catch up. But I thought we would cope with those things. And we would pick raspberries. We all loved raspberries. Every August, we would go out on Platt Road to a berry farm and pick raspberries to make jam. We would scrape the pot, lick the spoon, fill the jars and give each other red kisses.

And then, I still do not know how—maybe there are moments of grace in life. There must be because something shifted, and I knew what to do. I reached around to Ken's body and extended my open hand. He took it and I was grateful; that's the word. I was grateful. We made love like it was a truce, neither one of us really happy with the terms, but we made the effort; we concentrated on that, and then we slept with the faint sound of explosions still coming from downstairs.

Chapter 31

LOS GHETS

Sung spoke German and that puzzled people. Still puzzles them. They had preconceptions, of course. The German language and the Korean face didn't make sense: *Why was this Korean kid speaking German?* If they asked, he replied: *Ich war noch Korean geboren. Ich bin Amerikaner.* Of course, that never explained what they wanted to know. Why German? There was no big story. It was the language offered in his middle school. He acquired the spoken language of German as if it were a remembered dream. He could speak the language like a native. He spoke German from sixth grade on.

But he rarely passed a written test.

"Stupid," he yelled. "I'm a goddamn stupid idiot. I can't get it right. A simple past participle and I can't remember it. Everybody else did. It isn't fair," he yelled. He glared at me and tossed the failing test in my direction. He was a freshman in high school, a no-nonsense high school that had a dress code and random locker checks. It was far from what the older two had experienced, far from the self-paced learning I espoused. But I was ready to sign on.

People shrugged if I complained about the yelling. All teens yelled. Yelling was no big deal. Well sure. Sung was not a kid who left us discussing a grim future with a psychiatrist. He was an achiever, except for math and memorizing facts. He worked to make honor roll in the no-nonsense school of his. He played freshman football. His team would practice in nearby Riverside Park. I'd drive down Broadway to Maiden Lane. Sung and his buddies would be waiting, sweaty and rank. They'd crowd together, a couple in the front seat, three in the back. We'd head uphill to our house where they'd shower and pillage the refrigerator. "Thanks, thanks," they'd say, swilling blue Gatorade from bottles, microwaving frozen pizza. Sung had good school experiences that allowed him to enjoy a lot. We relished them. But those times he exploded, we were left askance, the way a really bad storm makes you wonder if your house will stay standing. Like the time he was doing German homework and struggling with verb declensions. I heard him muttering and growling, knew that things were not going well. And then—so fast—I heard glass shatter. He'd thrown a book at the dining room window. Ken grabbed Sung and pinned his arms. Skinny guy or not, Ken was strong. "What in God's name did you think you were doing?"

Sung looked scared, maybe shocked by the ease with which he could shatter something. He cleaned up the mess in silence. Chunks of glass hit the wastebasket. Cold came into the room. Ken got busy taping up cardboard, looking for a window repair place.

"I think you should get rid of me." Sung lay on his bed with the dog beside him.

"No. No." We rubbed the dog's belly, the two of us. "We didn't get rid of your sister and she has problems. We love her. She's part of the family. So are you."

He knew he was out of line. He probably worried that he'd go off to lockup next. No matter that we assured him that his problems were different kinds of problems.

"He better pay for that window," my sister, Rosie, cried out when I called her. "You don't want him doing that kind of thing."

Of course. Of course he would pay for the window. But why throw the book at the window in the first place? He was studying a foreign language to make honor roll when he threw the book. He was not getting high, hunting trouble, stealing.

I left Sung in his room with the dog, worn out, almost asleep. I found Ken in the overstuffed chair we had lugged from Cleveland. We had a sofa by then, but Ken loved that chair. I squeezed in next to him. We fell asleep together. A slight chill slid through the patched-up window but we slept anyway.

After that, things were so good for a while that I relaxed. When to relax, that was always the question. I picked the wrong time. It was dark and snowy outside, relentless Michigan winter.

"Fucking homework. Fucking shit. Who can get this?" The sound came from downstairs. I wanted to sleep but I knew how it would go: Ken would tolerate the yelling for a while, then he'd try to soothe Sung, then he'd get to yelling himself, leave Sung, and come to bed. He'd go to sleep with a pillow over his head. But that would never work for me. I couldn't find enough pillows. And anyway, the scene was always on repeat. Just like before and the time before that, he would be there, our youngest, standing outside our bedroom door, pounding and yelling until he cried. That night, I didn't think I could stand it. I pulled jeans on over my pajama bottoms, a sweater over the top, and went downstairs.

"Shut up. Shut up. Just shut up!" I yelled and it felt good to do that. I understood just then how anger functioned for Sung. It displaced fear. It shut down everything else.

I grabbed a coat, scarf, and hat, shoved my hands into my pockets, and walked out into the January night toward lights and an all-night CVS drugstore where I hoped to find people living easier lives. I was halfway there when I heard running behind me, panting, and calling. It was Sung, bare feet, no jacket, running after me. "Don't leave!" he called. "Don't leave!"

I turned and yelled back at him. "I want to. I want to leave all of you." I kept walking.

I knew Sung had been horrified when we took his sister off to Grand Rapids; abandonment was his worst fear: abandoned by us or left at the bottom of the heap in school. I knew that and I didn't care just then.

He stood there at the bend of the road, where Pontiac and Barton intersect. I heard him sobbing, the same sound he'd made under that dresser when he was new, the trapped-animal sound. It was freezing out and my son was begging me not to leave him. God!

I did not want to leave any one of them. What I wanted was some ease. I wanted a house without shouting, a room where the windows weren't smashed, a family together and, most times, happy.

I went back and pulled him to me, had him stand on my boots, to keep his feet from freezing. I opened my coat and pulled it around the both of us. "Sung, honey, I love you."

"You hate me. You wish you never got me."

"No, I love you! I love every one of you!" Life without Sung yelling and screaming, smashing windows and slamming doors, life without cash going missing, a daughter not caring whether she lived or died. It would be nice. I wanted it. But I did not choose it. I chose the kids, chose them before I even knew them.

"Sung, we love you. I remember when your dad came walking up to me at the pool, holding your picture. You're ours. Still," I added, "you have to work on the anger and yelling."

"I'm a dick sometimes," he said. "I know. I'll try." He would have promised anything right then and meant it. He looked as if he'd been given absolution. We headed back home with Sung hopping along yelling about cold feet, but that was all right, almost a happy scene. And anyway, there was Ken with the car come to look for us.

"Why did you take Anita to that place?" He sat in the back seat of the car on the short ride home.

"Anita wasn't safe with us. You know that."

"But parents are supposed to keep their kids safe. It's their *job*." We reached home and Sung got out of the car. Ken unlocked the door to the house and said, "It is our job. And that's why we sent Anita away. That's why I came looking for you and your mom. We do our job."

Well, Sung was right. I had taken my daughter away. I told her *forever* when she came to us; I promised, and then I took her away to be locked up. Some nights I woke dreaming about her. I looked at the moonlight reaching in the window and thought about places she had been. Places with knives, guns, drugs, ratty mattresses on the floor. Lockup was a choice we had made for her safety. I repeated that until I slid back under into sleep.

For a while out there on that icy sidewalk, I wanted to keep going in any direction other than home. I always came back though, to the place called home.

Chapter 32

GREEN MEN

It was Anita who thought of buying green plastic figures one summer day. She was still in lockup, but was allowed off campus to go shopping with me, having improved from sullen to "making attempts to cooperate." She spotted the green figures at the mall. They had spindly arms and legs, bulging black eyes, and were bendable. They looked like strange green men. We had finished a session that morning and I had been honest about the effect of Anita's troubles on Sung. He had nightmares, I said. Was often unsure that he wasn't messing up. "It isn't that I think this is all your fault," I said. "But it has been hard for him." She cried. We ended the session and left to go to the mall where she saw the green men.

"I know he's not a little kid," she said. "But still, don't you think they might help? What if we bought them, and he could bend them or even rip them apart if he wanted to? He could be angry with them. Maybe he'd feel better," she said. She stood there eager and, yes, amiable. It seemed like one of those mythical signs we had often looked for! I felt a surge of joy and hope.

We scooped up six or seven green figures. Anita sent the green guys home with me and told me to let Sung know it was her idea, that she was still his big sister, and he was her little bro. I was so glad for that bit of almost normal that I drove back home in the rain, not once gripping the wheel sweaty-handed when the semis merged. There was hope.

I gave the figures to Sung, who lined them up on a shelf in his room, twisting them into various poses, one bent over backward, one face forward, another on its side. He seemed to like the ability to bend them at will. Maybe they did help his frustration. Probably he liked knowing that his sister thought of getting them for him. Anita was triumphant when Sung came with Ken and me next time.

"Ha, little bro. Don't say I don't know how to help you." She gave him a cuff on the shoulder. He picked her up, lifted her off the floor like a scene from a chick flick. He was way bigger than she was, my Korean boy with a linebacker build. He kept her there for a long minute, whirled her around, almost dropped her before he set her down on the table in the group dining room, like she was the main course, right in the middle of the table. The two of them looked great. She leaned against him, laughed so hard she cried, wiped her face with the edge of her shirt, blue denim she'd scammed from her dad on his last visit. Ken noticed the shirt and laughed at her, told her she looked better than he did in it.

She did. She looked so beautiful it made you catch breath. Can you look that beautiful in residential treatment wearing your dad's shirt and high tops? Can you laugh? Cuff your younger brother on the shoulder, be spun around by him? She could. They were laughing, the two of them, those kids . . .

"Hold it," I yelled and looked hard at them. Anita and Sung, laughing. I didn't have a camera. No matter. I had them hold still and let the moment be.

* * *

No one I knew wanted to think that people who lived in a regular house on a regular street living a regular life—nothing so out of the ordinary—could have such troubles. We read the paper, voted in elections, contributed to school fundraisers, nothing more than a regular life. But that didn't seem possible to people. They preferred to think that you had to live in the wrong place or do the wrong thing, in order to have bad problems. Should we have sent Anita to a different school? Would it have been better if we had lived in the upscale section of Burns Park instead of the north side of town? Maybe she would have had less chance of trouble then. We understood why they thought that way. We thought that way ourselves some days—like we had come in contact with a terrible virus and failed to take the proper measures. "It's almost as if you two want me to say it's your fault." That's what Anita's psychologist in Grand Rapids said to us. Her voice betrayed a measure of annoyance. What parents wanted to be responsible for their child's trauma? But, to us, it made sense. If we had failed to take proper measures, then we had the answer! What we had to do was take proper measures and things would be better.

But figuring out the measures would be something else entirely.

Mostly the counselors, especially the young ones, loved Anita. They acted as if they had found exactly the troubled teen they had spent years studying to help. Anita could be so cooperative, so charming. She was lovely. She was sweet.

True. True. But how did we end up here? That's what I wanted to know.

"Maybe, maybe," a young counselor said, "maybe, you don't understand the confusion of adolescence?" She was intent on helping us. So sincere! Probably in her midtwenties, somebody still learning the ropes. We needed to be *more tolerant, more understanding.*

Anita sat still, in her silent mode. I figured she knew she had done a con job on the counselor, or maybe it wasn't even that. Maybe she had simply used her public face. That was the safe choice. She would never show her private face in public.

"I understand more than you know," I said. Or did I yell? I pushed back my chair and left the room. The young counselor came running after me, but I shouldered her away, held my anger like a gun I wanted to fire: *Sweet! Don't understand! I understand all right. She's sweet enough to send me right to hell. What am I supposed to do in hell?*

I found a worn basketball lying at the edge of a funky old court—I shot hoops and wondered if Anita didn't have a right to her faces, one for us, one for the psychologists, one private, one public. Maybe all the kids did. Who of us readily volunteers our worst selves to public view? It made reality hard to explain though, my reality anyway. If I told people the face that Ken and I saw, they recoiled in shock, as if we had ruined the painting of a Renaissance master.

Picture this, for instance. Anita came along to Saint Marys with me; the two of us went back to visit. The idea was to have her learn, slowly, how to integrate with family again. So, Ma and Anita sat at the table and cracked red pistachios between their teeth. Red coated their lips and tongues. Shells circled the pink Melmac cups of Red Rose tea.

Ma tossed me a pistachio. Just a month before, she had sent me the Prayer of Saint Ann, the patron saint of lost children, and she had included a note:

Dear Mary,
These things work out. Use the prayer. I do.
Love,
Ma

"Have a pistachio," Ma said as she tossed a few in my direction. "You know you love them." I liked pistachios. It was Ma and Anita who loved them. "Honey," she said to Anita, "stay a little girl for as long as you can."

Anita smiled and spit out a shell. The face she turned to Ma was her public face, a kind and loving face. She would never hurt Ma by letting her know she hadn't been a little girl in a long time. My father came into the room and said, "Hey, little girl, you're back again." Well, she was a girl and wasn't a girl. Back and forth, back and forth, that's how it went.

There was red on my daughter's mouth, from the pistachios, nothing bad, but I wanted to reach across and wipe that red away. Ma cracked another pistachio, chewed and spit the shells into the pile on the table with easy abandon. I drank my tea and looked into the cup like one of Ma's kitchen women, like I thought I'd find something there. I looked up and saw my mother and daughter, piling shells between them. It seemed normal; it felt *reasonable*, what I should be seeing, and I had no idea how to keep that scene in place.

Chapter 33

BROKEN GLASS

After a year in rehab, my daughter came home to stay, not for a weekend visit, not for a trip to Saint Marys either. We were scared; we wanted her back whole and happy, but would she stay put? We wanted her to *stay put*. Anita said she wanted to *stay put*. We had a final session with the psychologist before we left, Ken and I and Anita. We met with her and the rest of the support staff. Anita assured everyone that she wanted nothing more than to go home and stay home. She missed home. She wanted apple crisp again, her own bed, maybe some movies. It sounded good. The staff sent her off with a card they'd signed and a book of inspirational quotes, one for every day of the year. She talked nonstop on the way home, planning all the things she'd do. She wanted to have friends over. Nice friends. I could make spaghetti. She sounded as if she'd been gone on a long trip and was eager to reconnect. I was hoping for something more earnest, in line with the seriousness of the situation, but what would that be? She must have been nervous, looking to find her way back home. She had therapy scheduled for twice a week. That was in addition to family therapy, which was once a week. There wasn't a way to pretend she'd been gone on a trip. Although if making spaghetti and having nice friends over would help, fine.

 Two weeks after she came home, she blew off her therapy session and was gone for two awful days. Like her safety lock was broken and she couldn't do a thing about it, a statistic of recidivism, one of the 40 to 60 percent who fail to maintain their gains. We groaned in remembered pain. The thing about someone who is missing, no way to find the person, is that everything seems possible. If a person moves, you miss the person and you try to picture the person in the new place. Maybe drinking coffee in Seattle. If a person dies, you grieve and you miss the person, but still you assign a place, a photo, a grave marker, ashes scattered over a special spot. When you don't know anything, you imagine everything.

* * *

Sometimes she left me a note when she took off, sometimes not. Sometimes a phone message, or maybe no phone message, depending. If she left any tangible evidence, it was in another language, an atonal one—*Gone shopping.*

Which meant,

she was or was not having her nails done, painted half moons in blue;

she was or was not buying cigarettes and wine coolers;

or, she might be off with someone;

likely off with someone.

Seventeen by then and trouble's friend.

And I still took her back when she returned, although I was not supposed to.

Let her experience the consequences of her choices. That was the advice of every person who had ever given us advice. It was the final word from her psychologist in Grand Rapids. And it was the position that Ken wanted to take by then. "Let her go if she wants to go so bad." He said that when I cried. He was weary of tears. Who could blame him? He was hurt and mad that the girl he loved seemed to prefer any place to our place.

We had been given a game plan. We were supposed to

lock the doors, turn out the lights, and go to sleep if she took off. We were not supposed to go looking for her or wait up for her. I could have done that if I had been drugged. Otherwise no.

In that place we inhabited, I looked at the evidence my daughter left lying around, minutiae: hair in the sink, a nail paring, the way bed covers were turned back. I held her picture up to the light and looked at her teeth, the turn of her head.

My Bengali babe—she had X written all over her, a love story gone wild.

In the late summer of the year after Anita came back from rehab, we moved from the green house to the house on Broadway. We had been looking to move the whole time Anita was in Grand Rapids. Sometimes, when she came home on weekends, she went house hunting with us, not very happily. No one was happy to be house hunting. Only me. I couldn't live in the green house any longer. It was a good house. We had had great times in that house, picnics on that picnic table Ken built, birthdays with pancakes for breakfast, candles in the pancakes. It was the place where Ken and I had established home. The house the kids had come to. But, every time I looked out a window I remembered strange men in the front yard all over again. When I went to the living room, I remembered the police standing there, telling us there were lots of teen girls who went missing. Two policemen with thick black shoes. Or I saw the officers warning us to get her away.

The kids protested. They liked the green house; even Anita, who left it so often, liked it. They liked the wild black cherry trees, the old milk chute, the old tree house. But I couldn't stand it anymore.

"I have to go," I said to Ken. Different rooms, a different piece of sky outside. A different street. It might be better. I might not feel scared all the time. Ken wasn't convinced, but he agreed, willing to try anything that might help. We looked at places like Stockbridge where the billboards advertised farm implements. Stockbridge was about an hour from Ann Arbor, a long commute, but tempting. It seemed like such a safe place. But there were things we loved about our town, no matter that some places radiated pain. And there was Sung. We didn't want to make his life harder. He'd be the only Asian face in school if we moved to Stockbridge. We couldn't do that to him. So we moved to an old house on top of Broadway hill, not so far from the green house, but far enough to make me feel better, logical or not. Anita had been back home with us for about three months by then. Some days she'd sit under one of the wild black cherry trees grieving the upcoming move. Some days she'd remind me she wasn't all that far from eighteen, a legal adult. She'd live where she wanted to then. Exactly what I feared.

On the day of the move, the rented truck was in the driveway and there were Anita's things to be packed, but no daughter. She had taken off again and she had not left a note. She had been in her bedroom just that morning packing. Then between the time we left to get the truck and the time we returned, she was gone. She probably left right after I pulled out of the driveway with Ken. So, maybe eight o'clock. Where would she go so early in the day? The greenhouse window was full of loose change, old makeup, a can of hairspray, a few dead plants, and her journal. Stuffed animals, clothes, a Detroit Lions jacket were heaped in a corner of her room. The bedcovers were pulled off her bed.

Ken picked up the jacket and sniffed it like a dog. Then he drove off. By then it was about nine o'clock. I continued packing. Ken's brother John had come to help us move. He was quiet and sympathetic. We loaded the truck with the first round of boxes and John drove off with Minh and Sung. I stayed behind packing up for the second run.

Ken never knew how he happened to spot her, appearing out of nowhere, crossing over the Broadway bridge coming from downtown. He had driven all over Ann Arbor looking for her, no daughter. He'd come home, helped me pack more boxes. Helped move the boxes to the truck and went out for a second look. It was afternoon when he spotted her.

She was alone, walking over the bridge. Where had she gone? Like she'd tell. Ken jerked the car door open and told her to get in, brought her back, and handed her over to me like she was something he wanted to be done with: if I wanted her, I could have her. She looked like she was nearly used up. She had been gone for hours by then. I told her to pack. We'd take her stuff in the car. I didn't ask questions I would get no answer to. She tossed her things into garbage bags, hauled them out to the car.

Let's get out of here. I don't want to be in this place anymore. But, as if she'd read my thoughts, she said things wouldn't be better anyplace else. I was crazy to think so.

My daughter was definitely a statistic of recidivism.

Ken looked back when we drove away, at the empty house, the old milk chute, the seven wild-cherry trees. I didn't.

* * *

Our first night in the new house, somebody broke the greenhouse window of the old house and spray-painted Anita's room with fat looped letters that made words I couldn't read, but knew meant trouble. Only her room. Everything else was fine. We found the mess the next day when we went back to make a final run through. Who had Anita been with? What had happened? It had to be people she knew who had done it. Were they after her? Were they just out to scare her? Things had been bad. But this!

"Whoooee," said Anita, the girl who had eaten red pistachios with my mother. Ken turned to her, put his hands on her shoulders, his face right up to hers. He shook her, not brain-damage hard, more like he was trying to shake loose what reason she had left in her. Minh and Sung stared.

"Are you crazy?" he shouted. The sound of *crazy* filled the empty room.

Crazy, I'm so crazy. Oh, Patsy, I thought. *I'm near crazy.*

"Are you trying to get yourself killed? You could get us killed! Die if you want to, but you aren't going to bring us down with you." She let her father yell. Let him shake her, no protest.

It can be hard to pick a worst moment if your life is littered with them, but I think that moment wins. I looked at her—shoving some broken glass along the floor with the toe of her high top—and I wanted to die with love for her. But I didn't. I gathered my courage and I made myself say it. "No more, Anita. You have to go."

She tells me that she could not believe I said that: *No more, Anita. You have to go.* She was sure I'd always open the door for her. Even when I took her off to lockup, mad and scared as she was, she knew I held the door open for her return. I always said, "This is home. You're home, honey." Well that was the promise, wasn't it?

It was a worst moment for her too, and she still thinks of it, still struggles with it.

It isn't easy to explain myself even now. Why did I say, "You have to go," right then? Why not sooner, or never? What made me say that: "No more, Anita, you have to go?" There was the broken glass, the mess, the way she kept taking off. There was that. But it still might have been possible for me to cope, to plead with Ken to cope, just a little longer. I might have done that. We had already been through so much, were, in a way, inured.

She doesn't like to hear it. But I tell her how it was: I saw the faces of three other people I loved. They looked like they were prisoners and I held the key. I had not looked at those faces clearly in a long time. Her face was always in the foreground. I looked beyond her that time. I could lose her, never see her again or see her dead, but I could not, even if I were willing to ruin my own life, drag three other people into ruins. They loved her too, but they were scared. I looked at those three people and there was only the time it took to open my mouth and say what I knew I had to say, *no more.*

We hired somebody to clean up the mess.

Chapter 34

CHOCOLATE KISSES

The intake person at Ozone House, a local refuge for troubled teens, a place that prided itself on its ability to work with teens, looked at me and almost recoiled from my desperation. "Take it easy," he said. "Take it easy."

They had a room and they were willing to work with her. He assured me that it could be a turning point. I wanted to believe him.

Ken said I could do whatever I wanted; he was still mad enough to leave her on the street. But he came along with me when I drove her to the new place. I wanted people to see that she had a *family*, even if she kept leaving that family.

I thought she would be furious. Thought she would charge me with abandonment again, but no, she was—resigned. Maybe, she said, it would be better if we weren't together. If she lived at Ozone, I wouldn't be around to tell her how to live. She could make her own choices and we could keep in touch. Could she come over for dinner sometimes? It seemed as if she could never decide how far away she wanted to go. Take off. Then come back. Hate us. Then ask to come to dinner. But dinner was fine with me. I wanted her to come for dinner. "Come," I said. "We'll have masala dosa." I'd pick her up at Ozone on the nights she came to dinner and drive her back. Maybe it would work. By that time, our friends knew the basic story. John and Mary Ann had even gone to Grand Rapids to see Anita when she was in lockup. But now I was going to have to tell everybody more of the story: "I've told Anita she has to move out. She's at Ozone House." They were kind. Our families and friends found little presents—you could have called them house-warming presents—to give to Anita. Small things like a tote bag for her to carry her shower supplies in, a soft yellow throw she could use on her bed. People loved Anita.

We left her there. She had a duffel bag full of jeans, tank tops, and cigarettes. But first, I went upstairs to see the room she would share with another troubled teen, like I was checking out her college dorm. It was a nice room, with two twin beds, plaid coverlets in purple and mint green, a desk. I felt as if I should go looking for a beanbag chair, maybe a toaster oven. They could rent a movie, have a grilled-cheese sandwich. It could be like dorm living.

She waved from the porch. She was not far away, less than a mile from us. But this wasn't lockup. This was a place for teens who did not, as the intake worker said, *manage well with their parents.* No one would do more than note whether she was in for the night or not. After curfew the doors were locked. Where would she go if she missed curfew?

Would she try to come home to us? What would I do if she did?

Some weeks I saw her, some I didn't, and sometimes not knowing what she was up to was better than knowing. But then, several months after she moved to Ozone, she called crying and said the pain in her stomach was *so bad*. I was into the car and out the driveway before she added a single detail more. What if she had an ectopic pregnancy, a ruptured appendix?

Soon enough, she was stretched on white sheets, an IV dripping into her vein. She said, "It could have happened to anybody, don't you think? I mean lots of people get infections." I looked at her huddle.

"Sure," I said, but oh she valued herself so little, cared not much at all what happened to her. She was too easy. *Easy.* I tried using the word *easy* to describe my daughter. I ran the word through my mind, jabbed a mental needle in and out of the letters, poked the letters this way and that, said the word over and over until it was not so bad, until I said the world like *pipe fitter, sales clerk, gas-station attendant.* I took her photo out of my wallet when I was alone and wrote *Easy* on the back with a soft lead pencil. *I love you, easy girl.* The IV drip clogged, then resumed its flow. She would need maybe a week of the drip to be on the safe side.

She complained a little. "This stuff burns," she said, "like holy hell." The nurse who inserted the drip told her that it would burn. It would not be comfortable, but she needed the IV. She had an internal infection that could spread to her entire abdominal cavity, an infection common to young women who were easily mined. The nurse was circumspect and said it was an infection common to *sexually active women*. She never, once, implied *easy*. She warned that, if the infection were left untreated, Anita might not be able to have kids, later on when she might want to have kids. She was a good soul who wrote notations on the chart, then explained what they meant. She pointed to the door. "You have a visitor," she said, "with flowers. Lucky girl." A guy stood in the doorway holding Kroger roses.

He was wearing a black leather coat with black fur lapels— maybe real fur. He nodded to me. He eased toward my daughter's bed and put the roses down on her stomach, leaned over to give her a kiss, taking his time. She introduced us. "This is my mom," she said. "Mom, this is Steeler."

I remembered Steeler. Remembered seeing a black Camry and the guy who got out of the car. He came to pick her up after she had dinner with us one night. That had been a few weeks ago. I remembered him taking a chamois and giving the Camry a rubdown in our driveway. Then he held the chamois lengthwise and pulled across the toe boxes of his patent leather shoes. Anita sat on the porch waiting for him and took a cigarette from her purse. She inhaled deeply and sighed with satisfaction. She held the cigarette between her first and second fingers and her blue-moon nails were jazz against the white paper. She looked at me watching him, saw my eyes narrow. She frowned. "I'm on my own now," she said. Which was mostly true. "But just so you know, he's not the worst."

He stood just inside the hospital room and put his hand out in my direction. I felt a ring on his pinkie finger, a gold thing that might have been real or not. I sniffed the roses and put them in water while Steeler ran his pinkie finger around my daughter's neck. He eased down on the bed and took her free hand in his, bent the fingers back and forth in rapid motion, took her hand and stuck it in his pocket.

"Baby, baby," I wanted to yell. "Watch out. Look out."

Instead, I leaned forward and spooned Fudge Ripple into her. She swallowed, her eyes at half mast. I looked at Steeler and tried putting *kill* in my eyes, while still being careful because, *who knew?* He left quickly enough, no desire to hang around. "See you, babe." Wagged his fingers in my general direction.

She fell asleep, the IV drip going into her, her left arm hanging over the side of the bed.

The doctor was less careful about appearing judgmental, a young staff guy probably doing rotations. He frowned and warned her about risky behavior, then turned to me. "You're her mother. That's what this says," reading the intake sheet like it was full of bad marks.

"You better rein her in." He left, and we didn't see him again.

"Don't be negative," Anita said to me. Four days had passed, and she was still sleeping on white sheets, the last IV drip going into her. I unwrapped chocolate kisses; foil wrappers piled up on the nightstand. She took my hand and put it on her stomach, said she felt better, a lot better. She was glad I came to help; she wished it didn't hurt so much. I wasn't sure what she meant by that. We napped together, the smell of chocolate kisses in the room.

Chapter 35

Z24

Ma hardly ever called to talk, but when she did, she continued to remind me: *Little kids have little problems. Big kids have big problems.*

Well, Minh was a big kid already, a nicely stretched Vietnamese-American male, who had some big problems along with his height, which was normal American male height, five feet eight inches tall. He'd made it out of high school. He wasn't stealing so much anymore. A few bucks if I forgot and left my purse around, and he was short on cash. I'd confront him and he'd have to pay me back. He was paying some rent, which we put into a savings account for him. He was working his barista job. So there were good things. The problem was he seemed unable to consolidate the good things. Like he was afraid of them. I knew he grieved for his sister. His current and most pressing hassle was the car parked in our driveway, the red Cavalier, the special racing one, a Z24. Minh found the car in a used-car lot, made some kind of down payment, and drove off thrilled to leave the rust bucket Chevy behind.

The Cavalier was flash, fireworks—red, convertible roof—smooth and sexy, exactly the kind of car babes jumped into. It was polished and stroked by Minh who used a chamois, never a rag, and called the car *baby. My baby.* He asked us to take his picture polishing the car, then gave Anita, and then Sung, a ride. He took Ken for a spin and then me. His eyes glowed behind the wheel. He drove the car for six months, washed it and rubbed it down every week. Then the phone calls started. *May I speak to Minh?*

At first polite people called. Then people who were not so polite, people who were angry, who demanded he return the phone call ASAP. I gave the messages to Minh, but Minh ignored them and drove off, honking as he pulled out. "This can't be good," said Ken.

We were awakened by the dog barking. We looked out to the driveway where we saw two guys with white T-shirts and guns, standing around in the light from the lamp at the top of the garage, hooking the red Cavalier to a tow truck. It was summer. We had the windows open and could hear them. They worked like undertakers, careful not to damage the body. One guy swore softly when he jammed his finger up against a winch line. I couldn't make sense of it at first.

Ken rubbed my neck with his fingers and said: "They're repossessing his car."

I didn't know it would look like that. Men with guns in the middle of the night? Another bad scene. How many would there be? I went to Minh's room and shook him awake. The Vietnamese-American dictionary was on his nightstand, a take-out cup of coffee, gone cold, next to it. "Get up," I said, "they're taking your car."

He pulled his jeans on and zipped them going down the stairs. We watched him shake hands with the gun-toting guys, his grip long-fingered. We heard his voice—it slid across the asphalt and caught one of the guys by the ankles, but did not disrupt the process. He smiled at them. "Let me show you something," he said. He opened the trunk of the Cavalier and pointed to something inside.

Then the three of them leaned their weight against the tow truck and looked at the sound system Minh had created. They were almost like friends talking about the car and the great sound system Minh had. The guns stayed in their holsters, not needed at all. And even though the guys were supposed to get the car and go, they helped Minh jimmy the black boom boxes from the trunk of the car. They heaved the boxes out of the trunk onto the driveway where they lay like small black coffins. Amps, a snarl of black and red and green wires, all innards, no bones.

Minh tugged the black boxes off to the side, sat down on top of one, and had a smoke, orange fire like a small eye searching. When he came back upstairs, Ken stopped him and asked for the details.

"I'm relieved. You don't know how hard it's been to keep that car. At least there won't be any more phone calls." True.

He did not look sad or grieved, and he got to keep his sound system. He loved the red car, but it was trouble. It not only had an oil leak, but the driver's side door was jammed and the fuel pump needed to be replaced. This was what Minh said as he went back to bed and pulled a pillow over his head: "What's gone is gone."

When he came down next morning, he drank the blueberry smoothie I offered him, saying "Thanks."

"Minh," said Ken. "You need a system of money management. We'll go over the details tonight." Minh agreed, always the polite one, but the two of them had gone over details before. It seemed as if Minh thought the plan Ken laid out—savings, expenses, discretionary income—took too much time. He couldn't wait. What he wanted might disappear the minute he turned his back. It wasn't that he was a lazy person, lying around on the couch, expecting the world to take care of him. He worked hard at his job. But he couldn't manage the money he earned.

Even when Minh was a kid, we had to take him to the bank

and practically force him to put some of his allowance into a savings account. It puzzled me because it wasn't as if he lacked for the usual things. But he needed the best things, the most things. And that wasn't greed. It sounds like greed, but it wasn't. If you asked to borrow his sound system, he'd agree, cheerfully. If you wanted a coffee when you were out with him, he'd buy you one. He was a generous personality, but he was unable to bide his time. The classic interpretation would be that he was trying to fill an empty space inside of himself. And maybe he was.

For the rest of the summer, he got around on the old blue Huffy that had been stored in the loft of the garage. He pedaled back and forth to his job, a full-time barista at the deli-coffee shop, biking downhill and over the Broadway bridge, his ponytail a dark fist behind him, a flag of mourning.

Chapter 36

CEREMONY

I finally got a full-time job, a real professional life. I had, unlike my older son, been content to wait, fiddling around, taking one measly course at a time while I worked as a clerk in a kitchen-supply store selling garlic peelers, olive pitters, and blue Le Creuset pots. I did that when the kids were younger. Maybe around late elementary and junior high. The kids loved it when I had that job. They paid no mind to my schooling. It didn't seem real to them. Whereas, the store where I worked was right down the hill from our house, and they could stop in to see me sometimes. When I worked Saturdays, Ken would bring me a coffee from Zingerman's.

Then I stopped fiddling around and went back to school full time at Eastern and got the master's degree. After that, I was hired as an adjunct, the star grad student in the creative writing program who talked her way into a job. And then, finally, by 1996, I was teaching full time. I was a professional with a job that required me to pay attention. I taught Intro to Lit and I was glad enough to do that.

Dee had an office down the hall from me and she taught Intro to Lit too. We'd meet between classes and talk about teaching while we drank lemongrass tea until we had to go: we had classes to teach, papers to grade. Most of the time, I could move into my teaching space and leave other concerns behind. I could do a good job.

That October, Dee's class was finishing *Beloved*. My class had come nearly to the end of *Ceremony*, the complicated masterpiece by the Native American writer Leslie Marmon Silko.

I loved teaching the book and the issues it dealt with: racial identity, loss of tradition, hard choices, estrangement, healing. Teaching the book, for me, was like a ceremony in itself. I had my class sessions carefully structured, all of them leading up to the ending of the novel. I was always prepared for the students to be distressed by the ending. If they did their reading, they knew that in the end chapters of the book, Tayo, the biracial protagonist, has to watch Harley be tortured to death. It was never an easy thing for Intro to Lit students to understand.

These students weren't any more ready to understand than my other students had been.

"I hate the book."

"How can Silko write stuff like this? Harley was Tayo's friend!"

My handwriting is dreadful, but I scribbled their comments on the board. They squinted to decipher the words: responsibility to a friend, murder, abandonment. And my favorite, the one I could recognize as something I might have said: "There must have been some way for Tayo to save Harley."

"You can't just let somebody be killed like that," said a student who had shaved her hair off, for Locks of Love. She sat there with her lovely bald head a beacon in the late afternoon light. I brushed chalk off my black jeans and leaned against the desk. My students were from Ypsilanti, Howell, Detroit, Bellville, places that did not offer silver spoons to newborns, just hard choices that often enough left their lives hanging in the balance. My daughter hung out in some of those places.

"Have you ever had to let someone go? Have you ever been in a situation where you couldn't save a person?" Of course they had.

I drank tea from a chipped green mug and waited while

they talked about brothers, sisters, parents lost to drugs or alcohol, family members who were in prison or dead from a drive-by.

They could understand losing a person when they thought about it. But they were still angry at the way things turned out in the book.

"Harley intended no good to Tayo," I reminded them. "Look on page 242. Harley's job is to lure Tayo to Emo and Pinkie so that they can kill him. They hate Tayo because he is biracial and acknowledges both his worlds. When Tayo escapes, Emo and Pinkie retaliate by beating Harley to death with a tire iron. They want Harley's screams to lure Tayo out of hiding. But Tayo realizes that Emo and Pinkie intend to kill him. So he stays hidden. He chooses to live his biracial life. Silko wants us to see this as honoring the ceremony of life."

A girl with brown hair and hazel eyes waited for me to recognize her. "People want to think that things are simple. They like to think that things are black or white," she said. "Just for example," she added, "I'm like Tayo. I'm mixed. I'm part Ojibwe, German, and Irish. When I go to the Native ceremonies, I feel as if people resent me. I always think that if I disowned the white in me, my life would be simpler. But I can't. My life is a mix." She cried.

The class was stunned. One guy, maybe midtwenties, making it through school hardscrabble, two jobs and child-support payments, said, "Well, those people are giving you shit. You shouldn't disown anything. Be who you are. Isn't your name Amanda? Live your life, Amanda." A general assent went around the room. Amanda smiled.

I loved those moments of connection when the students seemed not only to get a point, but also to make use of the

The Year The Trees Didn't Die

point. My students came to class badly prepared most of the time, struggling to work and go to school, racked with debt, many of them single parents, catching what information they could on the fly, but moments like that I prized. I left class happy.

A week before midterms, I was in class working to define the intersection of ritual and ceremony. I turned from the board where I was scribbling again and saw her in the doorway.

Her hair was loose, down to her shoulders, no frizz. She wore a blue-and-cream jacket, black jeans, and her high tops. She was still living at Ozone. I stopped myself midsentence, went to the door, and motioned her in to take a seat. The class looked around. She smiled. "A visitor," I said.

I finished class, one half of me talking about ceremony, the other half watching the doorway to see if anybody else would show up, some kind of thuggy guy. But nobody showed up and Anita seemed fine, so I chatted with the students who moved out the door eyeing the girl in the blue-and-cream jacket.

"What's up?"

"I just missed you, so I caught the bus over here. I asked the secretary where you were."

"You asked the secretary? You knew what floor my department is on?"

"You wrote it on the blackboard in the kitchen. I saw it the last time I was home to eat with you guys. I can read."

I had no idea she'd noticed.

"So you missed me? That's nice. We can go get a treat. We'll go back to Ann Arbor together."

I was incredulous. I had been sure Anita was in trouble and came looking for help. But she had no reason other than to see me. My daughter took a bus to see me! It takes forty-five minutes to get to Eastern by bus. She got off. Walked to the building where I teach. Took the elevator to the sixth floor. Asked the secretary where I was and found me. This was a girl who didn't do things like that. She could go off any old way, yes. But she would never take a bus alone or ask for help unless she had no other choice. She looked pleased with herself. The stuff of a normal life for most people, but a wonder for the two of us. I hugged her, and we walked over to the student center.

She slid her jacket off, fiddled with a bit of paper left on the table. Folded it into lengths, then folded it again until she'd made a boat, sipped at her Pepsi and ate some chips. It was nice just then. Two people enjoying each other, the woman admiring the girl's paper boat, the girl smiling, no hard choices to be made.

We walked to the car. She turned on the radio, hard pounding music. I drove home the back way, past the Huron Hills golf course, through North Campus, past the deer feeding at the edge of the woods. She pointed them out. "Careful," she said. "You don't want to hit one."

Then she asked, "Why do you like to teach?"

"I like work that matters. Being a parent matters. Teaching matters. It's not like they're the only choices though. Your dad and I just want you kids to have work that matters. Whatever that work is."

She turned her head to look out at the deer, still visible. Another doe had joined the group.

"You're smart," I told her. "You can do lots of things."

"I hate reading. I'm not like one of your students." She still didn't like that I was teaching. Plus she had struggled, learning how to read. A person who had struggled to read in a house full of books. But she was an ace at math. She grasped mathematical concepts, spatial relationships, no problem. Even without homework or study, she did fine on her math tests.

"Lots of people don't read. Lots of my students don't read. They watch the movie instead."

She laughed at this. "Maybe you're right. But still, watch out for the deer."

And I did, driving home from work with my daughter, in a small part of life's ceremony, an unexpected joy.

Chapter 37

GLORY GIRL

That same year, Minh got to meet his brown-skinned woman. Not his mother, for sure. But he didn't mind. He was on the blue Huffy, biking over the Broadway bridge. She walked along carrying a bag of groceries from Kroger, beans and rice, mostly healthy food. Nothing my oldest son was likely to want to eat. But, they recognized each other as friends of friends. He got off his bike and they watched purple martins swoop under the bridge. She thought the Huffy was cool. She admired his ponytail and his laddered rib cage. She slid onto the back of his bike, wedged the sack of groceries between them. Gloria, that was her name. He called her Glory. "Glory, Glory, my Glory girl."

Not long after that, maybe a month or so, he raced up the driveway and told us that she was what he had always wanted. She laughed belly-up, he said, and she had brown skin—at least partly brown—and she liked him. He sat on the edge of a chair, his leg jiggling with excitement or nervousness; I didn't know which. He said all this before he gave us a bear hug, packed his duffel bag, and headed out the door for a life with Glory. "We're moving in together. She's what I want." Just like that.

He was barely out of high school. He had no real money, no car, no real idea of where he was heading. He was walking into snakebite country with no snakebite kit, but what chance was there he'd listen?

Maybe one of us tried shaking him. Maybe Ken gave him a shake, the same way he shook Anita once: *Is there any sense in your head?* But maybe not. Ken wasn't, by nature, a shaker. He came from a family of reasonable people. Me? I probably tried to find a way that it could be okay, pretty sure that our chances of preventing Minh from taking off were next to none. He looked so happy, so convinced. We cautioned him, pointed out pitfalls, suggested giving the idea more time, discussed the work of married life. But in the end, the best we managed was a hug from him: *Hey, hey, it's going to be all right. Come on. Let's have a hug.*

I was not one to turn down his hug. Would anger have been better? *I insist that you hear me. If you leave this house to go live with her, you are on your own.* Keep the door open. That's what I believed. I still do, but there were so many times I wanted to slam the door shut, bolt it. Maybe erect a barricade. Ken felt like that too. But we didn't.

They biked over the bridge into an apartment on Easy Street—they loved the name—between State and Division. And not long after that, maybe six months or so, Minh came in the door to say they were going to be parents. I looked at him, a kid still, and felt my stomach lurch. Parents? We went outside and sat on the porch step. "I'm going to be there for the two of them," he said. "I want to be like you guys."

A good moment. Mixed with a not-so-good moment. I knew it was true. He would be there for them. But what else there was, he had no idea. Still I allowed myself to believe somehow. Something about Minh's eternal optimism, the same quality that had him smiling at us when he came off that plane, soothed me. And pretty soon, the two of them showed us a baby, a soft-boned baby they laid in a corner of their brown sofa on Easy Street. A little girl they named Gloria for her mother; everybody called her Mookie; Anita gave her the name one night when we were eating General Tsao's chicken on the side porch, takeout from Lucky Kitchen.

Sung held the baby and Anita smooched at her a bit and said, "Hey, Mookie." And there it was, not her birth name, but her love name.

Then, pretty soon, all three of them, Minh, Glory, and Mookie, had dark ponytails. Their voices howled pleasure summer nights. They curled around each other while they slept on the pull-out bed of their brown sofa, the mattress soft as sliced bread underneath them, their bones leaving no imprints. And they stayed that way for a while, happy, living on coffee with cream, and taco takeout.

Mookie grew, of course, and eventually she walked in the back door and pointed to her socks that were mismatched, a purple and pink, or blue and green. We enthused over her mismatched socks and small jeans. It was great having that child in our lives. I shrugged when friends said they wouldn't want a grandchild; their kids (the same age as mine) were too young to have a child, and they didn't want to be grandparents. I *was* a grandparent.

Then, just that fast, or maybe it was happening all the time, the jet stream moved off somewhere, and a blast of arctic air screamed in like a fighter plane. So quickly, they weren't on Easy Street anymore. We didn't hear from them or see them for weeks. When I tried to call, the phone was *out of order.* I feared this was like Minh's Z24.

When we found them, they were on a street I had never seen before, in a house with a snarling dog on a chain in the yard, nothing at all like Easy Street. The dog pulled at his chain and barked at us when we climbed the steps. I knocked, Glory opened the door, no welcome, and we walked in.

Mookie sat on the floor of a bare room. Their dishes, the brown couch, even the blankets and the Huffy, they had left with the Easy Street landlord, until they paid back rent. Minh had left the barista job and taken a telemarketer job to earn more cash, but he couldn't make the sales quota. "I can't get the patter down. I can't talk fast enough."

"Minh, take it step by step. Get a job that's a regular job, not one that promises you'll be rich in six months. Then stick with the job while you plan for what you'd like to do." Of course that was Ken talking, the guy who had had the same science job for years by then, who wrote articles that were published in journals, book chapters, a step-at-a-time guy. Never a guy you'd find in Minh's situation. No. He was the guy who had said, "Let's write. Let's get to know each other," that time I would have gone off with him, still a girl, still in school. He hadn't changed. He still counseled patience.

Minh was impatient. When he saw Glory, it was *POW*, and they were off on his bike. Minh looked at Ken as if Ken *didn't know*. A nice man, his father, but not someone who could be expected to understand the situation.

Glory looked at us like she thought we had sold her bad goods, raised a son who talked nicely, but didn't do the job. She moved a grocery bag of clothes, socks, and shoes from the chair and told me to have a seat. "He better learn to make some money," she said. "I'm tired of this." She looked at me when she said that.

"Money is not his strong point," I told her, defensive. "Maybe you two can come up with a plan." I was sorry she was tired, but he was such a good guy!

She said she wasn't his mother. She was Mookie's mother. He needed to make some real money. That didn't sound good.

Ken slipped Minh two twenties. But they couldn't stay full on two twenties. They needed milk, pink-frosted Pop-Tarts, whole plates of noodles smothered under thick red sauce. They needed their skin to be stretched wide and shiny. They needed the skin of well-fed people, happy Americans.

    We waved good-bye and walked down the steps past the growling dog.

Chapter 38

SPLIT

Minh and Glory split soon after our visit. When I told people I was sad and surprised, they said, *Why are you surprised?* Meaning, of course, that it was to be expected. The two of them too young, nowhere near ready to be married. But I was surprised. I had hoped for, what? I had hoped Minh would make enough money to keep them in Pop-Tarts. I had hoped that they would make a plan together. I was a great one for making plans. I wanted it to work. They must have wanted that too. Those words they said to each other sometimes, *Glory girl*, *Minh love* . . . the way Mookie snuggled between the two of them . . . it could have worked, given a miracle. But it didn't.

What happened was this:

One morning the phone rang; it was barely seven. Minh was on the other end, and he sounded bad; he was coming over, he said, and bringing Mookie. They were fighting, he and Glory, and he wasn't handling it well. Panic crackled through the line. When he got to the house, Mookie fell in the back door, a sobbing little girl wearing Minh's T-shirt and a pair of pink big-girl underpants. That child, an Afro-Amer-Asian mix, was a complete success—every bit of her worked, bones, skin, and all. She was a sweet soft bag of cotton candy. Ken picked her up and offered toast and a runny egg, her favorite breakfast.

"We're splitting," she cried. "We're splitting." She was three. She didn't know a lot. But she knew they wouldn't be together anymore. Minh held an unlit cigarette between his lips and looked around for a light. "In the garage," I said. "Next to the charcoal. That's where the matches are." He shook his head, dismissive. "I'll wait. We're done," he said. "Glory and I are finished. She wants to leave and take Mookie." So. Things weren't good *at all*.

Gloria wanted the life they had at the start, the Hop-In coffee, taco takeout, fun. Minh had been using a pawnshop to manage. He'd pawned his CDs, his CD player, a camera, the Timex Indiglo watch he got for Christmas. What could he have gotten for that? He stood in the kitchen, leaned against the counter, and told us about pawning things. He stood in the same place, had the same posture almost, as when he told us we couldn't fix his problems anymore, back when he used parking meters as his personal ATMs.

I shivered and pictured my son going to a pawnshop. He walked of course. I was sure of that. I had not seen his bike in a long time, doubted he ever got it back from the landlord on Easy Street. Somebody else was riding the Huffy.

He had probably worn his purple jacket when he went. It had his name on the front in script: *Minh*.

If it had been cold, he walked with his hands in his pockets, no gloves. Somewhere on the stretch of sidewalk edged with party stores, a gas station, and Dunkin' Donuts, he pulled out a hand so he could smoke because he claimed that smoking was the only thing that kept him from going crazy. He had smoked on the way to the pawnshop.

I held on to Mookie, hot with anger. Although there was probably nothing that could have been different, given that he and his brown-skinned woman jumped on that Huffy and rode off, no helmets, bad brakes; still, what about the little girl?

He turned to the girl.

"I will still be your daddy," he said to Mookie. His voice choked. "I won't go anywhere." She wouldn't look at him; she made a cave in our bathrobed laps and cried. I stroked her hair; it smelled of cigarette smoke. Then Ken made her runny egg and she ate it.

Not long after that, Gloria moved out, taking Mookie with her.

Minh talked about lawyers and fathers' rights, but he needed a good lawyer. The best we could do was someone who made a stab at it. In the end, Gloria got Mookie, and Minh got visits. He moved back in with us, a mostly silent shape in the kitchen and back bedroom. He wore black and he cut off his ponytail and shaved his head again. His skull looked like the surface of a strange earth.

He talked about life in New York, Boston, someplace that wasn't Ann Arbor, and I wondered if he would take off. He said he might feel good again living someplace with lots of lights and lots of Asians. He sat in front of the platters of cabbage noodles or soy-sauce chicken I put in front of him, but he didn't eat. He used his chopsticks to pick noodles up and put them down again.

He bought a tank of beta fish and watched their blue-and-yellow shapes move through water. "It's comforting," he said. Sometimes, Ken or I sat with him and watched the fish, like maybe they could help us figure something out.

For a long time, he looked like a forgotten person. He smoked so much the driveway was littered with the small white arms he scattered there. He wore the same outfit day after day until I pleaded with him to change his jeans and toss his shirt into the laundry.

He drank.

One morning, I lined up all the bottles he had stashed in his bedroom and put them on the kitchen counter, a long row of forty ouncers, wine coolers, Jim Beam. "You're a father," I yelled.

"You have to do better than this. You need to take care of your daughter. You need to *be* a father!"

"You have no idea," he said. "It's easy for you." Not true. But I knew he thought so. We had our marriage; we had each other. We had kids. He had lost it all. Thin and hungover he stood in his unwashed jeans, his black shirt, clothes he'd fallen asleep in. "I've lost everything," he said.

I dragged him out to Bed Bath and Beyond with me, the only thing I could think of then. It was something we could do. Not a court fight, not a plea to stop drinking. Just a regular shopping trip. He leaned against a wall of pillows while I bought featherbeds. I wanted us to sleep on clouds. He seemed puzzled by that, but he was willing to go along with it, like his father that way, a nice guy.

Back home, I demonstrated how great the featherbeds were. "Just feel the softness." I pushed down on one with my hands. "They'll be great for winter." I lay down and made angel wings. He tried his out to oblige me. He slept on it for a week. Then he said he liked a hard surface. I put the featherbed in the closet.

The thing was, on a day that seemed like any other day that we were plodding through, he ate a little. Ken made his eggplant dish with everything fresh from the garden, the eggplant, the peppers, the tomatoes. Minh had some of that and said it was good. It felt like something I remembered, that slow movement from near-starvation into life.

Then one night, Minh and Sung watched a Pistons game. I heard the two of them hooting at calls. *Okay*, I thought.

I had learned a little about happiness, about taking what there was. On days when Mookie visited, if Minh fell asleep on the couch while his clothes spun out in the washing machine,

I had Mookie try on my skirts and shoes. She put on my red heels, asked me to get her into a black velvet skirt. I put it on her and held it up with a scarf tied around her waist. She pulled necklaces from my jewelry box and draped them over herself. We woke her dad to have him see her. He whistled softly, still half asleep.

Chapter 39

BABY SLUG

One January day about a year after Mookie was born, Anita and I went to lunch at Shehan Shah. I picked her up at Ozone House. The IV and hospital stay were in the past, something she counted as bad odds beaten again. We drank tea and ordered tandoori chicken, allo gobi, and papadam. We cracked fennel seeds between our teeth.

"Excuse me," she said, and went to the bathroom. When she came back, she shoved a piece of paper across the table. It landed just outside the corner of my white paper place mat and looked like a picture of a slug, grainy, something curved in black and white.

"Say hi to your new grandchild."

The waiter was pouring more tea. He nodded in the direction of the picture.

"Oh my," he said, "a baby, a little Indian baby."

"The father's off to California," she said to him. "The dick."

But she said that the way I'd call her a klutz—sweet fault.

Once the waiter left, I word-assaulted my daughter. I told her the father was a prick. (Steeler, I thought.) I used steel-toed words—ghetto lounger, male stud with semen for gray matter. She cried quiet tears that splotched the slug's picture, but I ignored them—cheat, slime ball, son of a bitch, asshole. I was crazy mad. This would be harder than Minh being a father. If she had the baby, Anita would be a mother. A single mother. Two of my children parents? No.

Any hope there was for her to have a life seemed as faint as the picture of the baby slug. The waiter returned, refilled the teapot, and slid to the side of the wall to watch and listen. It was an interesting talk all right. He kept his eyes on the statue of Ganesh across the room and listened.

The home pregnancy test was positive, so she took the bus to Planned Parenthood and they confirmed it. She waited to tell until she had the sonogram and could show me the baby, a little boy. She thought that would be a good way to tell; I could see his picture.

It didn't feel possible. *No, that's not my daughter's baby.* And yet, what could have been more likely?

"How will you raise the baby?" I asked her. My voice firm, almost distant. Her eyes spilled tears again. I couldn't picture it. How could it work? She was way too young and needy herself. It was true she had a job at a high-end store where they sold produce and bread and expensive things in jars, lovely bouquets of flowers. She had made it out of high school what with the courses over in Grand Rapids and help from Ozone. Then she found the job and she was great at it. Truly great. Customers loved her. She double bagged for the older customers and helped them carry their groceries to their cars. She remembered special requests. She knew the names of the regulars. She was a standout. *But the job was new. How would she keep the job when she was pregnant, sick sometimes?*

She broke papadam into bits and chewed. "I want to enjoy this," she said. "I like eating out and I don't get a chance to very often." I couldn't eat. The waiter looked sad about that. I drank my tea. When we left, he boxed my meal and some papadam. Anita said if I didn't want it, she'd be glad to take it. She wasn't mean about it.

On the way back to Ozone, I made a stop at the drugstore for some dental floss. Anita went over to the baby aisle and picked up a plastic teething ring, one of those things with tiny animals floating around in liquid. She twirled the ring around her wrist. "Look," she said, "this would feel good to chew on. Let's get it." She was still small, still beautiful, still loving, still my daughter. But, what should I do? What was a teething ring though?

I told her I'd get the teething ring, no problem, although it wasn't needed for a long time yet, but she needed to start looking at the real needs, diapers, diaper cream, a crib. She hunched her shoulders and walked away. I bought the teething ring. I handed the package to her in the parking lot, and she said she supposed I was right, but she couldn't think about cribs yet. Was she really going to need one? She didn't think she could be a mom, being a mom was so hard. How hard would it be? She pushed herself against me, her Lions jacket up against my white down jacket, the one that made me look like a polar bear.

How could I not laugh?

She should have known, looking at me, how hard.

She asked me to come into the examining room with her when I drove her to her next appointment. She wanted me to talk to her and distract her. I watched while she stretched herself out on an examining table—let someone search around inside her, a female nurse who practiced safe sex or was married and had married sex.

Not someone who went off to a bathroom in a restaurant and came back with a foggy picture and said, "Say hi to your new grandchild." Casual like, almost as if daring me to be upset.

No, that nurse searching around inside my daughter was probably not a person who walked around in Lycra and net. That person wore blue drawstring pants and slipped a gloved hand into Anita one more time, just to make sure, taking her time as if she were rearranging things in there, then she told us everything felt fine, which was good. Anita mentioned some back and hip pain, and the nurse said the ligaments were stretching to accommodate the growth of the baby, a good thing they did, she explained. Otherwise Anita wouldn't be able to manage a baby growing; it'd be like growing a plant in a pot too small. She withdrew her hand, removed the glove, and washed up.

"See," she said, drying her hands on a paper towel, "Mother Nature knows how to do these things. Your body is a great machine." She tossed the towel into a white wastebasket for someone else to empty. I pictured road graders; that was machinery. I tried to picture my daughter's body as a well-functioning machine, but it seemed like Anita's body was a machine I never got the knack of running, a machine I didn't know how to fix.

All of that baby-growing business was good, said the nurse; it was nothing bad, nothing to really grieve about. I believed that. It was a *baby* we were dealing with, not a murder. Our daughter was alive and she was growing more life. It could have been way worse. We even had time on that visit to listen to the heartbeat.

"Isn't it great? Listen. That's the baby's heart." The nurse gave us the stethoscope, and we listened through the wall of my daughter's belly, a steady beat like someone underwater pounding the sides of a pool.

"Will you help me have the baby?" she asked when the nurse left the room for a minute. "Will you be there when I have it? Do you know anything about having babies?" I told her I didn't know much since I never got too far along, but I'd be there. I was not likely to give the job to anybody else. Her dad would be there too, the one who counseled taking the long view. Always the calm guy. Always the guy to decide what was worth the fuss. "Nita," he'd said when she told him, "at least you know you can get pregnant." I loved the gallows humor.

"Honey," I said, "I'm glad you want us to be with you." Which was true.

She said a strange thing then: "You always use words."

Maybe I did. Maybe, considering her life so far, I used too many words. Still, some words stayed on my tongue—things I never said, but thought: *What if your Indian mother came right now, the one who knows about babies? The mother who had you? Do you think she'd do a better job?*

"You're white. Maybe white people believe in words. Brown-skinned people are more action oriented." She bit off her words jagged and sharp. I was white.

Well I was. I was like eggshell skin, the luminous sheath of muscle, teeth. She was brown, dark, opalescent, a fistful of wet leaves. And my brown girl would have a baby sliding down headfirst, a baby who would look like her, bend her bones back and come out between her legs to breathe what air there was.

The nurse came in and gave us phone numbers for possible consultations. She didn't say *adoption* and she didn't say *abortion*. She said *alternate plans*. I was glad for that. We headed out into the February snow, scrappy stuff in a ball-bearing sky. I drove home down Huron Parkway and put the numbers on the counter beside a bowl of winter fruit, oranges, bananas, apples, pears.

Anita, my brown-skinned girl, made toast, a cup of tea, and went upstairs to watch reruns, her day off work.

She loved watching *Little House on the Prairie*, the part where Laura comes running across the field. She hated it when they showed Laura grown up, teaching school, wearing her hair pulled back. But she was going to have to grow up now; I could almost hear Ma say that, in her sad voice, to me, to Anita.

* * *

It isn't as if I have anything to tell her, I wrote to my sister Rosie, trying to explain about Anita and the baby. Rosie knew all about teen moms and dads. She and a friend drove a truck into the Pennsylvania hills and set up a kind of mobile distribution center to help kids like that. She brought things that were needed, jeans, jackets, baby clothes, underwear. Patchy-looking kids came out of patchy-looking houses. The girls, like mine, mostly young and pregnant, the guys thin-fleshed, wearing high tops and jeans. Girls and boys, both, scratched around like mountain cats. They searched through the piles of clothes hoping for a denim jacket or something in black leather, something to make them look like they weren't teen fathers and mothers. Nobody ever took hats, even in the coldest weather. "It will keep you warm," said my sister, pointing to a cap. They didn't want warm. They wanted to feel even if it hurt; feeling convinced them they were alive. Like Anita.

My sister wrote back and sent me pictures of the boy and girl parents, their round-eyed babies looking pinched inside their stretch suits, sad babies, as if they already knew they would not be the ones to win the prize. Never hold a bouquet of roses, wear a real gold ring.

Not those babies.

In that same letter my sister said that I should write what was in my heart. Well, there was a lot in my heart, but I didn't know how to describe it: Anita was upstairs on the couch watching TV. Mookie ate taco shells like cookies, left crumbs wherever she went. Most days Sung yelled and sometimes I dreaded seeing his dark head coming in the door.

I brushed the dog to concentrate on small things.

The probable father of the baby slug, he was far off down the highway, driving his black Camry with antilock brakes. He was listening to something on the radio, some kind of song that made him slap the steering wheel and take a drink from his insulated mug of coffee.

* * *

"It's not so bad," I told her. She turned down the volume of the TV and looked at me. "It's not so bad, a baby. It's not like murder or car theft. Lots of girls have babies. The baby won't eat you. Lots of girls are moms."

"This baby is going to change my whole life!" she said. She was right. The baby would change her whole life, all our lives. She did not want an abortion, though; the thought of someone sucking out what was inside her gave her the creeps. Her birth mother had had her. Anita wanted to have her baby. She didn't know what to do with the baby once she had it though. How would she manage? She looked at me. We went down to the kitchen to make tea. I didn't know. It wasn't as if we had piles of cash. There was her job of course. Maybe she could get a room someplace decent, just one room. She needed to find a room somewhere for her and the baby. She could come home for meals and laundry. It might work. But how would she be able to afford day care? Would I be day care? Could I be? Should I be?

She sat on the green kitchen stool, her small feet in black Nikes beating against the rung of the chair—THUMP THUMP—like the small fist of the baby's heart pounding her wall. "Do you think I should?" She meant give the baby up for adoption.

I pictured her wrapping the baby in a pastel-green blanket

with a hood, little brown rabbits stitched around the rim of the hood. Standing somewhere downtown in her black pants and tank top and offering the baby to a nice waiting couple, a couple searching for a baby.

"Nice baby with dark-brown skin. Available to loving family. No drugs in this case, just sex."

That's what she might have said.

Chapter 40

BROWN BABY

Anita had to make the choice. If she chose to have the baby adopted, I had to agree. Anyway. *Didn't I believe in adoption?* Maybe it would be like when *we* got *her*—an eager family, outstretched arms.

But I didn't want her to let the baby go, although I didn't want the main job either. I couldn't be clear about a thing, and, sometimes, I was so angry I could have—what? Let her manage alone? She had moved back in with us until she had the baby. Where else could she go; where would I want her to go?

Defeated by my girl and a baby slug.

"This is what I know," she said to me. We were driving home from a checkup. "I could pass my mother on the street, and I wouldn't know her. I don't know my mother and I don't know my father, so what kind of life is that for a kid? 'Here you are, baby, this is what I have: two people who agreed to take me, and two brothers who don't look like me.'" She peered down at her stomach as if she were addressing the baby.

"You are my mother," she said, pointing to me, "and you are my father," she said to Ken, jabbing him with her gloved finger—by then, we had stopped to pick him up from work. "But," she went on, "you aren't the first ones. Who were the first ones? What am I giving this kid? What if I knew, though?" she added. "What would be different? That's what I want to know." Not knowing was a floating feeling. She hated it, didn't want her baby to float through life.

Later she grated sesame seeds over her noodles and forked them up. Her hand held her fork as if it were another hand. "I wouldn't know her," she said, keeping her eyes on the forkful of noodles. "I am struck by that. I would not know my own mother."

She lifted noodles to her mouth. I saw the mark on the little finger of her right hand, the one she caught in the screen door one day when she tried to chase the sparrows away, this kid who had been so afraid she ran inside if sparrows were in the yard.

I kept my eyes on the plate in front of me. Anything I said could have been counted against me, so I waited and after she had gone to bed, I wrote a note:

Dear Anita,
Please brush and walk the dog. It is your dog.
Love,
Your Mother

She named the dog Sugar when we got her. She might have been twelve then. She gave her bits of toast when I wasn't looking. She played with her and walked her. When she took to running off, she left her to us to care for. Sometimes, newly pregnant, she napped with her. The bed smelled like dog. Anita smelled like a combination of dog and cigarette. She had been told to give up the cigarettes, but some nights, she took the dog, stood out back under the garage light in the lumped snow, and smoked. The dog sniffed at old piles of droppings, found bits of birdseed and bread crumbs. Smoke clouded Anita's face, steam escaped from the dog's anus when she squatted.

They were a picture there in the night, the brown fur of the dog, the brown face of the girl, a gray jacket that I didn't recognize. She watched the dog scrabble in the snow, took a few more puffs; then dog and girl came up the back walk. They went to sleep under drifts of black and dog hair. The dog stirred and moved nearer the top, sighed and stuck her legs out. They both breathed from the stomach, muscles expanding and contracting. I watched Anita and counted, one, and inside her, two. One asleep, one growing, plus the dog, Sugar.

* * *

"We don't have a lot of demand for infants of color," said the social worker. "Which is a shame," she added, scribbling on her notepad, "because brown babies are so cute." We had made it to a consultation about the future of the baby. I had nagged for weeks at Anita until she picked an agency by shutting her eyes and stabbing a finger at the list the nurse had given us.

We sat in a purple-gray building that shed its purple-gray cast over everything, walls, furniture, magazines, even the caseworker.

The worker turned her pen in her fingers. Her eyes shone with sadness as if they had been slicked for the occasion. "It is a shame," she said. "I wish *I* could take your baby. I bet you will have a really cute baby."

I wanted to break that woman's pen in two. Instead, I grabbed Anita's jacket, grabbed Anita, and pulled her out the door, slamming it behind me. If I had turned back, I suppose I would have seen shock in the worker's eyes, maybe even hurt—my reaction not at all what she had expected. It wasn't what I expected either. Who was I so mad at? The worker? Myself? Anita?

It was the well meaning of her remark that scraped against me. We had come to the meeting because we needed to make a choice, but it felt as if our lives were lost in purple-gray offices with well-meaning people who saw us as next on the list.

My daughter cried in the hallway and said she would not have her baby *taken* by anybody. She would not let her baby be a not-wanted baby waiting for a home. I hugged her and considered. "Anita," I said, "honey, I don't know if that woman's right. She probably meant well; I probably overreacted; I don't know. I can't tell you what to do, not this time; it isn't like warning you away from trouble. This is a baby we're talking about. You have to make the choice and you have to believe in your choice."

There was her future, the difficulty of single motherhood. There was my future too; no matter what she decided, it would be a different future.

This was what she said to me standing in that hallway: "I am keeping my baby, end of discussion."

My mood swung up and out, as if we were taking off to someplace good. It made no sense, but there it was. Euphoria. Like the first time I saw Ken, Minh's arrival, the time Anita accepted food from Ken, Sung's bathtub soup. I had no idea how things would work. There were all kinds of reasons why things might not work. But, right then, I was glad. We headed out to a coffee shop on Main Street and ate peanut-butter bars layered with chocolate. We sat there a long time, her stomach growing bigger by the minute.

Chapter 41

BABY FOR CHRIST

And it was after that—try to imagine this—she pulled off her black Reeboks and got up on the ridgeline of the roof in red high heels, six months pregnant. Not in actual fact, of course.

What happened was: she opened the door one day when she was home lumping around the house. A young guy in a gray suit stood there holding tracts. He took one look and recognized my daughter and the baby-to-be as what he was searching for. He handed his tracts to Anita and talked to her in a voice that was eager. She was just the person Christ wanted, he said.

I tried shooing him away, but Anita put her hand over her stomach and listened to that guy. I feared him and his zeal. Anita wanted that zeal.

That night the moon came through my window, lighting the room. I rolled away from it and scrunched up next to my husband. He reached around and pulled the covers up over my shoulders. He was warm, stable as the heat from the furnace, no flash, no rush, but a steadying warmth transmitted that lulled me back to sleep where I dreamt and woke, heavy, as if I'd been swimming in a lake of rocks, every one the size of a baby.

He wanted her to dedicate herself and her child to Christ, a complete and total giving over. In return, she would have a rebirth. She would *know* who her real father was.

She intended to do it.

Some days she fretted that the baby wouldn't be healthy; she'd smoked when she shouldn't have, drank. It was all too likely she had messed up her baby. She took to clicking on her

Bic lighter and holding the flame of it close to her belly, like she was trying to see in.

A bare week after she met the door-to-door salesman for Christ, she was reading tracts like they were love letters. She walked around with one all the time. Short steps, carrying-a-baby steps, her bones cracking, her hips slipping this way and that. She started attending meetings and no longer smoked, drank coffee, wore lipstick, ate sugar or certain meats, busy creating a clean mind in a clean body. It was a relief to have her not smoking or drinking, to have her look *healthy*, but the rest of the stuff . . . She said it felt good to be wanted.

* * *

Face to the wall, she lifted her shirt and asked me to rub something in to stop her back pain. I remembered rubbing her back before. She was very pregnant, although still so small, it was hard to tell. She looked as if she had put on a few pounds. She didn't look pregnant. But she was. Her back hurt a lot of the time. I found some cream and rubbed where she said it hurt. Traces of her old life, leftover scars, were visible.

"You know what?" she said. "I am always on the lookout to see what's going to come out of the wall. I'm a jumpy, nervous person."

"Nothing is going to hurt you," I said. "Nothing will come out of the wall, okay, baby? Okay?"

But pretty soon something would be coming out of her. Someone would say, "Bear down, push, push." And she would, just like those women in Saint Marys.

The spring Anita was pregnant, we spent Easter in Saint Marys.

Everybody went along on that trip.

Minh took the lead driving his beater car. Mookie waved as they passed us by.

When we stopped for a break, Sung switched cars to ride with Minh, listening to angry young men on Minh's improv sound system, the same one those guys helped jimmy out of the Z24. Later he came back to us and offered Anita a foot rub; she took off her shoes and propped her feet on his lap.

That felt okay . . . It was not the full glory of that moment coming home from Independence Lake, but still, I would have said *good enough*. Ken pressed down on the accelerator a bit harder and we headed into the hills. Semis lunged past; I shut my eyes now and again.

I-80 skirted all the scrappy places—Clarion, Hazen, Dubois. We turned off to take the shortcut past Hazen, over the old Kersey road to home. Plastic bunnies were tethered in yards, tied to trees, on the roofs of houses. I felt the old mix of love and regret. I'd never live there, but I'd never let the place go either. We counted bunnies until we pulled into town.

* * *

At Easter dinner Anita loaded her plate with potatoes, green-bean casserole, and Jell-O salad. Nobody mentioned the difficulty of surprise babies.

Everyone went for a drive after dinner to see the Kinzua Creek and the spring runoff. We were all of us walking a railroad trestle, high above green water, in the hills—a family—mother and father and kids, sisters and brothers, my father, my mother, and the baby-to-be, the one inside our daughter.

Chapter 42

A GOOD BABY

So then she had her baby. She pushed and strained and she had Darius, a baby sliding out headfirst onto the hospital bed, covered in creamy white vernix, so that for a split second she thought she had had a white baby. Ken joked with her, "Look, honey," he said, "I put a hex on him."

The nurses exclaimed over the name. No one they knew was named Darius, but maybe someone she knew was? She didn't answer.

Then she said to me, because she was still zonked and couldn't quite focus, "Are you sure he's brown?"

"He's a little pale right now, honey," said Ken, "but don't worry, he'll darken nicely." She held him on her stomach; he yelled and then went quiet, like the whole business of living was too much effort.

We were happy, then we were not—rocks were crashing down on all of us. Darius, sweet baby-for-Christ, was too small. He had a *poor sucking reflex* and he didn't cry hard enough. That was what the doctors said and with that, they took the baby away and hooked him up to a respirator, inside a little plastic cage where he could be touched only by reaching a gloved hand inside and sticking it on his chest, a chest of heaving ribs that were like pencil lines on a map.

We had to use antibacterial soap, and don masks and gowns before we could go in to see him, clueless aliens. Days went by like that, a whole week. Anita was discharged from the hospital and every day we went back to sit in the neonatal intensive care unit watching green lines on the screen go up and down, waiting for the red light to flash, the sensor to beep. The bottoms of his feet were sliced open to insert tubes. They used the finest of needles, thinner by far than any needle I ever used to stitch a line down the ripped seam in my dress, so thin they reminded me of the hairs on my daughter's head, only silver, not black.

She looked at him and said it was her fault, she smoked and she drank. "Baby," she whispered, "hey, hon, what are they doing to you? Mama's here. We'll get through this."

"We find," said a doctor who came by in scrub green, blond hair, clean-shaven, muscular, like somebody you'd find pressing weights at Liberty Sports Club with a white towel around his neck, "we find that young mothers in your circumstances often have this trouble with babies."

I was halfway home before I thought what I might have said to that. "Ass," I might have said. "Ass. I find that men like you are a pain in the ass."

Anita said nothing. The doctor was just one more guy swimming across her line of vision, a guy who wanted her baby. A guy who wanted more tests, a long thin needle up the spine because who knew what might have happened in the months she carried the baby? Plus there was no genealogical history. I wanted to tell her, irrationally or not, to pick up her baby and run. The girl I had tried for years to keep from running, right then, I wanted her to take the baby and run. I didn't say that though. She agreed to the tests.

We listened to the doctor say that Darius was a good baby. "He's a good baby. He hardly cried through the whole procedure." Anita cried. We left the good baby in neonatal intensive care and sat in the dark of a movie, something Ken took us to, something with Julia Roberts smiling in it. The two of us cried together. It was almost nice there in the dark with my daughter, crying for the same reason, together.

Two weeks later, I was so glad I shouted. The tests were negative. Baby Darius managed to extricate himself from the tubes, the needles, and that little plastic box. He was small; that was his problem, nothing else was wrong with him, nothing that could be discerned. *Although, he was so small.* We liked his size fine.

Anita and Darius slept in the back green room with the border of stenciled roses, the same one Minh had returned to for a while after his breakup. Sugar slept with them at the foot of the bed.

Ken rocked the baby when he cried, rocked him and sang "Go Tell Aunt Rhody," the same thing he'd sung to Anita as a kid, with the same cracked voice.

Anita came in and said, "What a song to sing, 'Go tell Aunt Rhody the old gray goose is dead!' Why do you sing that song? It's nothing like a lullaby."

"It's what I know," said Ken. "It's what I can sing, the best I can do."

Chapter 43

BAD MATH PROBLEMS

It was a Saturday in late summer. Sung was still in high school, Anita had either had Darius, or was about to have him, Minh was sharing a sublet with a friend, coming home for meals and general maintenance. Josie and I met for breakfast and catch-up at the Northside. We talked about our families and the unbelievable times. Who *could* believe those times? No one but someone like my friend, Josie, with her adoptive family. She said she felt as if she had spent forever trying to keep her kids from capsizing. "Why is it so hard?" she asked me. "What will they say when they're grown up? Will they blame us for their troubles? I did that to my parents. I suppose all kids do. It's so demoralizing sometimes." I wondered. Maybe my kids would blame me: too lenient, too protective, too worried . . . I didn't know. Just that morning Sung had been upset with me.

"You always want me to be good," he said. "You don't want *me*." Angry about life again, frustrated. Well, I did want him to be good, Sung, my straight-arrow kid.

I had only the weakest protest: "Sung, I love you." In truth, when I turned to Sung those years and asked "What do you need?" there were times I didn't want him to need a thing.

There is a framed picture of his grade-school basketball team upstairs. He has his arms around his buddies who all wear basketball shorts, cool-looking nylon basketball shorts. Sung has the right shirt on. It's red and says *Northside Tigers*. But he is wearing regular summer shorts, not proper basketball shorts. It doesn't look as if he minds. But he must have. Probably the day I was supposed to buy him basketball shorts, one of the older two had a major crisis.

I didn't want him to have a major crisis, not any kind of crisis if that was possible. *Be okay, Sung. Don't mess up.* And both of us, Ken and I, were extra vigilant, like we had been careless with our money and were counting every nickel and dime. When Sung finished middle school, we chose a no-nonsense private high school. *A school with structure, that's the ticket*, we thought.

He was angry; "Not fair, not fair," he yelled when we told him.

"It's a prison," he yelled.

"It's not," said Ken. "Prison wouldn't cost us a small fortune."

Sung laughs at his anger now, claims he'll send his kids to the same school. But now is a long way from then. He struggled with the academic demands in that school. Which was fine in the end, but I remember one night when Ken wrote down math formulas for Sung to memorize. Sung had to nail the formula for quadratic equations for class the next day. "Look, Sung, study the formula and say it five times. After that, we'll see what happens."

$$x = \frac{-b \pm \sqrt{b^2 - 4ac}}{2a}$$

From where I sat in the kitchen, I heard the pencil scratching across the paper, heard him muttering, heard the chanting, "x equals minus b plus or minus the square root of b squared minus four ac, all divided by two a." Five times. I sat in the living room and said it with him, under my breath.

Ken kept silent and scooped ice cream into bowls. Finally, finally, many more than five times later, Sung *could* repeat the formula for quadratic equations, could even do a problem. I know the formula myself. I can repeat it if I have to: *x is minus b plus or minus the square root of b squared minus four ac, all over two a.*

* * *

She looked like a picture in a guide to the Far East. She was hyphenated too, Thai-American. Minh stared when he first saw her, still checking for clues to his lost mother.

But she was born here, in the States, and she was not nearly old enough. Her name was Grace, *Grace*. She was hired to be Sung's math tutor and she walked into our lives like, well, grace. She walked Sung through quadratic equations until he didn't even break a sweat remembering the formula. She taught negative numbers and other messy math with a mix of firmness and Butterfinger bars. She broke off bits of the Butterfinger bars every time he worked a problem. He slept happy and smelled of sweet. She exuded confidence. I was so glad to have her that I considered asking her to move in with us. We took a picture of her with Sung one spring. They stood outside, by the lilac bush, and held an algebra book together. Sung was triumphant; he had passed a math final with a B. We loved Grace. We kept raising her salary, brought her cups of tea, and told her that she *had* to move in with us. She laughed at us.

And, of course she left. She got married. It was mostly okay though because Sung was getting ready for college. He was finishing high school, had managed the ACT test, and had a spot saved for him at Hope, that small school on the west side of

The Year The Trees Didn't Die

Michigan. His brother was glad for him. His sister was glad for him. We were, I think, if I'm honest, more than glad. Receiving Sung's college acceptance letter felt like getting a successful parent mark. Although we had always said that we'd be happy with whatever the kids wanted to do; we never wanted to put the Ann Arbor pressure of a maize and blue PhD on them. I don't think I'm sorry about that. Maybe if we had been more focused on achievement, all the kids would have had an easier time academically. But that wasn't our style.

I grieved for Grace leaving. Everyone was happier when Grace was around. Every week I thought—if things got bad and Sung reverted to yelling—I thought, "Well, Grace will be here on Wednesday." Wednesday was the day everyone in the house cheered up.

We went to the wedding and gave her an electric rice cooker. She left our life for the most part, but we thought about her from time to time. "Listen," Sung said to me one day, a few months after the wedding, when Grace had called to tell us she was pregnant, just like that. "I still can't do the three times table. Grace needs to drill me all over again." It was true. He couldn't say the three times table. But he was headed off to the college he wanted, so he had succeeded, the kid who ran after me barefoot in the snow, the kid I walked away from and returned to.

Ken had something to say when Sung told about Grace and her baby and the three times table.

"Sung," he said. "You've made it a long way."

Sung looked at him, cautious. He always wanted Ken's good opinion, always needed more positive, more than Ken could easily give.

Ken persisted though. "It hasn't been easy," he said. "We went at it tooth and nail lots of times. But you are a good son,

Sung. Math is kind of like your dragon, and it's not the only dragon you'll face. I will always try to help you. I'm in it for the long haul and you make me very happy whether or not you master math." He gave Sung a squeeze. I could have died content, right then.

"Okay," said Sung. "Okay." He smiled and squeezed his father back. There they were, two men I loved, a math-whiz husband and a math-blank son. And I had learned something from Grace: too much sympathy makes a person unable to fight. Probably Ken knew that all along.

Chapter 44
FISH SOUP

In the summer before Sung left for college, the three guys, Ken, Minh, and Sung, placed bets all the time: on preseason football, a pickup game of hoops, whether or not somebody could call a coin toss three times in a row. The prize was always ice cream, a double scoop of mint chocolate chip at the Washtenaw Dairy, the place where we went to sit outside and lick sweet until it was gone.

We loved that Sung was going to college and at the same time, we took nervous breaths. Would he be okay? He was so intense! It seemed that he was reasonably secure with his place in the family. He knew how to jiggle the thermostat when it got stuck, pour hot soapy water down the so-so kitchen drain, buy bi bim bap from the Korean deli, make sweet-bean pancakes, one of the only Korean desserts we liked. He didn't yell nearly so much and most nights he slept without nightmares. He was fine; he really was.

But. What if I hadn't been so lost with the problems of the older two, been more able to concentrate on Sung? Would he have struggled less? Would things like math have been any easier? Well, he had learned how to succeed, that was for sure. Sung was a winner. He said so himself sometimes. "I'm a winner," he said—when things went well.

But, if I wanted to bet on a winner, would I bet on Sung? What bet would I place on Sung? I'd bet on his goodness, his strength, the fierce sense of justice he had. I'd bet on that, no problem. I'd bet on his brains. He was smart, that was certain. Everything else, whether or not he'd do okay in college, whether or not he'd get derailed somehow—well, who could say? But then, what parent could say?

Before he went away to school, I told Sung a story, a going-away story about the Hmong of Southeast Asia. It wasn't my story, something I made up. Like so much else in my life, I'd read it and then borrowed it. I wanted to pass it along to Sung, the kid who felt for so long that he was *in addition to* in the family.

"Sung," I told him, "I read once that if you ask a member of the Hmong tribe how to make fish soup, they will take hours to describe the making of the soup. They'll begin by describing the life habits of fish and won't end until they've worked their way through the catching and cleaning and filleting. They will also find it important to lend general information on the making of the pot the soup is cooked in. The Hmong see *everything* as part of the story, Sung. Remember that. The Hmong know about connections. Nobody is alone. We are connected. You need to know that. This family needs you. You are part of our story."

He listened and said, "Okay. Okay, *Mutti*." Sort of like he was soothing me, and maybe he was. I laughed and let him be. I couldn't make sure that he'd be fine by telling him a story, although I had tried to.

Maybe all that anger and frustration that Sung experienced is part of everybody's story? Maybe, if the Hmong are right in their view of the world, we all have a share in it, Sung's story. It started at Green Meadows. Before that, really. His story started with his mother. Well, even farther back. It started with *her* mother. The story would have to include the father too, the person hardly ever mentioned. Sung's Korean mother and father were children. Then they were not. They met, they were probably young, like my older two who became parents. And sometime after that, a baby was born. The baby was left on the back of the bus. Moses. He was found and taken to Green Meadows. Eventually, Ken showed me a toddler's picture one summer day when I was eating ice cream with the two older kids. We looked and that was that. The story goes halfway around the world and back again.

On a ninety-degree day, a few days before he left for college, Sung biked up the hill and came through the door, sweaty, glad for the iced tea on the counter. He went through his mail and found a brochure for a Motherland tour, a group of adoptees going back to Korea. I asked if he would like a trip to Korea at some point. He drank his tea in a long gulp and stared out the window at clumps of basil falling over. He was quiet for what seemed like forever. Did he think I was hinting that he *should* go? "I don't think anyone will remember me over there." That's what he finally said. He was matter of fact. Or maybe I wanted to think so, didn't want to think he was sad.

Slow, I thought. *Go slowly for once.*

I said, of all our children, he was the one who had the best chance of finding something out. Korea had records; we could help him find his birth parents if he wanted. We would do that. It was okay. He shook his head, "No. No thanks. You guys are what I want."

"It's okay to want both," I said. It *was* okay to want both.

I would always want to be *the real mother*, *the forever mother*, but at the same time I wanted him to be complete. He laughed at me then, his high-angst mother, and went off to his computer. His voice carried back to me, frustrated, like he was the parent, tired and ready to end the story, wanting no more of it, telling me that his hands were full. "I'm just trying to make it: go to college, get a job, live."

Living took all he had. The part of the story that was back there in Korea, maybe he would hear it one day and come back to tell us. Maybe not.

Chapter 45

LIKE CHRISTMAS

It was a triumph! A triumph, said Rosie. She rejoiced with me because Anita, like Ma, turned out to be a baby lover, a very good thing. Maybe Ma put something in that oil she rubbed on my daughter's back when they stretched out in the sun. Because, against every expectation I had, in the face of the resigned doom of my friends, after Darius appeared, things got better for Anita. For us too.

I didn't understand. What I thought would be the final break—Anita would run off and leave me with the baby, or end up on the streets with the baby, or lose the baby—never happened. Anita saw the baby as a reason to survive: she had to be okay; her baby needed her. Anita was a mother. Things turned around for her and for us.

She *mothered* the baby. She snuggled him and played with him and didn't complain when he cried. I heard her feeding him in the middle of the night, the wail, the stirring, the dog moving, then quiet. She got up mornings and went to her job and took her baby to a good sitter. She was careful and cautious and loving. Everything I wanted her to be for herself, tried to be for her, she was for her baby.

When Darius started to crawl, she crawled around the floor with him. They fell asleep together in the back room. There was a crib, but most mornings when I looked in, there were Anita, Darius, and Sugar, together on the bed. Once, I walked in and let myself touch them, still sleeping, safe. I called out to Ken, softly, and he came in and stood with me. We took in the scene like immigrants arrived on the shore of their chosen country.

She did not immerse her baby in Friends Lake, which the tract guy wanted her to do. She ignored the guy, asked Sung to be godfather to her baby, and had Darius baptized in the same church we had had her baptized in. Sung came home from college for the occasion and held him over the baptismal font. He held Darius and told him that he'd make sure to be around for him. If Darius had troubles with math, he'd get him a Grace, and if he had any ideas of running off, *no way*. Sung loved being a godfather, and he got Darius the best present of the day, a red Radio Flyer wagon, the one with wooden slats and an extra-long handle for pulling. There was a white-frosted cake decorated with yellow-icing roses. Phyl had made it and she carried it on her lap the entire way from Cleveland to Ann Arbor.

Ma and Dad, Rosie, all the Saint Marys clan came; the Cleveland family came. Everyone was glad and excited, eager to share a good time. We hadn't had company in ages. I had fun making runs out to Sam's Club. I even had money in my wallet when I checked out. I bought gallon jars of olives, institutional-size bags of chips. It was a party.

Darius was loaded down: there was the Radio Flyer wagon, hand-knit sweaters, blankets, books, pull toys, all of it. Ma had made him an afghan. She sat in the living room holding him, and exclaimed to all of us that she was holding a baby again. "This is a treat," she said. Anita joked that pretty soon he'd lie out in the sun with them.

Minh took the picture: Ma held the baby on her lap; Anita sat next to her. Eager spring light covered the three of them that day.

* * *

I was glad we had the party and Minh took the picture because just that quick, Ma was rushed to Pittsburgh in an ambulance. She'd had a stroke. Rosie called to let us know.

* * *

"Ma, do you know who I am?"

"Of course I do. Mary, get my shoes from underneath the bed and get me out of here." There were tubes in her arms, tubes in her nose. Her feet were faintly blue. I wanted to find her shoes and go off with her, but it was not going to play out that way.

I had loved her and left her to go off with a guy from the city, made my life as different from hers as possible, made sure I never fell in love with having babies—although there *were* the children, my sometimes-compulsive need to love—and then she was flat out like she was doing a run-through for her coffin.

"Mary. Mary. It's like Christmas," she said. "It's like Christmas." She said that to me, very clearly, like she had been thinking about it and she had got the answer right. "Death's like Christmas. It snuck up on me!"

And before I could tell her: *Wait. Don't die. You could go out in the sun again. I'll go with you this time*, the light left her eyes. She was still breathing though, so Dad kept praying fast and hard like he thought he might nail her down. I watched my mother die, the hard work of her breathing, the sheer physical effort. I had rarely seen her happy unless she was holding a baby, but at the end, I saw her smile. My mother smiled while she was dying.

A friend, a fervent Christian, told me she believed death was a sacrament, a hard, but beautiful sacrament.

The thing was, my mother loved the sacrament of birth.

* * *

The kids came for the funeral. Minh sidled up to me and said, "Sorry." Anita brought Darius wrapped in the afghan Ma had made him. Sung forced himself to take a quick look at Ma in her rose-colored dress, her head on a pillow, face up.

There was a spray of roses from the kids.

It felt odd to be comforted by my children.

* * *

I thought if I loved hard enough and followed guidelines, I would end up as a good mother. I'd never go to bed in the middle of the day or hide my face. I'd always be fully present, a good mother. But after Ma died, I was confused. I missed her in ways I had never imagined. I never thought she had been a good mother, but what if she had done the best she could? What if she was the best mother she could have been? Always focused on the kids, I never imagined missing my mother. She had, after all, often been a shadow mother, like my children's other mothers. But when she died, I lost direction. I had no one to point to and say, *See? I still love these kids, even though it is hard. See?*

What makes a good mother, anyway?

Ma was somebody I patterned myself *against*, not *like*, and then—I never expected it—I saw that she had been the loaf of bread I both wanted and refused. Even as I said *no*, I held onto the loaf she offered. I understood with new rawness what my children must have felt. Is there a word for shamed loss? Because I was ashamed. I had used her as an example of what I would never be while I kept returning home and eating her bread. Like my kids who mourned their birth moms and at the same time declared that they would never give *their* baby away, an amalgamation of hate and love.

What does it mean to be a mother? Was I a real mother? I had not kept my children safe. A mother was supposed to do that. What about my children's mothers in Vietnam, India, Korea? Those ghost mothers who lived behind my children's eyelids? My mother who went into the ground in beige lace? Her mother who died long before she could fully mother? So many mothers!

Chapter 46

LANDING IN FOG

One night not too long after Ma died, I was driving home from work. I had taught late that night, not finishing up until nearly ten. It was early fall, the night was warm, the car windows down. I pulled up at a red light and waited to make a left onto Geddes, the same route I had taken with Anita when she came to see me at work that time. Maybe I was thinking about her. Maybe it was the sound of an ambulance coming up behind me. Maybe I was sad, missing my mom. I'm not sure, but something happened: my body felt as if it had convulsed in on itself and, before the light changed to green, I was terrified.

But why? There was no threat anywhere around me. Still, I was terrified. There was no clear thought in my head other than to get out of the car and run. As if some terrible danger surrounded the car. I had to force myself to sit still and wait for the ambulance to go past, the light to turn green. My heart pounded, fear came over me in waves. I drove the rest of the way home, just barely. I didn't know what to say to Ken when he opened the back door for me, had no idea how to describe what had happened. He says I didn't look any different when I came in the door that night. I carried my papers, put my sweater on a hook, kicked off my shoes.

"I think I'm losing my mind." That's what I said. I remember saying that because that's what it felt like to me. "I think I'm losing my mind." We say that often enough, in a casual way when we misplace our keys for the third time in a week, when we're on overload. We don't mean it. I meant it. Ken looked astounded. I saw his eyes widen, although things seemed slightly distant from me, almost unreal. We sat in the living room with cups of tea. I didn't know what else to say, and I don't think he did either. He held me rubbing my back and neck until he dozed off. I got up from the couch and paced the floor. I swallowed more tea. I couldn't think of what to do. Every part of me was screaming, *Get out, get out, get out.* But where to? Everything pressed in on me, the dark, the walls, even my skin, the fillings in my teeth. Things that normally gave me comfort—books, Ken, the house itself—didn't seem to be real anymore. Eventually the night turned over into morning and I looked in the bathroom mirror trying to see who I was. I saw a woman whose skin, hair, and eyes had taken on a lank texture, a slightly muddy cast—as if I had been walked on by someone wearing steel-toed boots.

Weeks went by like that. I went to work. I taught my classes. The fear would abate a little while I taught or if I went for a run. Then it would come back full force. I was afraid all the time. If I slept, exhausted, I jerked awake, heart pounding, my body in a cold sweat. What had happened?

One day when I was home alone, I fingered the bread knife, a very nice Wusthof knife with the blade running all the way through the handle; it had heft. I laid it against my arm and it rested there, like a steady friend. It felt impossible to continue living with so much fear, no idea what was wrong, sure that I had lost my mind. When you become scared enough, you aren't likely to call for help because you *are* afraid. The fear feeds on itself. You are sure that someone will take you away and lock you up. Just like I did to my daughter. What else could a reasonable person do with you, someone so completely irrational? Ken asked me why I was so afraid. I didn't have an answer. The kids eyed me and looked sad.

Ken grew gray circles under his eyes, but I never asked, "Are you okay?" I couldn't. I didn't have the energy to care anymore. He suggested going out for coffee, trying a movie. I ignored him and pulled covers up to my chin. I felt a little bit safe under the covers. Sometimes, I lay in a white tub filled with hot water, so hot my skin turned red, and watched Ken looking at me. He stood next to the tub while I stretched out in water. I shivered no matter how hot the water was. I looked back at him. He seemed grainy to me, out of focus. Everything was out of focus.

Who was I? Who was he? Would he still want to go off with me? Did we know how to roll around on a bed anymore, lower ourselves into a red porcelain heart? Was that red heart still around? Did Honeymoon Haven still exist? Could we still pull children down from the sky?

I wore the same gray sweat pants and top every time I could, soft things that required no effort, that were baggy and easy.

"Mary," Ken said, when he came into the bedroom and found me under covers again, going into the third week by then. "I don't know why it's so bad for you now, when it's finally getting better, but you need help. I'm scared for you. Besides, you have a family that needs you. We need you!" I remembered that once I had stood in that room, yelling at him, wanting him to be a savior. He had been clear then that he wasn't a savior. I remembered that *he* was under the covers that time. *I* was the one standing. I remembered how I had yelled at my oldest that he was a father; he should behave like one. But all that seemed long ago. I rolled over and shut my eyes. He pulled the covers away and took hold of me. He walked me to the car, and put me in on the passenger side. He drove off with me to get help, an odd retake of the Anita scene. "We're getting help," he said. "I called someone and he will see you. If you don't like him, fine, we'll go somewhere else. But you have to try." I nodded. I didn't mind. Didn't care.

"It will take a while," said the psychiatrist. Ken sat in on the meeting. I wouldn't go in alone, afraid of the doctor too. I explained the situation and as much of the past as I could. "You have a mess here," he said. "I don't know which of you looks worse," he pointed to Ken, nodded toward me. "Look at it like this, Mrs. Koral. It's like you held a cup and it's overflowing now. You could cope while you had to. But now your life has calmed down and your body and brain are allowed to react. You have a combination of free-floating anxiety and panic disorder. You look as if it's been hell, one panic attack after another. But I can tell you this"—his voice exuded confidence—"you will get better. You will get better," he repeated, his brown eyes looking at me straight on. They *appeared* to be honest brown eyes. "You have to hold up the bottom, though," he said. "I can't do it for you." He meant that I was supposed to use the knife for bread. Maybe even eat some bread. "I can't keep you alive," he said. "If you think you can't stay away from the knife, we need to use the hospital."

I could stay away from the knife. We left with the doctor's confidence between us, like another child we held. Ken smiled at me and I could half smile back. I swallowed pills. I finally slept and then I began to eat. At first, because I said I would, and then because it was a normal thing to do. One day, I put on a new pair of jeans and a blue-striped shirt. Ken kissed the back of my neck when he saw me and suggested coffee.

We walked downhill to Zingerman's. We drank coffee and looked around to see who was there. There were other people in the world who laughed and drank coffee too. Those people were glad enough to see us. It was all normal stuff and it felt like a full-blown miracle.

It was then I saw Mui. She was serving up coffee, a barista who seemed lots more confident in her not-new-any-longer world. She had some gray in her black hair. She had kids I knew, who were about the same age as mine. We hadn't seen each other in ages. At the worst of times, I would not have wanted to see her. She was a bit like Mother Teresa to me, someone I felt accountable to. I had, after all, taken a child from her mother country.

She came out from behind the counter and wrapped her arms around me. She knew our story. Anita had told me once that she'd run into Mui at Briarwood Mall and Mui had followed her around reading her the riot act. "She wouldn't stop," said Anita. "She kept following me and going on and on, telling me I should listen to you guys." Anita laughed telling me that, as if Mui had some kind of most-favored-nation status. I wondered how Mui had learned our story. Ann Arbor was small enough for her to have heard though.

And then, there she was, holding me. "You are a good mama," she said. "You are a good mama." She hugged hard as if she were trying to get her words inside me. We cried together in the middle of Zingerman's. But it was okay. Mui had always made me feel good about myself, and it wasn't any different this time. She accepted what there was and made no big deal of it. It was okay with her if I parented one of her country's children. My family could almost disintegrate, some of us here, some there, most of us in bits and pieces, and Mui seemed to understand how that could happen. Maybe, because she knew that sometimes there is only the unexpected. She gave me a final hug and went back to her work. I moved off to join Ken, and she called out to me one more time, "A good mother." I was back in the world again.

* * *

Almost hesitantly, like we didn't know each other very well and were afraid of moving too fast, Ken and I planned a trip. We thought to fly out to California and get some sun. Maybe in a place with full light, we could see each other again, we two who had said *yes* so easily.

It can be hard to plan for fun if you've honed your skills on sad. I got stuck on deciding what clothes to take. I had my jeans and I had sweats, hardly what a person would wear out there in the land of slinky tank tops. So, like the time I went shopping for a new-mother dress, I left to go shopping for—a what? A survivor dress? Anita came along and helped me pick out another yellow dress, a slinky thing this time, not the simple sundress I wore when I went to meet Minh all those years ago. I was really skinny, so I looked pretty good.

I was nervous. I walked around the house as if I would never see it again. I cried looking at Ma's funeral cards, Darius's Radio Flyer wagon, the water mark on the dining-room table where someone had put a glass of iced tea down and forgotten the coaster.

Ken had his packed bag and tickets in hand; he waited at the door. "It's time to go," he said, "time to go." Oh, I remembered hearing that before. This time was different though; things were going to be fine. Sung would be all right; he was a big guy, said Ken. I knew that. Besides, he added, Anita was around with baby Darius. She'd keep an eye on him, her little bro. She planned to make bulgogi with him. Things were all right!

Go, the kids said, *go. We'll be fine. We're past all the dumb stuff.* They meant it.

They wanted us to go and come back happy. They wanted us to get a life.

We bought the wine the attendant offered, toasted each other, and flew west. I was never a good flier, always silently urging the pilot to concentrate, trying to keep the plane in the sky, but the wine relaxed me, and I risked a look out the window. A few magazines, another glass of wine, and we were nearly there.

And then the pilot's voice came over the speaker. "Well folks, we're almost there, but it seems that there is a bit of fog, so we might have some trouble landing."

People looked at one another.

"Uh, oh," the guy in the aisle seat said. He'd been reading a book about investments the whole way. He looked over to Ken and me, put his book away, and got up.

"Folks, I'm going to have to ask you to be patient about this, we may need to circle a while, or even detour. Flight attendants, please check seat belts and prepare for landing." The fasten-seat-belt sign blinked on; the flight attendants went up and down the rows. We fastened our belts and prepared for landing. The guy in the aisle seat came back, craned his head to look out, and said there should be *something* visible, at least some lights. Nothing was visible.

I glanced at Ken who looked straight ahead, not especially worried, but not looking out the window either.

I felt us go down, heard the landing gear heave into place. Then, zoom, we climbed what seemed like, but could not have been, straight up.

Whoa, said the passengers, *whoa!*

Call buttons pinged on. One of the flight attendants, the tall one with brown skin and hair, said in a very stern voice, like she was reprimanding bad children: "We're climbing at the moment. We cannot answer calls! Safety concerns need to be paramount!"

The pilot tried again: landing gear in place, then down, down, followed by a sharp climb. I felt my heart thunk hard; I gripped the seat and waited: *smash, smash, smash.* That's what I waited for.

I didn't want to die in the fog, in San Diego Bay. I didn't want to die at all.

The third time the pilot went in, the aisle guy uttered a curse or prayer: "Jesus Christ!" But there was nothing to do. If the pilot was intent on ramming it in, we could only hope.

"Folks, it looks like we'll have one more go at it; the fog comes and goes. So, we'll try again. Hopefully this one's a winner."

"My God!" said the guy. "I'd jump if I could."

Me too, I thought. *Me too.*

But there was calmness inside me. It was not at all the way I had felt for years, on edge, scanning the horizon, emergency measures and call buttons at the ready—I understood. At that moment, there was nothing to do. I let go of my grip on the seat, took Ken's hand, and held it lightly, not begging him to save anybody. It was okay.

The plane descended once more, kept on going, hit the tarmac, and thundered forward, nobody saying a word and—finally, finally we came to a stop.

We were alive. Was the pilot a hero? Was it a miracle?

"There you are folks, a landing, at last. We made it to San Diego."

The plane erupted in a cheer; the tall stewardess patted a few passengers on the back as she moved forward to stand by the cabin door with the pilot.

It had been scary; it had caused trembling and apprehension, but we had made it. Who would understand it? No one except the people who got off the plane with us, chattering, best friends to each other right then, saying: "I didn't think I could survive one more try." But once we left the terminal, we walked off ready to believe it could not have been any other way. *Of course, we were alive.* Maybe it's always that way, a nebulous line that we want to believe we can walk with impunity.

"I don't know," I told Ken when we finally got into bed—it had been a long night, but I still wanted to talk it over.

How close had we come, after all?

But Ken figured this: "We made it, Mary. That's what matters. We made it. We're alive, and the kids back home are alive too." His answers were always in his actions. I always wanted words. I took his hand and pulled him to me, skinny, cautious, careful guy, my guy who had been in it for the long haul.

We rolled around on the bed, happy to be together. After he slept, I let myself think awhile. I thought about what could have happened: dead in the bay, burned alive on the tarmac. I played with disaster, my old best friend. But then I turned away from it. I felt the smooth sheets on the bed, took a bottle of water from the minibar. Disaster had not happened. I picked something else to stay with me as I fell asleep, an old memory, one I had not thought of in years. It happened the day we took the kids to tour the Jiffy Mix factory in Chelsea, Michigan.

We had driven out in a heavy snowstorm, Ken, the three kids, all of them young then, and me. Nobody else was out, but Ken had promised the kids, so off we went. When we arrived, the receptionist was so excited to see us, she gave the kids a whole plate of sugar cookies, made from Jiffy Mix, and glasses of orange drink. Fussed over them. We toured the factory, just the five of us. The kids loved watching blue-and-white boxes of Jiffy

Mix come off the lines, corn muffins, brownies, biscuit mix. They left loaded with samples.

Ken fishtailed at stop signs, but it didn't much matter; he went slowly and the roads were deserted. I never once gripped the seat or worried that we would end up in a ditch. Everything was fine.

There in that city full of fog with everything fine, I turned to sleep with my city guy. I let my arm rest against his back, no gripping. I pictured our three kids back home in Michigan, two of them with their kids. They waited for us, confident that we would come back to them, our suitcases full of surprises.

Chapter 47

SURVIVORS

When people learned we were adoptive parents, they always asked if we would adopt again, even if they didn't know what happened all those years. They were curious to know if family worked when it wasn't shaped with blood, one set of genes to the next. "So, would you adopt again? Has it been what you expected?" They waited for an answer holding a mug of coffee halfway to their lips if they met us at a party, a bag of chips or bunch of lettuce held above the checkout counter if they saw us at Kroger, always slow motion, the sequence of their activity suspended.

Because adoption is still not the norm. And what happens then? Does a person feel glad about the choice? Or, and they waited for this, wondered, is there regret? Was I sorry that I never had a child *of my own*?

When we totaled the trouble times, we added up ten years. Ten years! Ten full years, complicated, often dreadful, and, then, gone. Most of those years, we felt like ancient pilgrims headed to a shrine, crawling on our knees, living on a bowl of gruel a day.

Somehow, we had got to another place; it wasn't a perfect place, but it wasn't bad either:

There was Anita who went out so far on thin ice, I imagined her funeral any number of times: Ken and I weeping together, white roses and violets on her casket. Anita still small enough that we bought a child-size coffin. I imagined all of it: the funeral home, the service at the grave, the drive back home.

It still gives me shivers, and if she's angry, doesn't call, or if she's sad, the scenes flash by in a rush: *She was lost, almost gone. My daughter nearly died.* But, she made it back, skittering and sliding over that barely-there ice; she made it back—with a baby! And she met a good guy on the way. She met Bob, who is exactly what she swore she'd never look at.

A quiet guy a lot like her father.

She loves the guy, but she is puzzled sometimes when she tells about meeting him. She can't figure out how it happened because—she remembers what she said about guys like her father, and—can you believe it? She ended up marrying one. She doesn't know how to account for that, and neither do we. But who cares?

Bob is a chef who uses knives to cut melons, not skin. He has never pointed a gun, or rammed his fist at anyone. Plus, he keeps feeding our daughter things like salmon with cherry sauce, grilled shrimp, and fresh tortellini. He lured Anita with food, just like Ken lured me with those pictures of Honeymoon Haven, the platters of piled-high shrimp.

When Anita started dating Bob, she came home with her stomach full of food, no bumps, bruises, drugs, or bad times to report. She didn't think she could hold out against him; he was good with Darius, and he drove down the highway without needing to duck. His car didn't even have tinted windows. She shook her head, and her hair came loose from the spray on top of her head, whirled around her face like a small tornado. "This is one I can bring home," she said. "He says he'll cook a meal for you. What a change from my normal. Can you believe it?" We couldn't, but we hoped.

That weekend, Bob brought his chef gadgetry over to the house and made a feast. We all sat down to beef tenderloin in teriyaki sauce, garlic potatoes, and Caesar salad. We took time to study him, then we licked our lips, coated with teriyaki sauce, and crossed our fingers underneath our napkins. "Please," we thought, "please." That guy fed our daughter; he didn't eat her. He fed us too. He smiled at us, and it was a smile we could believe in.

"Oh, boy, sister girl," said Sung, full of beef and garlic potatoes. "This one's a keeper."

"Anita," added Minh, "I don't know how you did it, but you found a good one."

Darius wore a tiny tux for the wedding and walked down the aisle with them.

At the reception, Ken gave the first toast. "To my only daughter," he said. "Years ago I asked to be your best guy until the right one came along. Now, I'd like to dance with you before you take off with your guy." They stepped out onto the floor. Anita joked to Ken that the first song should be "Go Tell Aunt Rhody."

Nobody could believe that the girl who nearly killed herself one way and another danced with her father on her wedding day. Bob had carved an ice swan as a centerpiece for the buffet table, but I swear I saw an angel.

And there's Minh who works in a car shop selling tires, and loves the cars that people bring in. He cares for them with respect, and his customers see that. A whole Asian clientele asks for him by name. He takes web design classes on the side. So he has plans.

"May I please speak to Minh," customers ask when they call the store. Minh loves that he has a name that's so distinctive. When he was young, he sometimes complained about his name. But once Mookie was born, he gloried in it, as if she gave him permission to be who he is, a Viet-American. He and Gloria have all kinds of fights over pickup times and clothes and who allowed what. But for stretches of time, there is peace. He gets to see the Mookie girl weekends and holidays. There's edginess. The mom sometimes talks about moving to California. We wonder when we're nervous, what if she said, "So long, Viet guy, good luck to you. I have her, and I am not bringing her back"?

So, Minh is not *completely* happy, but lots of days he is *pretty* happy. We go to movies together. We sit there eating from the same bucket of popcorn, a small row of us in the dark.

Recently, he met somebody who taught him Korean for *Hello* and *Let's go on a date*. Soon goes for walks with him, and they eat ramen noodles with egg and soy sauce. They slurp the noodles from white bowls with red-lacquered chopsticks. Minh told me he thought his learning Korean suited our family. "It's like us to stir the pot," he said. "Sung speaks German, and I'm learning Korean."

He still speeds through life, still has that tendency to grab and go, but having a child, learning how to speak Korean, seems to have eased him a bit, as if he might believe that life won't slide out from under him. One time we watched the two of them, our son and the woman who eats ramen noodles with him. She leaned toward him, her long black hair in a tail behind her. She offered him noodles from the red-lacquered chopsticks. He took them in.

Why not?

We asked for a bite of noodles, and they were happy to oblige, glad that we wanted a taste.

And Sung. His professors loved Sung. They cheered when he brought glory to the German department by winning a Fulbright his senior year.

He sent me the first hint of the news by email: *There's going to be a surprise!*

His brother and sister were glad. They were fair and generous. *You worked hard, little bro; we're glad for you.* And, it wasn't hard to be glad for him.

Chapter 48

THE GRADUATION: PART TWO

"Are you an adoptive family?" she asked. I was surprised that she used those two words, *adoptive family*. Those words suggested a knowledge that most people did not have. I told her yes. We were. Then I waited. She teared up. I didn't understand, but I offered her a napkin, the best I could do right then. She pulled herself together and took a shaky breath. "You're like a sign," she said, and reached into her purse. I couldn't be a sign for anyone, but I kept quiet and waited. She reached into that navy-blue purse and pulled out a picture of a little boy. A toddler. An Asian toddler, almost exactly, it seemed, the same age that our Korean-born son was in his picture all those years ago. Surely it was a referral picture she was showing me. This was her son.

He was standing in the middle of a room that could have been a playroom. There were some balls and push toys. There was an Asian woman nearby. I looked at the little boy. He wasn't familiar in a physical sense. But I knew that little boy very well, the dark hair, the eyes, his look of confusion, edginess. He was flying home to the woman and her husband in a couple of months, from Korea.

The story sounds like Ma's smile when she died, a story no one can believe. But, it's real. Ask Ken. Ask the kids; ask anyone who was with me that day at Sung's graduation.

We looked at each other, that woman and I, like we had a language all our own. Like we had planted flags to claim our own. I held her close for a second. She was a stranger I loved just like that, and she loved me back.

I never expected it, was prepared only to defend myself

and my family from her, but then I mostly never expected what happened. She couldn't believe her boy was coming. And I couldn't believe that our family was whole. We were there in that room in one piece, all of us. Like Ma used to say, *we lived to tell the tale.*

We could hardly *stop* telling the tale. There was so much to tell. Should I have warned her about boulders? They could flatten her. Should I have told her that little boy's birth mom was a ghost, not a bad ghost, but somebody to deal with? I might have said she would feel, sometimes, that the whole idea of adoption was impossible. Who needed so many hassles? Because, even though blood and flesh don't make family, still there is blood and flesh to deal with. She didn't know; she didn't have a clue, holding onto that picture for dear life.

She had better not be a wimp. I could have, at least, told her that. But I didn't. None of it was the right story then. Her husband was patting her on the shoulder. She pulled him forward to meet us. He looked wary, a little like Ken, another cautious, careful soul, unsure about the adoption business, the strange people she wanted him to talk to, but he was a good guy. I could tell that just by looking. He'd jump on the roller coaster with her. They would hold their breath going up and scream plunging down.

Ken shook his hand, in one of those guy-to-guy exchanges, and I heard the guy ask if he'd adopt again, waiting for the answer, hair trigger.

She turned to listen, waiting too.

"Well," Ken said, in his careful way. "It wasn't what I'd call easy. It was hard, but"—he waved his hand around to circle all of us—"here we are." He smiled around the circle too. He looked at me. *What do you think?*

Yes, I thought.

I loved his calm certitude. Who'd have chosen the pain? Not me. But still, we *were* there in that room. For that moment, we were there in that good place, all of us.

Was that enough? I smiled at him again. He knew: the kids, they took us places we never would have gone to on our own. Some times were great—I've never known kids so able to love, that love coming out of the sky the way it did! Some times were wretched—like a week's worth of rain in a mud hovel, third-world country, no food, no heat, lost passports, and rebel forces having taken us hostage, demanding concessions from the government while they held knives to our throats.

And there was still no guarantee, no bulletproof glass, safety net, goggles, steel-toed boots, anything at all that would promise more good moments.

It was all too likely that Sung would be lonely and frustrated in Austria. He'd lose his Euro-rail card, worry about finding a woman, and be sure yet again that he was a loser, no matter how disbelieving we were that he could think that.

Anita would be uneasy when she walked down the street with me. Sometimes, someone would call out to her, "Hey, baby. Hey, pretty girl." Somebody she knew from another time, still waiting. Sometimes she would be silent on the other end of the phone line, crying.

Minh would struggle to believe in his father's one-step-at-a-time theory. He'd always have the tendency to rush headlong into things, as if we'd kept him from something he needed in years past.

Ken and I would fight, not over the past; we made peace with that. But there were other things: the small children of our children. We'd debate about them for sure because we never knew. There it was, a person never *knew*.

So, was it enough?

It was. It was enough to be there, all of us together. It was more than enough.

I looked at the couple holding onto that picture thinking they had everything in the world. I believed they did.

I breathed easily, calmly, confidently, like I'd always had the guarantee, safely in my pocket.